# Contemporary
# Jewellers

# Contemp

## Interviews wit

# orary
# Jewellers

## uropean Artists

# ROBERTA BERNABEI

Oxford • New York

English edition
First published in 2011 by
**Berg**

Editorial offices:
First Floor, Angel Court, 81 St Clements Street, Oxford OX4 1AW, UK
175 Fifth Avenue, New York, NY 10010, USA

Berg is an imprint of Bloomsbury Publishing plc.

**Library of Congress Cataloging-in-Publication Data**
A catalogue record for this book is available from the Library of Congress.

**British Library Cataloguing-in-Publication Data**
A catalogue record for this book is available from the British Library.

ISBN    978 1 84520 769 4 (Cloth)
        978 1 84520 770 0 (Paper)

Typeset by Apex CoVantage, LLC
Printed in the UK by the MPG Books Group

**www.bergpublishers.com**

Dedicated to Michael, Violet and Stella

# Contents

# Plates and Illustrations

## Plates

## Illustrations                                                       *Page*

# Preface

This book was conceived as a research tool for those interested in European contemporary jewellery. It therefore presents a series of interviews with twenty-five of its outstanding jewellers. The purpose of these discussions was to reveal the creative, conceptual and technical working practices that underpin their jewellery. Consequently, each jeweller's practice is represented through a transcript of the interview with photographs of signature works. The book is an attempt to build an unfiltered repository of contemporary jewellery knowledge, disseminated through the words, visions and artefacts of its primary exponents.

The original stimulus for this book emerged whilst teaching critical studies of contemporary jewellery at *Le Arti Orafe* jewellery school in Florence in the 1990s. I observed the difficulties my students faced in locating direct source material from contemporary jewellers and especially in reading their ideas without the influence of interpretative analysis. Although interviews with jewellery artists have been published before, these are invariably located in monographs or the occasional exhibition catalogue.[1] Thus, the idea for a single tome was born.

The interview format enabled the jewellers to express themselves directly, without any intermediary. My role as interviewer was to guide the dialogue towards a distillation of their practices. In so doing, I attempted to remain as neutral and invisible as possible to allow each artist's voice to come to the fore. In selecting jewellers, I focused on those pioneer practitioners who were at the forefront of contemporary jewellery's emergence and subsequent jewellers who have continued the development of this language by broadening its formal vocabulary or through innovations in materials, technique or concept. Of course, it has not been possible to include interviews with some of the major pioneers of contemporary jewellery because sadly they have passed away. A more complete version of this book would have included interviews with influential luminaries such as Friedrich Becker, Onno Boekhoudt, Marion Herbst, Hermann Jünger, Giò Pomodoro, Reiling Reinhold, Emmy van Leersum and Helga Zahn.

The interviews were compiled between 2000 and 2009, and each conversation lasted approximately two hours, with some requiring a second sitting to update or expand the initial transcript. Wherever possible, I interviewed the jewellers face to face, and since the advent of VoIP (voice over Internet protocol) software, I also exploited video conferencing over the Internet. A few interviews were conducted via an exchange of letters or e-mails because direct contact was not possible. Transcriptions were then made word for word and edited in collaboration with each jeweller. The priority during the editing process was to distil the fundamental qualities of each jeweller's practice, including their approach to form, content, technique, materials and their views on jewellery's role in the world and its relationship to the body; along with a brief chronological exploration of the evolution of their jewellery. The pan-European backgrounds of the contributors meant that seventeen jewellers bravely consented to speak not in their native languages, but instead communicated in English. Inevitably this resulted in some subtle attenuation of nuanced thought. Similarly, interviews with some jewellers were conducted in languages other than English. For example, those with Giampaolo Babetto, Bruno Martinazzi, Mario Pinton and Annamaria Zanella were recorded in Italian and then translated into English. Despite the care with which I attempted to maintain the sense and ethos of their words, dislocated from the cultural context of their origins, some small loss of meaning may have occurred.

The book is divided into four main sections: the introduction describes the context surrounding the emergence of contemporary jewellery; this is followed by the interviews and images of key works; thereafter the conclusions summarize the main findings; and finally a contemporary jewellery resource contains a bibliography and listings of artists' Web sites, jewellery galleries, museums, journals and jewellery Web sites. The structure of the book is intended to facilitate a cover-to-cover reading or alternatively to allow the reader to dip in and out, to read about specific artists or consult the listings where appropriate. It is hoped that the universality of certain aspects of the interviews in terms of design method, form generation and harnessing creativity will render the text of interest to students of disciplines beyond jewellery such as three-dimensional design, product design, crafts, applied arts history, fashion, textiles and fine art.

Prior to commencing the introduction, it is appropriate to acknowledge the support, assistance and participation of those people who have been instrumental in the book's completion. First and foremost, I would like to thank Giò Carbone, director of *Le Arti Orafe* jewellery school and academy, who gave me the initial opportunity to teach my subject in a professional environment and who, perhaps more importantly, encouraged the germination of my idea. I would like to express my admiration and gratitude to all the participant artists who generously and enthusiastically committed their time and energy to the project. Without their openness in sharing their thoughts, ideas, discoveries, techniques, methods and even secrets, this book could not have come into existence.

Generous research input has also been provided by the staff of Bilston Craft Museum and the Matthew Boulton archive at Birmingham Central Library. I thank the generous providers of images, including all the jewellers; various institutional contributors such as the Victoria and Albert Museum, the British Museum, the Museum of Decorative Arts, Paris and the Danner Rotunder, Munich; Aurelio Amendola and finally Eva Jünger who digitized her photos of her uncle Hermann's jewellery. Additionally, I would like to thank the staff at Berg Publishers for their support throughout the commissioning and publishing processes. I also acknowledge the generous support of Loughborough University and its School of the Arts, which has enabled me to pursue and conclude this idea. I have been aided by the editorial advice of Andrew Stonyer, and Glenn Adamson of the Victoria and Albert Museum. Penultimately, I wish to thank my family for all their help and support during the long road to fruition, especially Michael Shaw; with additional thanks to Mrs Margaret Brown and Mr and Mrs Shaw. I would like to dedicate this book to my daughters, Violet Angelica and Stella Celeste: the new jewels. Finally, I thank all those interested readers who have chosen to explore this book and trust that it will provide starting points for further research into contemporary jewellery.

# Introduction

This introduction aims to distinguish the objects we now refer to as contemporary jewellery from past examples of the medium. This entails clarifying some of the key characteristics of contemporary jewellery's approach to function, content and materials. These characteristics are used to distil the ideas and philosophy of twenty-five of the most prominent European contemporary jewellers through the interview format. However, to understand the history of contemporary jewellery and what it might be, it is useful to commence by exploring the broader history of jewellery and how and why it came into being. Therefore, the introduction explores why humans have chosen to decorate their bodies with jewellery and contains a contextual and historical analysis of its production. Given the geographical locations of the participant jewellers, these discussions predominantly centre on the history of European practice. This is not, however, intended to diminish the role and influence of non-European and non-Western practice on the development of the jewellery language.

## Decorating the Body

Without the curiosity, desire or need to decorate the body, jewellery would simply not exist. So the original human act of placing some kind of pigment or object onto the body gave birth to jewellery. Beyond the initial curiosity of playful experimentation, the early motives prompting human adornment may well have entailed self-embellishment for its own sake or perhaps to help procure a partner. Other innate reasons become manifest at an early age; it is possible to observe in very young children their joy whilst creating impromptu bracelets by inserting their hands into open objects. They appear to enjoy the sensory pleasure of how the object moves when they move, its balance and momentum and the sensations it induces on the body. These reasons for body decoration extend into adulthood, where sensual pleasure and embellishment combine with the role of communication.

Alongside the personal stimuli for wearing jewellery, an altogether more public, contextual and functional set of reasons have evolved whereby jewellery is explicitly about the transmission of meaning. Certain kinds of jewellery have conferred status, declared fidelity and betrothal or manifested faith and belonging. In all these cases, the jewellery can create expectations on both the wearer and observer of how they should respond. Accordingly, if the act of wearing jewellery can change us in some way, it then follows that through this act of adornment we also contribute to a transformation, subtle or otherwise, of the meaning carried by the object. This relationship becomes increasingly sophisticated in proportion to the intricacy and complexity of the communicative role that one demands of the piece of jewellery. Therefore, a symbiotic relationship between object, wearer and observer exists.

Evidently, throughout human civilization, many reasons for wearing jewellery have developed, but when did this instinct commence? Current research supports an extremely long history dating back tens of millennia. In 2005, three ancient shell beads were found in two different locations; two at the Skhul Cave in Israel and one at a site in Oued Djebbana, Algeria.[1] Each of the mollusc shells was pierced with a small hole to enable them, it is supposed, to be threaded into a necklace or bracelet. Analysis of fossils found in the same rock strata indicates a chronology of between 100,000 and 135,000 years BC. This suggests that jewellery's nascent function and meaning is timeless.

As human civilization gathered momentum, a documented history began to emerge and can now shed light on the function and social significance of early jewellery. Generally, the latter has remained steadfast for centuries; ongoing examples include the engagement and wedding ring and their service to betrothal. Other somewhat less venerable examples now include the ubiquitous diamond stud on the pop star's or footballer's earlobe. Yet the latter is not so far removed from how ancient Roman gold rings glorified the wearer by confirming their status and power in society. For instance, in the late third century AD, the right to wear gold rings was reserved for certain classes of citizens such as senators and knights and not simply determined by one's financial ability to purchase.[2]

Roman jewellery was not only inspired by symbolism and status; other more pragmatic functions existed, including the key ring. It was a practical solution for securing one's keys – a tricky problem given that togas had no pockets. Fashioned from bronze or iron, they enabled the wearer to access storerooms and strong-boxes. Placing the key on the finger meant access was immediate and security was kept safe at hand. Jewellery has also protected wealth by serving as an investment; however, the invention and broad dispersion of coinage eroded this function.[3] Perhaps the most lasting Roman heritage is the engagement ring, which, as Shirley Bury observes, marked a shift in thinking, whereby 'gold rings came into increasing use not only as symbols of status and as seal-rings, but as tokens of betrothal.'[4]

Whilst the betrothal ring was a Roman invention, using a ring to confirm one's identity is believed to have originated in Mesopotamia, prior to widespread adoption by the ancient Egyptians.[5] Seal rings invariably consisted of a metal band holding a metal, stone or shell form on top, into which a moniker, symbol or image specific to the wearer was engraved or carved. These could then be used to sign and validate documents by mono printing or impressing them into clay tablets or soft wax. In other words, they stood for, and attested to, identity. Seal rings became widespread in ancient Egyptian society and were often engraved with scarabs that had a dual function of amulet and signet. Later, in Roman society, they could also represent symbolic allegiances to aristocratic identity and therefore bear a likeness of someone other than the wearer.[6]

Roman rings often signified the power of status; however, other pieces of jewellery ascribed higher powers. Certain jewels – emeralds, rubies, sapphires and diamonds amongst others – were believed to have religious, spiritual or magical powers that fortified the wearer.[7] In this way, adornment exceeded mere decoration in favour of talismanic protection. For example in traditional Italian jewellery, amulets containing red coral served this purpose, and even now the practice of protecting newborn babies with gold and red coral jewellery continues.[8] Alongside the more spiritual and quasi-mystical manifestations, jewellery also has embellished the teachings of religion. Since Christendom, biblical inscriptions have been engraved into jewellery to protect people, or, in the case of memento mori, to remind them of the precious brevity of life and the inevitable day of judgement.[9]

There are therefore a broad range of reasons for wearing jewellery, ranging from the socially complex to the purely decorative, from the talismanic to the commemorative, from investment to communication. Some of these reasons seem innate, and others have developed due to social conditions. Certain motives are public and others private, but what remains consistent is the human desire to change or reaffirm appearance, identity, perceptions, expectations, behaviour and feelings through the use of objects that decorate the body.

## Jewellery as Personal Expression

For jewellery to exist, someone has to create it – be it through the selection and adoption of a found object or entirely from scratch. This section of the introduction is therefore concerned with the realm of the maker and the potential for self-expression through jewellery. I contend the latter is one of the defining characteristics of contemporary jewellery, and the following text therefore charts the history of jewellery makers in developing their creative identities. Central to this development was the recognition that the act of conceiving jewellery could be a distinct phase, separate from its subsequent manufacture. The factors contributing to this are complex and intertwined, and their occurrence over many centuries clouds matters further. One of the first catalysts of change was drawing, which became a vehicle for the artist's thoughts, a guide for craftspeople and a means to communicate with any commissioner.

## Drawing

During the Renaissance, drawing became an important research tool that aided understanding in science and in the arts. Its effect on jewellery led to developments in form generation, style and the juxtaposition of materials, thereby expanding the confines of the language.

The subsequent invention of the printing press was similarly influential because it enabled a broad dissemination of jewellery designs through print.[10] Printing provided a stable and portable means of cataloguing designs, which were then collated into pattern books that formalized preconceived actions and individuated distinctly personal styles.[11] No doubt previous makers had given consideration to what they might make before picking up their tools, but these engravings bear first witness to what we would recognize today as evidence of a design process – in other words, a distinction between the thinking of planning and the action of making jewellery. This contention is further supported by the recorded appearance of known designers throughout Europe, including Hans Colleart, Erasmus Hornick, Daniel Mignot, Jakob Mores, Virgil Solis and Pierre Woeiriot, alongside artists such as Albrecht Dürer, Hans Holbein the Younger, Hans Mülich and Giulio Romano, who also produced some designs for jewellery that are still in existence.[12]

## Named Designers

An artist who consistently produced jewellery design of the highest calibre was Hans Holbein the Younger. His rendered designs were not those of the dilettante who lacks practical insight into the implications of actually producing the works. Quite the opposite, according to Hackenbroch, who maintains that Holbein's drawings 'show Holbein's complete understanding of the nature of precious materials and their handling'.[13] During his life, Holbein's designs became popular with a number of London-based jewellers, including Hans of Antwerp, Cornelis Hayes and Peter Richardson.

Holbein was first and foremost a painter, and whilst it is difficult to establish the precise influence of painting on his design process, some osmosis evidently occurred between Holbein's documentation of existing pieces,[14] his designs for fabrication and the jewels he sometimes invented to personalize a sitter's portrait. Intriguingly, the challenges of downsizing from large-scale portraiture to the micro dimensions and fine detailing required for jewellery would not have unduly perplexed Holbein, who, being an accomplished miniaturist, was capable of exquisite circular portraits not exceeding 5.5 centimetres in diameter. Indeed, perhaps operating within such limited spaces influenced the reductive nature of Holbein's jewellery designs, which are often characterized by elemental linear arabesques that sinuously twirl around a small number of stones set in regular patterns, as in Fig. 1. In

**Fig. 1**
Hans Holbein the Younger.
*Design for Oval Pendant, Set with a Ruby, Sapphires and Pearls* ca 1532–43.
Photo: © Trustees of the British Museum.

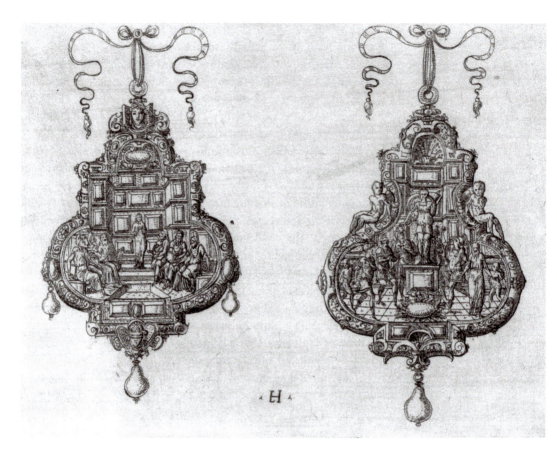

· H ·

**Fig. 2**
Erasmus Hornick. *Designs for Pendants* 1562. Published in Nuremberg.
Photo: © Trustees of the British Museum.

fact, his abstract designs might be described as compositionally compact, restrained and devoid of overtly decorative elements. Holbein evidently preferred to give prominence to the cut stones in their own right rather than making them the servants of narrative, as Erasmus Hornick did in his designs.

One of the most prolific designers of jewellery was Erasmus Hornick, who originated from Antwerp but operated a workshop in southern Germany for many years.[15] He published pattern books in 1562 and 1565, in which his pendant designs regularly featured asymmetric structures with human figures at the centre, all circumscribed by an architectonic framework, as in Fig. 2.[16] The sides of the designs are limited by two columns, which are often adorned by precious faceted stones, as in the pendant in the style of Hornick, Plate 2. Stylistically, the designs are dense and geometrically complex and may therefore be considered early forbearers of baroque decoration. Through this complex geometry, Hornick sought to balance all the elements into harmonious compositions whose figurative content was derived from the designer's knowledge of mythology, literature, religion and science. This was significant because it meant the work could not be effectively improvised during its production, but was instead preconceived and driven by the intellect. In other words, it was a reassertion of the storytelling that had previously featured in Classical and Roman jewellery, though, with Hornick, the narrative was conceptually formalized through drawing before the making commenced; the mind, therefore, preceded the hand.

In conceiving his designs, Hornick influenced the realization of jewellery by the manner in which he deconstructed them into constituent components. Whilst the architectural framework was almost a structural given, the inner content could be personalized according to the client's desires.[17] In some ways, this might be considered a precursor to the Industrial Revolution, when objects were produced in series and with the possibility of interchangeable parts.

The aforementioned deconstruction of designs through drawing was taken further by Hornick's production and use of lead patterns, similar examples of which can be seen in Figs 3 and 4.[18] These were either for complete works or parts such as pendant surrounds. The latter allowed greater input from the end user, because they could be moulded and recast, enabling additional modifications, or simply used in their original form if so desired.

**Fig. 3**
Maker unknown. *Jewellery Pattern* late sixteenth century. Lead. Germany.
Photo: © Victoria and Albert Museum, London.

Interestingly, working from one of Hornick's drawn designs still required a very high level of craftsmanship, whereas the use of a three-dimensional pattern slightly reduced the required virtuosity because the base structure and its geometry were pre-established. In other words, the design possibilities during manufacture were reduced. In addition, the introduction of lead patterns around this time may have conceptually devalued the act of making and, by consequence, increased the kudos and control ascribed to the originating designer.

In Germany, towards the end of the sixteenth century, a new approach to pendant design emerged that lessened the influence of Hornick's architectural motifs. Lighter, spacious and more structurally open designs were championed by designers such as Daniel Mignot.[19] This reduction in physical mass may have been in part due to economic conditions that required materials to be used more judiciously. Alternatively, experiments in drawing may have influenced the creation of the scrolling openwork jewellery typified by linear explorations of objects in silhouette, all overlaying tendril-like linear patterns. Certainly, these designs would have enabled a relatively speedy translation from drawing to object, because the planar base of the pendant could almost be cut out of metal sheet or formed independently using the drawing as a direct template. Afterwards, any three-dimensional figures could then be screwed in to complete the composition. An example of this nimble touch and weightless suggestion of volume can be observed in Mignot's design for *Pendants, Medallions and Studs,* 1593, Fig. 5. The rear of *Cupid Drawing an Arrow,* ca 1600, a brooch in the style of Mignot, confirms the immediacy of transforming this kind of drawing into jewellery, Fig. 6.

The exploration of open skeletal structures may have emerged through drawing – most probably through printmaking, because the sharp points of engraving tools would have inevitably lent

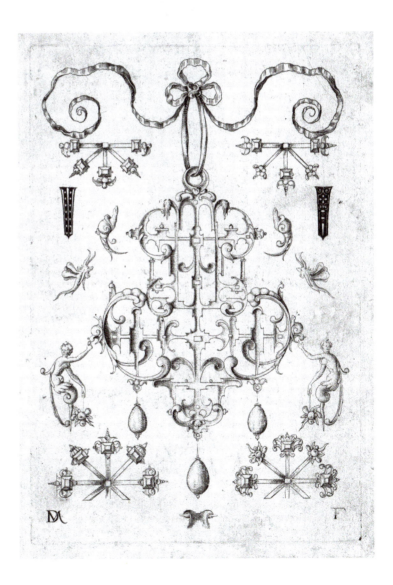

**Fig. 5**
Daniel Mignot. *Pendants, Medallions and Studs* 1593. Engraving.
Photo: © Trustees of the British Museum.

**Fig. 6**
Daniel Mignot (in the style of).
*Cupid Drawing an Arrow*
(rear) ca 1600. Enamelled
gold, rubies, pearls. Pendant.
Southern Germany.
Photo: © Victoria and Albert
Museum, London.

themselves to the articulation of line. Further parallels between print and jewellery making can be identified, primarily through their shared use of engraving. Indeed, the technical skill required to achieve certain imagery would be virtually identical irrespective of whether engraving plate for printing purposes or the metal surface of a piece of jewellery. An example of this is Virgil Solis's design for pendants bearing a linear arabesque pattern, Fig. 7. In this case, one could envisage the means of creating the design, the engraved printing plate, actually becoming the work itself.

## Pattern Books

If drawing was becoming an important part of the jewellery-making process, then the emergence of pattern books gave currency to the cult of personality. Pattern books were a drawn synthesis of a given designer's taste in jewellery; tantamount to a manifesto of the designer's aesthetics, sensitivity towards materials and technical preferences. Consequently, pattern books also could be devices for self-promotion. For instance, according to Yvonne Hackenbroch, the jewellery designer Jakob Mores sent

**Fig. 7**
Virgil Solis. *Two Pendants
with Arabesque Ornament*
1530–62. Engraving.
Photo: © Trustees of the
British Museum.

his sons from Germany to Sweden and Denmark to solicit new commissions based on his designs from 1593 to 1608, which were included in his book, *Das Kleinodienbuch des Jakob Mores*.[20] Pattern books therefore facilitated the commissioning process whilst also accelerating the role of jewellery trader – a forerunner to the modern-day gallery owner.[21] Some of these traders even speculated by commissioning designs themselves, primarily because it was a cheaper and more secure alternative to keeping large stocks of actual jewellery.

The drawings of Mores present an interesting case, because some of his designs were rendered in colour; this obviously indicated to the maker the colour of stones to be used in each piece. By contrast, jewellery designs made through engraving were monochrome and could therefore only prescribe form, proportion and surface decoration. Consequently, this left some scope for selecting materials and the colour of stones,[22] whereas strict adherence to Mores's drawings would have meant the complete relinquishment of any choices during the making process. The completeness of the designs, as in Plate 1, gives them currency as conceptual substitutes for jewellery, whereby the draughtsmanship is sufficiently adept to make them valued as works of art in their own right. The latter is important because it gives added impetus to the distinction between conceiving jewellery and the act of its making.

The vibrant qualities of Mores's chromatic drawings are indicative of the potential lustre and luminosity of metals and stones. The fact that they remain appealing now, and indeed must surely have seemed even more striking in their day, derives from their lifelike portrayal. The potential for drawing to be a believable substitute for reality had already been aided by Piero della Francesca's invention of perspective and its subsequent diffusion. The illusory projection of three-dimensional space could aid communication between any commissioner and the chosen craftsman, enabling design developments during the process of making. In fact, the importance of drawing is recognized by Cellini's discussions about a potential commission for a medal, recording how Michelangelo said, 'I will gladly sketch you something; but meanwhile speak to Benevuto; and let him also make a model; he can then execute the better of the two designs.'[23]

During the sixteenth century, it already seemed accepted that a drawing was a complete entity which could instruct how to complete a work. In other words, drawing became analogous with the process of making and thus evidence of the partial distinction between the act of conceiving an artefact and its subsequent execution. This meant that one person could design a jewel and another could manufacture it. Confirmation is again provided by Cellini, this time in the introduction to his treatise on goldsmithing techniques, where he discusses the attributes of his various contemporaries. One such individual was Antonio Pollaiolo, of whom Cellini noted how he 'was likewise a goldsmith, and a draughtsmen too of such skill, that not only did all the goldsmiths make use of his excellent designs, but the sculptors and painters of the first rank also, and gained honour by them...This man did little else besides his admirable drawing.'[24]

This multiplicity of roles in the creative process had advantages and disadvantages for the emergence of self-expression in jewellery. From a positive perspective, liberation from making meant that designers were no longer necessarily inhibited by the extent of their own manual dexterity, but were instead free to lay down extravagant and complicated challenges to the eventual makers. As Yvonne Hackenbroch suggests, Virgil Solis 'understood the needs of the goldsmith, and also how to tempt him to practice a surprising variety of techniques and to adopt new patterns'.[25] Naturally, there were also disadvantages from this division – mainly that makers might become fabricators who just copied with little or no artistic input. We now have antique jewellery from this period that is not identifiable in relation to a particular country or school, let alone an individual. The stylistic homogenization of jewellery was further encouraged by the standardization of skills sought by the guilds.

## Guilds

Whilst the advent of pattern books may have aided the burgeoning development of the jewellery language, an opposing force had sought its restriction. The inception of guilds throughout Europe gained precedence until the fifteenth century, when their influence increasingly began to promote the homogenization of style, and this inevitably had repressive consequences on the possibilities for personal expression in jewellery.[26] The guilds sought to protect members' rights through monopoly; however, enrolment also carried responsibilities to conform to both technical and assay standards and relatively uniform aesthetics. The latter meant individual nuances were generally unwelcome, and therefore any distinction between artist and artisan was also considered undesirable.

During the Renaissance, goldsmiths in Italy came under the auspices of the silk guild, together with practitioners of gold beating and gold thread making. Members underwent long apprenticeships which included training in multiple workshops, all organized by the guild to diffuse and guarantee technical skills. Progression would have required conformation to the guild's standards, which probably discouraged self-expression. Existence of the latter would have made an equitable distribution of work around the various workshops that much harder. To this end, guilds also limited the number of apprentices or journeymen a master might employ to control the quantity of work they could take on.

Counter to the guilds' stranglehold on style were alternate voices such as Cellini's, who argued that practitioners should possess intellectual and theoretical competences as well as the customary manual abilities.[27] The desirability of this dual capacity seems borne out by the apprentice jewellers who eventually became painters or sculptors of note, such as Andrea del Verrocchio and Lorenzo Ghiberti.

Cellini further distinguished himself by ignoring the jealous guarding, prevalent to his age, of the secret knowledge of goldsmithing, which was normally restricted to familial relationships. Instead, he openly described the intricacies of his technical expertise, perhaps admittedly for purposes of self-aggrandizement. However, the publication of this knowledge in a lengthy treatise on goldsmithing techniques,[28] whether altruistic or not, signified a relinquishment of technique as the prime value of artistic merit.

By revealing everything about the 'how', might Cellini have been asserting that the creative driving force behind an artefact was the will and vision of the individual? Were this to be the case, it would have been another important step towards contemporary practice, where jewellery becomes a vehicle for self-expression.

As well as setting out his stall as a major theoretician, Cellini was a gifted virtuoso maker who, according to John Hayward, introduced 'conceptions that are fundamental to Mannerist philosophy: the duty of the artist to express noble and beautiful ideas, the importance of the conception (*concetto*) underlying the work'.[29] Naturally, the latter is most important to the subsequent evolution of contemporary jewellery, though Cellini's vision had to wait almost two hundred years to be realized with the industrialization of Europe, which brought the next groundbreaking developments.

## The Seventeenth Century

In the meantime, the wider dispersion of pattern books throughout Europe continued apace in the seventeenth century. This meant that a given style of jewellery could simultaneously become diffuse in many countries, leading to a greater homogenization in the production of jewellery. Pattern books also served to spread the work and influence of the originating designer. One example of this was the diffusion of the floral style *schotenwerk*, which was first documented in 1621 by the Strasburg jeweller Peter Symony.[30] The style originated in the Low Countries, having developed out of tulip-mania, but it spread far beyond these geographical borders. Overall, pattern books became a visual story of the evolution of design and showed how jewellery had become ever more abstracted from the source of its inspiration, as in the 1626 designs for jewellery by Balthasar Lemercier.[31] Even then (as now) these books would have provided a research tool for the study of jewellery, which in effect gave impetus to the medium and its history.

In contrast to this reduction in variety was the continued existence of popular traditional and folk jewellery. The individuality of those items became stronger through the significance of their cultural identity, the latter fortifying their continued existence.

## The Industrial Revolution

As it did with most trades, the advent of the Industrial Revolution influenced the production of jewellery in Northern Europe. The changes were initially most acute in Britain, beginning from the mid-eighteenth century and subsequently affecting manufacturing in France and beyond. The primary change was of course mechanized production, which enabled the mass production of jewellery. Combined with new techniques and the incorporation of hitherto unused materials, it assisted the boundaries of jewellery to rapidly expand. These developments were accelerated by the emergence of a middle class with disposable income who were keen to purchase the latest fashions of what became known as costume jewellery. This marked a significant shift in the values ascribed to jewellery from symbolic, economic or functional towards qualities more readily associated with fashion.

Whilst the transition towards aesthetics denoting value was a major shift in thinking, it was less likely to have incorporated self-expression. This was mainly because early machines were fairly rudimentary, requiring designs to be conceived accordingly. Therefore, any drawing had to be readable by the pattern maker or engineer and consequently be explicit in form and dimensions. So, even though aesthetics had become one arbiter of value, it remained at the service of the machine. This stricture would no doubt have been enthusiastically enforced by industrialists keen to ensure the efficacy of their workshop machinery. Design and its communication through drawing had to foresee and accommodate technical problems, both to minimize losses during production and to enable speedy manufacture. Inevitably, this resulted in some regression in the general virtuosity of craft artefacts.

Another development that could be perceived negatively is that, unlike handicraft production, with the machine there would have been little or no opportunity for intuition and chance to intervene in the shaping of the finished object. What emerged was absolutely preordained during the design process, cementing the distinction between the design and manufacturing phases that had begun with Renaissance pattern books. An early example occurred in the 1750s, when the invention of transfer printing was embedded into enamelling. Some of the resulting jewellery and trinkets are still known as Bilston enamel after the Midlands town in England, which became a centre of production. The photographic reproduction of the source image meant that brushstrokes and the signs of the hand with all its warmth and idiosyncrasies were eliminated. Consider for example the chatelaine in Fig. 8, where the quality of the enamelled image is pristine to the point of perhaps being soulless. Intriguingly, it is a decorated ornament, but it is not decorative. Chatelaines were waist-hung objects that contained a range of tools often including bodkins, tweezers, knives, nail files, toothpicks and other assorted sewing or grooming implements.

**Fig. 8**
*Chatelaine* 1760. South
Staffordshire enamel. Image
courtesy of Wolverhampton
Arts and Museums Service.
Photo: Luke Unsworth.

These complex and functional assemblies were effectively tantamount to modern-day Swiss army knives or travel sewing kits.

## Material Developments

The increasing mechanization of many jewellery techniques broadened the range of materials available to jewellers and the ways in
which they could be used. The most notable innovations included
both cast and cut steel and the increasingly sophisticated application of glass paste stones in costume jewellery. This may have led
to a kind of jewellery that I describe as having metaphorical value,
whereby the metaphor was not sustained by a narrative or figurative equivalent but rather stood in for a more precious material.
Consequently, it signalled a redemocratization towards jewellery's
earliest origins.

One example of this metaphorical jewellery aimed to simulate precious cut stones using highly polished faceted steel. Attempts to replicate the visual qualities of diamonds and their response to light were central to this form of jewellery, which responded to the prevalent taste for diamonds in courtly jewellery during the eighteenth century. Commonly referred to as cut steel jewellery, it was inspired by the use of marcasite to substitute for diamonds. Mechanization greatly speeded its manufacture and enabled this hard alloy to be worked with surprising dexterity, as can be seen in the glinting and bejewelled head of the pin in Fig. 9. The designers of these pieces deliberately attempted to enable their steel jewels to sparkle brightly, thereby appearing to trap light in a similar way to diamonds. This dazzling effect was achieved by first cutting crude facets at varying angles and then polishing the steel heads to a high sheen. This process, along with the close packing of multiple heads, meant that light could be directly reflected back to the observer or wearer from a variety of viewpoints – a phenomenon much enhanced by the movement of either party.

The development of cut steel jewellery was aided substantially by advancing mechanization. For example, according to Clare Phillips, the Birmingham firm of Matthew Boulton was the first to use steam power to drive the polishing machines in the 1770s.[32] Boulton was a new breed of design entrepreneur and industrialist, and the title he gave to his centre of production in Handsworth, Birmingham, around 1765 gives an indication of the scale and ambition of his enterprise: the Soho Manufactory.[33] Its professionalism was mirrored in the extensive pattern books developed over

**Fig. 9**
*Hat Pin* (detail) 1700s. Cut steel. Probably Wolverhampton, United Kingdom. Image courtesy of Wolverhampton Arts and Museums Service. Photo: Luke Unsworth.

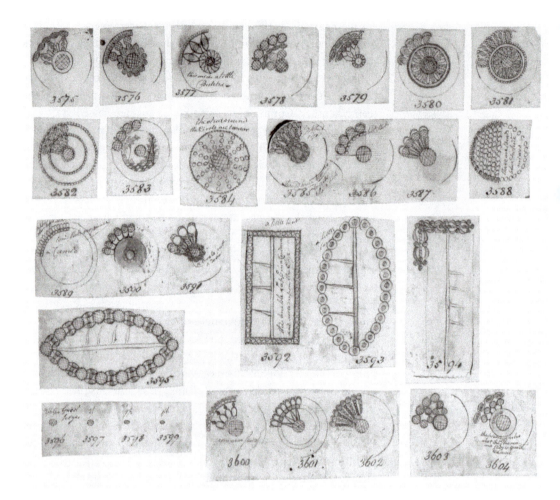

**Fig. 10**

*Design from Pattern Book*
(supposed to be for brooches
and buttons). Matthew
Boulton Archive. ca 1775.
Photo: Reproduced with the
permission of Birmingham
Libraries and Archives.

decades by the firm's designers. The delicate and beautiful drawings in these books give valuable insight into the preconceived
design of objects, as well as the consequences of the separation of
hand and mind.[34] The designs for jewellery often included indica-
tions for the plethora of steel 'gems' to be used to decorate a piece,
as can be seen in the brooches, buckles, buttons and pommels
in Fig. 10. Boulton eagerly sought innovation to help refine his
manufacturing processes, including those for jewellery.[35] Whilst
the steel faux gemstones were initially produced individually,
subsequent developments in machinery meant that multiple runs
of heads could be produced in batches, thereby eliminating the
laborious need for individually fixed rivets.[36] This obviously accelerated the mass production of jewellery.

A second example of metaphorical value in jewellery involved
the reintroduction of glass, albeit in a much more sophisticated

manifestation than its previous incarnations. Glass had previously featured in Roman and Anglo-Saxon jewellery as threaded beads, but the type developed by George Frédéric Stras was particularly hard and therefore receptive to faceting and polishing.[37] This meant it could imitate the brilliance of precious stones and take the sophisticated cuts used on diamonds, all at a relatively low cost. Machine cutting meant that glass stones of regular form and consistent dimensions could be produced in large quantities, thereby providing real choices that consequently accelerated jewellery design as a profession. Indeed, according to Judith Miller, in France, 'by the 1760s over 300 jewellers and designers belonged to the guild of faux jewellers.'[38]

Additionally, the mechanized production of glass paste stones at an industrial level reduced costs through economies of scale, with the result that this jewellery became affordable to a larger proportion of the population, especially the burgeoning and relatively wealthy middle classes. Of course, luxurious jewellery of the highest quality continued, as did symbolic jewellery that celebrated birth, baptism and marriage or marked acts of heroism and ultimately death. Intriguingly, their continued existence partly liberated costume jewellery from fiscal, symbolic or investment responsibilities. This jewellery could be entirely for decorative purposes and the embellishment of one's appearance. With increases in consumer spending, designs could be updated more frequently, meaning costume jewellery became associated with fashion and clothing. The high turnover of designs and reduced expectation that the finished pieces should last a lifetime helped liberate designers, encouraging them to be more experimental and extravagant.

Another relatively affordable material that was commandeered for the purposes of jewellery was iron. Berlin iron jewellery sought to replicate the geometry and qualities of one medium with another material: in this case, using cast iron filigree to simulate lace. The designs took inspiration from sources including architectural tracery, fruits, flowers and cameos. The delicacy, intricacy and sophistication of the resulting lattice designs meant that, in order to successfully sand cast them, the designer had to foresee the eventual placement of runners and risers and moderate their designs accordingly to ensure the molten metal would flow throughout the mould.[39] Subsequently, the sand-cast components could be mechanically assembled and varying juxtapositions of parts could be made.[40] This sophisticated production elevated a relatively cheap material through technical mastery and the design process. This enabled the designs and artefacts of individual designers such as Siméon Pierre Devaranne and Johann Conrad Geiss to become fairly widespread. Works such as Geiss's bracelet from about

**Fig. 11**
Johann Conrad Geiss. ca
1820–30. Iron. *Bracelet.*
Photo: © Victoria and Albert
Museum, London.

1820–30, Fig. 11, demonstrate the proficiency of casting that had been achieved and the effects resulting from combining voluminous forms and more delicate filigree elements. The willingness to pursue hitherto unseen designs in unusual materials through Berlin iron and cut steel jewellery may partially have derived from their evolution from existing trades and the involvement of skilled craftspeople who were not originally trained as jewellers.

As previously indicated, the invention of costume and steel jewellery marked a shift in thinking whereby the value of a piece was not exclusively defined in monetary terms. Rather, it subtly shifted to the veracity of the simulation of using one material to stand in for another, which therefore meant value was partially defined by what was done to a material. The production of what I describe as 'eye candy fakes' was also accompanied by events that almost seem like antecedents for the contemporary use of so-called poor materials. A case in point was that of the renowned Berlin iron jewellery issued in Germany between 1813 and 1815. The Prussian royal family beseeched its subjects to surrender their gold jewellery to fund the uprising against Napoleon's occupation. Donations were met with exchanges of iron jewellery, sometimes inscribed on the back with *Gold gab ich für Eisen* (I gave gold for iron). Filigree iron pieces were transformed into symbols of loyalty and patriotism through their connection with gold. Similar looting of golden heirlooms has undoubtedly persisted throughout history, but perhaps not without anything quite so symbolic given in return.

The Industrial Revolution obviously laid down vital foundations for contemporary jewellery by giving authority to jewellery design. What began centuries earlier with the emergence of pattern books was fortified by the advent of mechanization, whereby the machine stood in for the human act of making in the distinction between mind and hand. The potential for design to blossom was also greatly accelerated by the mechanical production of a huge range of glass paste stones and the invention of the gold substitute, pinchbeck.[41] These technological developments continued through the nineteenth century, further increasing possibilities through electroplating, jet (a black glass enamel) and Parian ware (a type of mouldable porcelain). It was also a period in which mechanized production meant it became advantageous to reinvigorate antique techniques such as filigree. The latter for example meant that large quantities of voluminous and visually heavy gold jewellery could be produced quickly and from relatively small quantities of gold.

These technological developments were widely disseminated throughout Europe through international expositions in the latter half of the nineteenth century. Notable amongst these were London's Great Exhibition of 1851, followed by the Universal Exhibition in Paris in 1867. These events provided a showcase for the promotion of new materials, forms and techniques across a broad range of crafts, design and industries; promoting new typologies such as mourning jewellery; initiating intercontinental trade and further validating mechanized production. Notwithstanding these developments and the advances they brought in jewellery, the initial fascination and wonder for non-handmade 'authorless' products eventually led to concerns relating to authorship and ultimately rejection by some critics and makers, including John Ruskin and William Morris, followed by the protagonists of Art Nouveau.[42]

## René Lalique

One reaction against the perceived lack of humanity of mechanized production in comparison to lovingly handcrafted artefacts was heralded by Art Nouveau in the 1880s. Its protagonists sought to elevate the decorative arts through a mastery of hand techniques. The jewellery of its leading light, René Lalique, was for instance the antithesis of the mass produced and was instead the pinnacle of handmade and exclusive luxury.[43] Lalique excelled by uniting traditional goldsmithing with glass elements to incorporate translucency and light into fantasies of his personal virtuosity. The sinuous whiplash lines in his jewellery are symbolic of his visual language, which constituted the personal expression not of sociopolitical or autobiographical signifiers but aesthetic preferences.

## 1920s and 1930s

In the late 1920s and early 1930s, several jewellers in France, including Gerard Sandoz, Raymond Templier and Jean Després, evolved distinctly personal styles. Sandoz is particularly intriguing because he represented a new figure in jewellery; he not only made jewellery but also undertook research, created manifestos and wrote about its production. Admittedly, centuries earlier, Theophilus Presbyter and Cellini had written treatises on goldsmithing;[44] however, these focused on technique and method, whereas Sandoz was more concerned with context and the social role of jewellery. One of his contentions about the value of materials effectively preempts one of contemporary jewellery's core principles: that the object as an entity should guide the selection of its materials rather than any canonical or economic prejudices. Sandoz wrote forthrightly on this matter in 1929, stating, 'let us have no preconceptions as to materials. Personally, I consider that before everything else, one must think of the line and the general volume of the piece of jewellery to be created.'[45] This is mirrored in a broader context by the manifesto of *Uniones Artists Moderne,* in which a group of jewellery artists who counted Sandoz amongst their founding members asserted that 'a beautiful material is not necessarily rare or precious. It is above all a material whose natural qualities or whose adaptability to industrial processes are pleasing to the eye and to the touch, and whose value derives from judicious use.'[46] In other words, the value of jewellery could derive from the actions of a sensitive maker, irrespective of any intrinsic material worth.

Examining Jean Després's jewellery, it seems he too shared Sandoz's opinion, because the constituent materials appear to have been selected for their chromatic values and the compositional relationships they could establish. Després departed from the floral and curvilinear influences of Art Nouveau, inspired instead by his mechanical past as an aeroplane designer. The allusion to cogs, gears and other machine parts can be self-evident, as in the *Crankshaft Brooch* of 1930, Fig. 12, which features an asymmetric design atop a pitted surface that is synonymous with sand-cast engine parts.

One final figure of note during this period was the jeweller Naum Slutzky, who had worked in the precious metals workshop at the Bauhaus. The influence of Bauhaus design ideology is evident in the lack of ornamentation in his elemental pieces, which are often typified by movable parts. Central to Slutzky's innovation was his virtually unprecedented use of materials such as chromium-plated or silver-plated base metals. Aesthetically, his work seems synonymous with industrial units or prefabricated

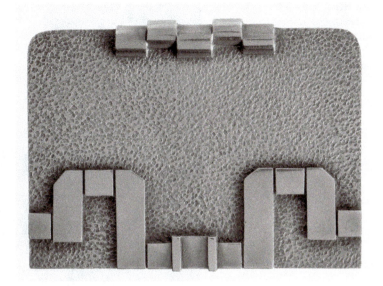

parts, where the repetition of an industrial tubular unit results in a refined and simple composition. This effect is visible in Slutzky's 1930 necklace, Fig. 13, where the simple geometry of the orthogonal pendant contrasts with the angularity of its chain.

Intriguingly, Slutzky's jewellery would seem to be acutely affected by being worn or not. So much so that dual states exist: when disconnected from the body, it may seem cold and somehow jagged, yet this seemingly harsh appearance is softened by contact with the body. In fact, it actually provokes a dynamic contrast between the sinuosity of the body and the geometric rigidity of Slutzky's work. Much in the same way as a Renaissance grid provides a harmonic counterbalance between curve and orthogonal geometry, the straight, zigzag and dotted lines of Slutzky's work overlay the body's fluid curvature. Whether simply a by-product of his fascination for the geometric and mechanical or specifically intended, Slutzky produced pieces indicative of a jeweller concerned with corporeal relationships and how jewellery could shape them meaningfully. This sensibility is indicative of certain types of contemporary jewellery that followed.

What unites these jewellers is how their work seems to reflect the broader context of its time of manufacture. The movement of line and resultant geometry is dynamic and complements the accelerating velocity that permeated life in the machine age. However, whilst the imbuing of social resonance is another step towards the expressive ethos of contemporary jewellery, these pieces still

**Fig. 13**

Naum Slutzky. *Necklace* 1930.
Chromium-plated brass tubing.
Photo: © Victoria and Albert
Museum, London.

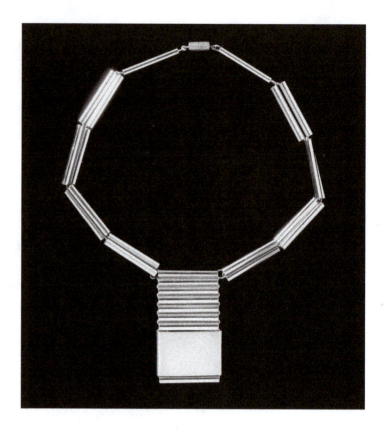

appear conditioned by traditional precepts of what beautiful jewellery should be.

## Postwar Developments

This section explores the history of jewellery after the Second World War and discusses how the jewellery practice that is generally considered to be contemporary emerged from the rebuilding of Europe. Inevitably, the ravages inflicted by the war affected all aspects of society and creative production within it. Whilst the resurrection of physical infrastructures could be initiated almost immediately, the reconstruction of artistic pathways took somewhat longer. After the inevitably slow recovery, an increase in makers occurred in the 1950s, and a range of subtly hybrid works emerged. Nonetheless, certain key practitioners initiated an approach that diverged from the functional notions of jewellery being wearable, valuable and decorative.

Whilst expectations about jewellery were not fully subverted in the postwar period, considerable challenges were laid down to traditional values. In the case of Sigurd Persson and Torun Bülow-Hübe, this often involved the production of sinuous abstract forms that were synonymous with modernist sculpture and produced predominantly in silver rather than gold. Max Fröhlich also created abstract jewels through elemental, curvilinear and sometimes kinetic geometries that seem indicative of mathematical figures. The value in these jewellers' works derived from the geometry and qualities of their formal languages rather than the commodity of its materials.

Another subversive strand of activity came from the wide range of fine artists who began to produce works in jewellery in the decade following the war. Amongst these were Afro, Arp, Braque, Dalí, Fontana and the Pomodoro brothers. Being primarily painters or sculptors, these artists were not preconditioned by the rules of the medium, and this encouraged an expressive freedom and spontaneity of form in their jewellery. This style, as in the case of the Pomodoro brothers, often manifested itself through the translation of the qualities of drawn, painted and sculpted marks into metal. Similar qualities are also evident in the jewellery of makers such as Ebbe Weiss-Weingart; her abstract jewellery during this period is typified by fluid textural surfaces that allude to molten alloys or even scrunched-up foil.[47]

As the 1960s progressed, the initial signs of a new kind of practice emerged in which the traditionally accepted norms of fiscal value, permanence, wearability, unrelatedness to the body, aesthetic beauty and decoration were directly challenged. Jewellers such as Friedrich Becker, Hermann Jünger and Mario Pinton began producing jewellery that subverted these precepts. This led to a gathering momentum that achieved critical mass with the addition of other jewellers in the late 1960s, who further confronted the previously sacrosanct characteristics of jewellery through content-driven work; exemplified by Gijs Bakker. At this stage in history, the work of certain jewellers loosely coalesces to imply two divergent branches of evolution. The first projects self-expressive content often relating to sociopolitical conditions, world events, body relationships or autobiography (jewellery as content). The second group incorporates a sensitive manipulation of materials, techniques and the formal relationships within a piece (sensitized jewellery).

## Jewellery as Content

As its name suggests, this category of contemporary jewellery is characterized by the meanings it encapsulates and projects. The integration of the makers' ideas and sensibilities about sociopolitical conditions, world events or autobiographical musings became central to defining the work's appearance – to the extent that some traditional values of jewellery, such as beauty and function, were almost discarded. Indeed, some of the jewellers appear to have deliberately adopted a confrontational and radical approach to the previously accepted norms of jewellery practice. That said, the reincorporation of content also returned body decoration to some of its signifying origins, when jewellery communicated specific information such as rank, allegiances or acts of heroism. Generally, the constituent materials of jewellery as content have been selected according to the underlying concept and to facilitate its successful communication.

Consequently, as the range of meanings in the work diversified, so did innovation in the selection of materials. An exploration of the human body also began to condition the work, placing increased emphasis on the relationships between the piece and the wearer. This has often manifested itself through jewellery of large dimensions, which extended beyond the traditional comforts and convenience of small-scale objects. A complementary exploration of jewellery for unexpected parts of the body has also persisted. The earliest exemplars, such as Gijs Bakker, Emmy van Leersum and Peter Skubic, helped bring this new kind of jewellery to fruition from the mid- to late 1960s onwards. They were swiftly followed by makers such as Onno Boekhoudt, Otto Künzli, Ruudt Peters and Bernhard Schobinger through to the more recent talents of Ted Noten and Christoph Zellweger. The following analysis of their works considers three themes: the body, value and jewellery as social commentary.

## The Body

Central to the measured exploration of the body in contemporary jewellery was Gijs Bakker. Whilst his early work appears to show some influence of the modern jewellery designs of Sigurd Persson and Torun Bülow-Hübe, a significant departure was marked in 1967 by a series of large, almost oversize, collars which frame the wearer. They were raised from aluminium sheets, and whilst an unusual material choice, perhaps their most striking aspect is their sheer size. Conceived to assert the individuality of the wearer, pieces such as *Shoulder Piece, 1967,* were intended to focus attention on the wearer's face through dramatic framing. Similarly theatrical pieces were conceived and made in union with Bakker's wife Emmy van Leersum, who described how she 'wanted to give jewellery the same importance as clothing, I made big objects which followed the shape of the human body. This resulted in the design of clothing as a unified whole.'[48]

Together, Bakker and van Leersum went on to collaborate on the frontier work *Clothing Suggestions, 1969–70*, Fig. 14, which consisted of several full body costumes with growthlike protuberances projecting from various body parts, such as the knees or elbows. Planar discs were also inserted into the body socks at differing heights to dramatically alter the profile of the body. The work commented on the role and value of clothing in ornamenting the body. van Leersum was actively aware of her radical approach, stating, 'I liberated myself from a number of restrictions concerning the traditional use of forms and materials...For me the idea is the most important element, the process of making the pieces comes second, too much emphasis has come to lie on pure craftsmanship in the course of time.'[49] Her comment asserts how determined these jewellers were to break away from traditional approaches to jewellery.

Taking a prompt from the *Clothing Suggestions,* van Leersum's subsequent works considered the body to be composed of simplified geometric solids. She drew particular inspiration from the conical

**Fig. 14**
Gijs Bakker and Emmy van Leersum. *Clothing Suggestions* 1970 (one-off). Polyester, nylon, cork, plastic, wood. Executed by Charles Bergmans and Tiny Leeuwenkamp.
Photo: Ton Baadenhuysen.

nature of the forearm, describing how 'the conic form of the arm intrigues me tremendously. The basic prefabricated tube is cylindrical, so I find systems to transform the cylinder into a conical form.'[50] The resulting metal tubular jewellery from 1970–5 was mathematically defined in advance by controlling the placement of subtle cuts, which then enabled tubes to be folded or bent into conical sections. Aesthetically, they appear very different from her preceding jewellery, having little or no surface decoration and precise elemental geometry. This difference is heightened by the jewellery's resemblance to autonomous and singular sculptures and its apparent lack of functional elements. van Leersum rejected the latter, stating, 'fastenings bothered me – they struck me as disturbing features, both technically and visually, so I either avoided them altogether or made them an essential part of the design as a whole'.[51] Her production of jewellery from nonprecious metals and transparent plastics meant more affordable pieces, through which she announced her rejection of the status symbol in favour of a more democratic everyday product.[52]

In contrast to the physical presence of van Leersum's jewellery, Bakker's next notable innovation, and there are plenty, was his ethereal *Shadow Jewellery* of 1973, Fig. 15. An arresting work in

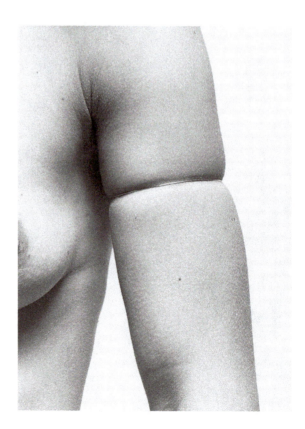

**Fig. 15**
Gijs Bakker. *Shadow Jewellery*
1973. Yellow gold 585 (limited
numbered edition).
Photo: Ton Baadenhuysen.

which the effect left by wearing the object is the work rather than the object itself. A constrictive metal ligature is placed around the circumference of an arm, a leg or the torso, which upon removal reveals its imprint in the wearer's flesh and reddened skin. Significantly, it is an ephemeral work, devoid of the generational permanence of jewellery that commemorates or serves as an investment. Bakker states it originated from the 'wish to make an invisible piece of jewellery, at last to find a form on the body which makes a change to the body. The changed body has to be more visible than the piece of jewellery.'[53]

Bakker's subsequent evolution concerned personalized jewellery, which was achieved by tracing the silhouette of a person's face, centrally, across its vertical and horizontal axes. Therefore, in the case of *Profile Ornament for Emmy van Leersum*, 1974, the resulting skeletal cage is not just made for an individual; it only truly fits one person, who, of course, is Emmy van Leersum. His concern for the body in specifics continued with the *Bibs* he created in 1976; these bore a photo of the wearer's naked chest, bringing the ordinarily hidden exterior to outside attention.

In some respects, Peter Skubic did the inverse of Bakker's bibs, taking what ordinarily remains external to the body and literally taking it inside. As the title suggests, his 1975 action *Jewellery under the Skin*, Fig. 16, entailed the insertion of a stainless steel implant under the skin of Skubic's forearm. This took the role of the body as a location for jewellery to an extreme, before a subsequent operation seven years later reversed the procedure.[54] As well as referencing jewels that mutilate the body, Skubic's gesture also

**Fig. 16**
Peter Skubic. *Jewellery under the Skin.* Implanted
4 November 1975, removed
27 May 1982. Stainless steel implant.
Photo: Harry Ertl.

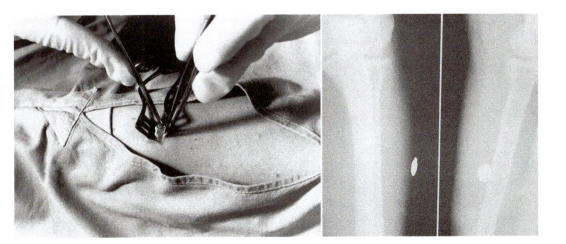

explored jewellery's frequent lack of visible presence – a matter about which he wrote:

> Jewellery can be invisible, when either worn in a concealed place, buried, or locked in safekeeping, or even be surgically placed and worn under the skin surface...The physical state of jewellery can be achieved by means of injury, such as through ornamental scars, tattooing, the filing off of teeth and today even through piercing – and lastly through an operation such as surgically inserting a decorative element.[55]

In 1976, the following year, David Watkins dealt with the body in its entirety by producing large ornaments such as *Hinged Interlocking Body Piece,* Fig. 17. It interacts with and encapsulates the upper body, treating it as the fully three-dimensional object it is. This contrasts the jewellery typologies that rest on the surface of a specific body part as bracelets and necklaces invariably do. The hinged linear structure jerkily maps out the solid components of the body, passing around, over and behind the upper torso, taking jewellery on a journey around the body. This roving quality was further emphasized by the wearer's movement.[56]

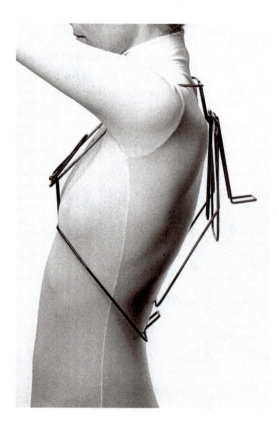

**Fig. 17**
David Watkins. *Hinged Interlocking Body Piece* 1976. Steel. Body piece. Photo: Michael Hallson.

Overall, these varied key works testify to the increasingly dynamic and charged relationship between the wearer, the body and the jewellery that began to emerge after 1967. Of major significance was how the jewellery actually started to do something physically to the body or affect the wearer's perception of his own body rather than merely resting where it was placed.

## Value

Some jewellers are quite aggressive in confronting the traditional value of precious metals and stones, and perhaps understandably so given the length of time such materials had been held sacrosanct. Bakker's previously discussed aluminium collars of 1967 were a portent of the relatively poor materials to follow. In fact, his *Stovepipe Necklace* of the same year was fabricated from standard units of industrial ventilation pipe, which subverted conventional expectations of what materials jewellery should be made from. This type of work achieved a kind of apotheosis with Giuseppe Uncini's works from 1968, which feature silver cages that were oxidized to look like iron and then filled with concrete. Their rigorous aesthetic and materials derive from the reinforced concrete used in buildings.[57]

Industrial materials are also crucial to the jewellery of Peter Skubic, who began working in stainless steel in the early 1970s. The constituent parts of the resulting works are often held together under the tension of springs, magnets and tied steel rope. These functional elements also give the work a theatrical nature, and, because there is no solder or welding, the act of making becomes a kind of conceptual revelation of its own production. Consequently, as interesting as Skubic's work undoubtedly is, it is not instantly recognizable as jewellery. It could easily be something else, and this is one of its distinguishing qualities. For example consider the brooch *Münchhausen,* 1980, Fig. 18, which might well be a mechanical part or found object.

Perhaps Lous Martin took the democratization of jewellery to its inevitable conclusion by selling a jewellery kit that the purchaser had to assemble. *Do It Yourself,* 1974, consisted of a flat aluminium necklace and bracelet, each with predrilled holes and a number of pipe cleaners. These were to be threaded by the buyer to complete the jewellery according to Martin's instructions. Naturally, the owner could follow the suggested patterns or create their own.

In 1977, Bakker again contributed to developments with a series of large neckpieces that were each composed of a laminated photograph of a bejewelled queen – a process through which sparkling and priceless jewels were transposed into almost throwaway materials,

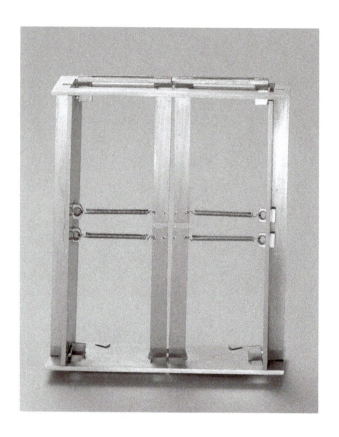

accessible to all. Bakker's work dryly chides, as he notes: 'I went to a shop selling royal memorabilia and got photographs of reigning queens…I then laminated the photographs in PVC and, for quite a reasonable price, you can have the feeling of royalty. You can be part of it.'[58] Perhaps the most iconic attack on the status symbol in jewellery, and the indiscriminate use of gold, was Künzli's *Gold Makes You Blind*, 1980, Fig. 19, which encapsulates a spherical bead of gold in an opaque black rubber bracelet. The patently cheap rubber contrasts the colour, lustre and value of that which remains hidden.[59] Künzli describes the work as returning gold to the geological darkness from where it came.[60] In some ways, the work represents a re-appropriation of gold, but it is also a sophisticated attack on preciousness, using gold to denigrate gold.

The durability of even relatively inexpensive materials still provides some sense of security. For example, whilst materials such as plastic or wood may not be indestructible or permanent, they can last for a long time. So, perhaps in seeking to identify jewellery that actively opposes the notion of value, we should look to genuinely ephemeral works such as Pierre Degen's self-explanatory *Ring in Bread, Jam, Elastic and Ribbon*, 1982. Other examples include

David Watkins and Wendy Ramshaw's paper jewellery and Susan Heron's experiments with light projected onto the body. Finally, self-destructing works such as Bernard Fink's ice ring *Eis*, 1996, or the *Siberian Necklace*, 2006, Fig. 20, by Ted Noten conclude the argument. Being made of ice, they both melt when worn; the former disappears for good, whereas Noten's necklace is irrevocably changed, revealing the mysterious content that was previously frozen within the giant beads of ice.

## Jewellery as Social Commentary

There are some makers for whom jewellery has become a vehicle for the delivery of content that often relates to prevalent social conditions, politics, major world events, philosophical questions or autobiographical documentation. Early protagonists of note include Bruno Martinazzi, Bernhard Schobinger, Otto Künzli, Manfred Bischoff and Ruudt Peters.

The first significant creator of this type of jewellery was Bruno Martinazzi. His jewellery often includes reconstituted fragments of the human body, which are combined with methods of

measurement to infer philosophical themes. These have included the creation of man, god and man's intelligence for example. The bracelet *Homo Sapiens,* 1975, features a thumb and fore-finger almost touching in a circle, as if pinching. The piece explores the evolutionary advantage humans gained from having opposable fingers and thumbs and how this has enabled us to create and use tools to shape the world around us. Martinazzi has also metaphorically used weights, rules and standard measures to stand in for geological timescales and molecular, continental and even cosmological dimensions, as in the necklace, *Misure,* 1977, Fig. 21. Literature has provided rich material too, including Greek mythology and tracts such as Homer's *The Odyssey,* alongside science and Kant's writing on the sublime. These fertile and varied sources have influenced many of Martinazzi's pieces, including the brooch *Mela,* 1972, which takes the form of an apple with a slice cut out. Figures, measurements and mathematical curves have been engraved into the polished inner faces. A complex work, it refers to notions of rationality and Newton's eureka moment of discovering gravity; one imagines it may also symbolically relate to the forbidden fruit of Adam and Eve.

**Fig. 21**
Bruno Martinazzi. *Misure* 1977.
White gold, pink gold, Levanto
red marble. Necklace.
Photo: Bruno Martinazzi.

The jewellery of Martinazzi appears to be nourished by a deep-seated rationale where the conceptual underpinning is implicit rather than explicit. In contrast, the jewel as an idea was formalized by the *Bond van Ontevreden Edlesmeden* (League of Rebellious Goldsmiths, or BOE[61]) in 1973 through their boxed manifesto *BOE Box,* where on its lid was written: 'The BOE is a group of four goldsmiths and one sculptor who wish, through the more personal presentation of their work, including the necessary information, to broaden the normal manner of exhibition, to make it a manifestation of ideas.'[62] The BOE was in part a reaction against the prevalence of the so-called smooth jewellery by jewellers such as Emmy van Leersum, which they believed to be characterized by restrained and minimal geometry.

There is certainly little reductive anonymity in the work of Bernhard Schobinger; rather, he seems a potent mix of shaman, storyteller, soothsayer and comedian. His works can often seem visually confrontational and have variously incorporated found objects such as a bicycle pump valve, miniature paint pot, toothbrush, colouring pencils or computer parts (see Plate 23 and Figs 85–87). His assemblages are frequently composed of items and materials not readily associated with jewellery, even going as far as to include meteorites, saw blades, broken bottles or shards of glass if they could potentially contribute to the manifestation of a given concept. Meditations on the contradictory and often violent world that surrounds us have included jewellery made in response to the Cambodian genocide for example. Yet, despite the gravitas of this content, many pieces exhibit considerable wit and irony. The subject of Schobinger's work can be as diverse as the materials that constitute it, including science, cosmology, belief systems and world events to name but a few. Overall, Schobinger's jewellery is challenging, elusive, romantic and thought provoking in equal measure.

Another jeweller whose works can be politically charged is Otto Künzli; perhaps more of a social analyst, he uses jewellery as a vehicle for his thoughts. His expressive language took shape in the early 1980s and is evidently the product of cognition and preconceived design, whereby everything about the work is put at the disposal of the idea. In other words, manufacture asserts the initiating idea. One early piece from 1980, *The Red Spot*, Fig. 22, commented on the pressures to sell in commercial galleries. Despite the technical excellence evident in his later works, on this occasion Künzli used a throwaway object in the form of a red

**Fig. 22**
Otto Künzli. *The Red Spot*
1980. Pin, rubber. Brooch.

drawing pin. The resulting object is disarmingly simple, but effective, with the work's production sustaining the idea of translating red-dot sales stickers into jewellery. Künzli has also extensively questioned the role of jewellery and the generally accepted conditions of its existence, as with the *Wallpaper Brooches* from 1983, Plate 14.

A distinct and individual language has also been developed by Manfred Bischoff, using a reduced palette of gold, silver, coral and ivory to create metaphorical works that originate from drawing, as in *Il Mio Casa,* 1986. More recently, the role of drawing has become explicit with pieces of jewellery exhibited upon their originating drawing. The latter, in combination with the work and its title combine to narrate the story Bischoff wishes to tell. This tends to include historical figures and events and philosophical considerations explored through universally recognizable symbols ranging from the infinity symbol to a television set. Were it not for the ever-present narrative content, his work could easily be associated with sensitized jewellery given the exquisite range of surfaces and textures he achieves in gold and silver; consider for example the exterior of the brooch *Kun,* 2005, Plate 6.

Beyond the synthesis of form and content, what is also interesting about this group of jewellers is how they have dealt with traditional notions of beauty. For centuries, jewellery had been synonymous with joy and beauty, largely achieved through a blend of gold and brightly coloured luminous stones. Whilst not necessarily rejected outright, these jewellers are by no means blindly adherent to the aforementioned doctrine. For the first time, a lack of harmonious proportions, brilliant surfaces or luminous colours, or what might even be described as ugliness, could be considered a desired quality if it helped encapsulate the work's concept. In other words, even aesthetics was to be subject to capturing and communicating the source idea.

## Sensitized Jewellery

Alongside the postwar emergence of jewellers whose work is defined by the concepts it projects, another group of jewellers was developing another strand of contemporary jewellery. This second group is characterized by a mastery of technique, with the work often being self-referential. The content or ideas portrayed by the work invariably, but not exclusively, concerns the internal relationships between its materials, colours and forms. Rather than being imbued with sociopolitical musings or autobiography – as jewellery as content can be – this work primarily deals with the sensitizing of materials into poetic artefacts. It is less revolutionary and operates more in line with traditional conventions, particularly in terms of scale and the aesthetic values of proportion and harmony. Its senior practitioners include Friedrich Becker, Hermann Jünger, Reinhold Reiling and Mario Pinton; and subsequently Tone Vigeland, Giampaolo Babetto, Robert Smit and Wendy Ramshaw; alongside more recent jewellers such as Liv Blåvarp, Giovanni Corvaja, Karl Fritsch and Annamaria Zanella.

## Friedrich Becker

One of the first major contributions to this category of contemporary jewellery comes through Friedrich Becker's kinetic jewellery. Its first manifestation was described by Becker as 'variable' jewellery, which meant that, by virtue of hinged and pivoting parts, the wearer could manipulate and transform the appearance of the piece. The multipart works date from the early 1960s and could be configured into an almost infinite range of geometries. An example of this is the brooch *Variabler Ansteckschmuck* from 1962, Fig. 23, which consists of a series of circular gold discs that can be rotated in relation to one another by means of spindles, each marked by a ruby. Various configurations of crescents and circles can be revealed by moving the discs around.

**Fig. 23**
Friedrich Becker. *Variabler Ansteckschmuck* 1962. Yellow gold, rubies. Brooch. Photo: George Meister. Owner: Die Neue Sammlung – The International Design Museum Munich. Permanent loan of the Danner-Stiftung.

A subsequent development saw the kinesis in Becker's jewellery derive from the movement of the body, with parts of a piece moving according to the orientation and speed of the adorned body part. The delicate balance and weighting of the internal mechanisms were synonymous with the precision engineering of watch manufacture. Therefore, he clearly employed machine manufacture at the service of his ideas. But his work follows the conventions of aesthetically significant jewellery, being of convenient scale and often incorporating stones and highly polished metals. Where it diverges and innovates is in enabling the wearer, and to some extent the observer, to enjoy a sensory experience of motion and the interplay of parts through technical wizardry. According to Becker, his jewellery involves 'freely swivelling pieces, turning on vertical and horizontal bearings, with centric and eccentric axes, with weights, with impulse balls of platinum; these are the constituents of my jewellery. As the wearer's body moves at random, the kinetic effect is heightened and new and varied sequences of motion take place.'[63] Perhaps most importantly for the advent of contemporary jewellery, they make the wearer an active and ongoing participant in how the work looks and behaves.

## Hermann Jünger

Jünger's work is a paradigm of how materials may be sensitized – in his case, through the successful translation of the sensuous qualities of his watercolour drawings into metals and enamel.[64] The link to drawing was reinforced in his brooches by his frequent use of a planar base from which additional elements were then built up on top, as in the brooch of Fig. 24. The resulting intersections of planes create a play of light and shadows that extend over the surface to animate the source drawing. Jünger's jewellery demonstrates a poetic humanity achieved, I believe, through a combination of its proximity to the drawn mark and painterly signs, the use of non-rigid outlines and the frequent union of multiple and seemingly unrelated elements in one piece. This unusual, unfettered and playful quality is evident in the necklace composed by multiple hanging elements in Fig. 25.

A cursory look at Jünger's jewellery may suggest it is allied to traditionally mercenary preferences for precious materials, given the frequent presence of gold and stones. However, whilst gold is indeed often present, Jünger's highly expressive touch subdues its appearance and softens its exuberance. This quality is often achieved through the application of enamel to gold surfaces. The resulting aesthetic, allied with the seemingly unrefined geometry and presence of imperfections such as holes, scratches and

**Fig. 24**
Hermann Jünger. *Brooch*
1998. Gold, amethyst, uncut
diamond, uncut ruby, sapphire.
Photo: Eva Jünger.

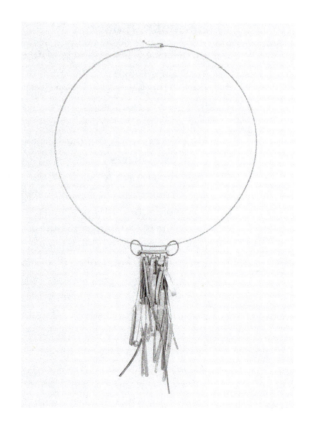

**Fig. 25**
Hermann Jünger. *Necklace*
date unknown, ca 1980. Gold,
silver, ivory.
Photo: Eva Jünger.

simulated wear, give an altogether different value from the merely economic or gold for gold's sake approach. My observation concerning the restrained qualities in Jünger's work appears to be confirmed by his following statement:

> Agates, garnets or rubies, lapis lazuli, granite or haematite pearls…it is the traditional appeal of their colours that makes them so attractive…Provided one does not allow their commercial value to hinder an uninhibited choice of these materials in grouping them together, one can achieve a more colourful appeal than the sum total of high polish, carat weight and flawlessness.[65]

It seems as though all the materials in Jünger's work have yielded to his humanity and the sensitivity of his touch. Confirmation of Jünger's belief in what might be described as the poetic soul in the making process is provided by his comments on technique, which he believed to be 'a far more complex matter than merely the practice and execution of perfect technique'.[66] He went on to assert that 'there are no formulae nor tables, not even recipes for the decisions which finally give an artistic quality to any work. Here everyone is on his own.'[67] Jünger was also influential through his teachings at Munich Art Academy, and together with Reinhold Reiling, his pedagogic ethos encouraged self-expression and the projection of identity through the jewel. Significantly, this philosophy has permeated the jewellery of many of Jünger's and Reiling's students, including Manfred Bischoff, Daniel Kruger and Otto Künzli.

## Mario Pinton

As with Jünger, Pinton is another exemplar of the jeweller who, through the sensibility of his touch, brings materials to life. The animation of surfaces was a vital concern for Pinton throughout his career, and there is a warmth and haptic lightness to his jewellery; one feels with one's eyes that these are delicate objects. This is partly achieved through the sensitivity of mark making and delicate lines that often map his surfaces, shifting imperceptibly from the evident to the almost invisible. Despite their subtlety, these marks modulate light and shadow on the surfaces to make his pieces vibrate, as in the square brooch from 1988, Fig. 26. Similarly expressive qualities can also be seen in Pinton's drawings; consider for example the exploratory sketches in Fig. 27.

**Fig. 26**
Mario Pinton. *Brooch* 1988.
Gold.
Photo: courtesy of the artist.

The geometric figure was invariably employed by Pinton either as a starting point or a framing device. Yet he often instinctively exploited gestalt psychology by intimating a shape and allowing the viewer or wearer to perceptually close the circle or square for example. Other characteristic devices include the subtle distortion of regular shapes or their surface division. The placement of a stone or two onto his relief surfaces is also a common feature, oriented to assert a particular geometric configuration or to demarcate an axis or meridian. Despite them being precious stones, they have nothing to do with ostentation. Indeed, working with faceted stones can be challenging because their intrinsically rich colour and strong light are difficult to control; however, Pinton, through subtle placement and the use of proportionally small gemstones, managed to stop the faceted stones from dominating.

In addition to producing jewellery, Pinton dedicated much of his life to teaching the subject. His influence therefore extended beyond the jewellery he made and into the practices of the students

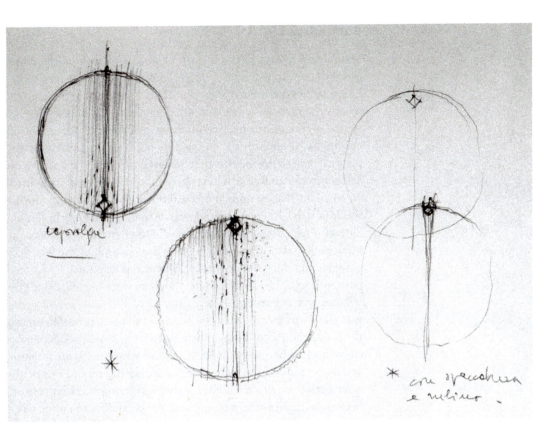

**Fig. 27**
Mario Pinton. *Drawing for Brooch* (detail) 1982.
Photo: courtesy of the artist.

who passed through the school where he taught in Padua, Italy. His impact on the jewellers, collectively known as the Padua School,[68] promoted the principle that design commences from basic geometric shapes and employs geometric structures to restrain or counterbalance the demarcation of shapes and spaces. This was in part transmitted by the use of grids to design two-dimensional shapes and boxed structures to project three-dimensionality onto the page during the design phases. This approach can clearly be seen in the jewellery of Francesco Pavan and Giampaolo Babetto, whose work is often contained by, or refers to, a geometric figure or skeletal solid inferred by structural lines.

What unites the jewellery of Becker, Jünger and Pinton is a curiosity for materials and a desire to animate matter through the consequences of working their chosen materials. Although their specific working practices differed, each contributed to new and rich possibilities in jewellery, seeking evolution from within rather than through referencing external events or ideas. In other words, the work's subject or content is the work itself and the formal relationships that exist within it.

## Summary

Several key events in the history of jewellery, such as the emergence of jewellery designs, pattern books and the Industrial Revolution in Northern Europe, appear to have helped set the stage for what is commonly referred to as contemporary jewellery. A brief synthesis reveals one major shift as the perception of value, which encompassed not only the commodity of precious stones and metals but came to recognize that materials could be imbued with aesthetic, spiritual and narrative significance beyond their fiscal worth. This was prompted by costume and steel jewellery during the Industrial Revolution and was further postulated by Naum Slutzky and others in the 1930s. Another major shift was the gradual division of the goldsmithing profession into the jewellery designer and the jewellery maker. This was precipitated by printed pattern books, in which jewellery designs were recorded and distributed via engravings. The existence of the jewellery designer was given further credence by the advent of mechanization during the Industrial Revolution, which meant that mass-produced jewellery had to be pre-planned. This distinction between thinking and doing activities, which were not necessarily carried out by the same person, sowed the seeds for jewellery as personal expression, because without some precognition, the possibility to imbue work with personal meanings is usually diminished. The latter almost certainly became central to contemporary jewellery, enabling the form of each work to be the expression of the artist's concepts, whether figurative or abstract. These ideas are then manifested through materials, which have been selected to accentuate the given concept rather than for any monetary value.

Since the late 1960s, contemporary jewellery appears to have become manifest through two primary approaches: the sensitization of materials and the imbuing of content. Jewellery as content reveals three primary subjects: the body, the perceived value of jewellery and its materials and finally sociopolitical, contextual and autobiographical meanings. Jewellery as content contains the most revolutionary work in terms of scale and medium, whereas sensitized jewellery operates closer to traditional precepts. The latter does, however, exceed these by heightening the investigation of internal formal relationships between geometry, colour, material properties and proportions.

Irrespective of which of the two aforementioned categories the jewellers adhere to, it is surely the case that contemporary jewellery commences when the expression of their concept, figurative or otherwise, becomes paramount. This means that the geometry, materials and aesthetic of jewellery are selected and developed with the sole intention of transmitting or capturing this concept.

I have discontinued my analysis of contemporary jewellery from the early 1980s onwards because my intention is to let the jewellers discuss these matters through their interviews. Therefore, readers seeking a more comprehensive chronology and critical analysis are recommended to consult the excellent anthologies by Peter Dormer, Helen Drutt and Ralph Turner that are detailed in the bibliography.

In the following interviews, the reader can assess which jewellers, if any, share my contentions. The interviews commence by asking how and why each jeweller began making jewellery and then proceed to explore the working processes and techniques each jeweller favours. Some questions are generic, and others are focused towards the interviewee's practice in an attempt to understand the various manifestations of personal expression and the formal and metaphorical languages that have been created. The discussions feature questions about the relationship between the body and the jewel, the relative importance of function and preferred jewellery typologies. Sources of inspiration, techniques and research methods are also considered, as are the influence of educators and the act of teaching, before the interviews close by soliciting advice for students of jewellery.

# 1

# Giampaolo Babetto

**Born: 1947, Padua, Italy**

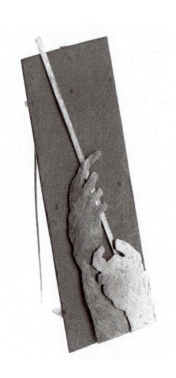

**Fig. 28**
Giampaolo Babetto. *Da Pontormo* 2005. White gold, pigment. Brooch.
Photo: Giustino Chemello.

RB: *You were a student of Professor Mario Pinton in Padova. What did he teach you during your studies?*

GB: A sense of harmonic equilibrium between all the components of the design process and the final object; otherwise it is not an artistic intervention and lacks any sensibility towards the materials. In other words, he taught me how to sensitize everything one touches.

*Other than Pinton, did anyone else help or influence your career?*

GB: One person who was very important was the gallery owner Alberto Carrain from Padua. It was a special relationship because I had an exchange of ideas with him beyond the purely mercantile. He came to see some of my jewellery and bought everything I had created, and this gave me faith in what I was doing. During that period in Padua one could see the works of artists who began to influence me – artists from Arte Programmata, Gruppo Uno from Milan, Gruppo N from Padua, Zero Group from Düsseldorf and the South Americans Raphael Soto and Contreras.

*What inspires your jewellery?*

GB: At the beginning of my career I was interested in repetition, arriving at the limits of materials and things. The early pieces of jewellery were born from observing nature, and as a consequence of my visual sensibility. The process is quite long; I appropriated to create a library of images, which then emerge whilst drawing freely. Once a thing emerges repeatedly, I understand that there is something worth pursuing, so I begin to work, and from this it becomes a piece of jewellery. This was at the beginning; thereafter I became interested in light, transparency, architecture and assembling forms kinetically. For example, a squashed geometrical figure, the flattening is functional – if it were too great it would no longer be functional. I attempt to give function to things if they must have it. In any case, I am interested in creating jewellery that makes one think rather than exclusively self-referential pieces. I have always been interested in architecture, and I believe that I attempt to create architectonic things. In my work, I do not look towards jewellery, but to art in general. I do not seek utopian jewellery; it must also be wearable. That which I attempt to achieve now is harmony between all the parts that constitute a work.

*Could you discuss how you create your jewellery, starting with drawing?*

GB: Drawing is very spontaneous and therefore suggests a method of working and diverse techniques. Drawing is the free part where

I work to find a cue. I have never done the opposite; that is, drawing from an object. Through drawing I try to liberate the form and enable it to become jewellery. In the end, however, my research is more complex because beyond drawing I feel the need to construct and make pieces. Having selected a suitable drawing, I begin working directly at the goldsmith's bench to create the object. During this phase, one can lose the freshness of the drawing, so I seek to align my work with the spirit of the drawing – adapting my techniques accordingly. Personally speaking, I do not use card for models but rather metal, I must file. The material must be stiff and elastic – then its personality can intervene; I don't like soft things.

In my work, there are things that I know and understand and others that I am discovering. Sometimes I work instinctively. When I have a drawing, I do not follow it absolutely, but use it as a guide. I never use material as it is, but always work it.

*Have there been distinct creative phases during your career?*

**GB:** Yes, the first phase was denominated by the ring with the red acrylic; the second phase by the use of very low carat alloys made by melting my mother's jewellery. The third phase involves the jewellery with ebony and geometrical solids that have been squashed, where there is an interplay of optical illusions. The fourth phase is the jewellery born from the works of Pontormo.

*Could you discuss the works dedicated to Pontormo?*

**GB:** For many years I have been attracted to his painting, especially by the use of forms and proportions, because being a mannerist he lengthened and deformed figures with elegance and tension. I created a series of jewellery extrapolating details from his frescoes. In some of the pieces I sought to get close to the colour of the fresco using differing tonalities of alloys. The frescoes in Certosa del Galluzzo have lost their painterly image, so one cannot see the drapery anymore, and sometimes all that remains is masses of colours. In these frescoes one senses the strength of the painter, even if you cannot see everything; you feel the inner soul, as if the spirit of the artist was inside the work. This is what I try to do with my jewellery.

*Where did the desire to use colour in your jewellery come from?*

**GB:** I have used primary colours since 1982. Influenced by an exhibition of Japanese lacquer that I saw in New York, I sought to use contemporary materials to simulate it, and then I used pigments from 1990. For black, I use niello because I like it as a material. I use it unrefined and it seems almost volcanic. I use red and blue as vibrations. Blue creates an imaginary space that draws you into the object.

*Do you feel a particular empathy for Japanese art, and especially the concept of eliminating the unnecessary?*

GB: Yes, but in Japanese art certain things are taken to extremes, and they become very aesthetic, very decorative. They are taken to the maximum of perfection. Personally, I believe in going slightly less towards the extremes.

*Why did you choose to combine materials such as resin and acrylic with precious metals?*

GB: At one point I made some designs with transparent parts. I like to use transparency because it permits a reading of the whole object, and, in order to create them, I thought about what materials might be suitable. I tried glass, but due to its fragility I found it too limiting for my work. In the end I obtained some acrylic – I engraved it and try to give it some material value. Only on a few occasions have I used it untouched and in its natural state.

*Geometry seems to be part of your language; what are the origins of this interest?*

GB: If we are talking about works with simple and rational geometry, I personally experienced this when I discovered works by the artists of Gruppo N, and maybe this is where my interest was born. During the 1970s, I attempted to express tension simply and poetically, and this kind of geometry suited my needs.

*In some of your pieces one has the impression that you are attempting to capture the void; is this so?*

GB: Yes, I have made some pieces to enclose the void – some closed forms to capture a bit of atmosphere, a piece of infinity.

*Could you discuss the concept of repetition and especially in terms of how you have used it?*

GB: I very much like to do one thing many times; it is something that makes me 'fly', as if one can always go a little further. I like limits, and I need a reason to do what I do. This has a connection to my life and the city where I live. I look for chaos, but in the end there is control. I look for the limits so as to exceed them in some way.

*You have spoken disparagingly about decoration; why?*

GB: Well, it's not that I don't like decoration; just that it's not for me and something I don't do.

*Has chance ever played a role in your work?*

GB: There was a series of pieces created between 1995 and 1996 that are like parts of the human body. They were derived from the effects that fire provokes on the surface of very fine sheets of metal, just a few tenths of a millimetre thick. I subjected their surfaces to an uncontrolled deformation thanks to the intense heat of the gas torch. Afterwards, I continued to work the sheets, striking and pulling them by hand. In other words, I worked the gold sheet as though it had a different consistency, such as that of paper. The next stage involved scoring lines on the rear of the sheet; these are engraved to create a ninety-degree channel allowing the metal to be folded over. Then I soldered the folded edges to create boxlike empty objects, which could either become a brooch, bracelet or necklace.

*When you adopted this method of working, to what extent did you allow chance to define the work?*

GB: I started from chance, but then almost immediately after the deformation of the surface I attempted to control the final outcome of the jewellery. An important aspect was to give the surface tactile value until the object became sensitized. This comes even if I use other techniques or materials such as Plexiglas or niello. For example when I work with niello, I use it as though it were a painterly material, therefore I paint with niello to create monochromes.

*With reference to your pieces where there are intersections of various planes created between 2003 and 2005, I noticed that there was a change in the finishing. Why was the sharp edge replaced by a rougher edge?*

GB: In certain cases the sheet was cut sharply, and in others I leave the finish of the edge caused by the hammering and rolling to give the plane continuity and a sense of the infinite.

*Passing from the void to interpenetrations of solids; how were the latter born?*

GB: These works came into being because I had seen some crystallizations, and they inspired me to ask how I could possibly translate them into a ring. Two interpenetrations of solids give me a ring. Thus, I made these pieces of jewellery; the mystery of a boxed piece of jewellery is that it encapsulates a void, whereas in jewellery with transparencies it enables me to read its internal structure. Thanks to the transparency, the observer can understand the interpenetration of solids.

*Is there any connection between your work and music?*

GB: Yes, but I'm not sure exactly how.

*What is your outlook on wearability?*

GB: Jewellery is a very particular thing; when it is worn it is stronger than when seen in the hand. It is enhanced when worn; I believe that this is its prerogative. There are very few jewellery artists that manage to create jewellery with this value; one of them for example is Peter Skubic. When his works are worn, they transform completely. Jewellery must have this characteristic; otherwise it's not worth putting it on. Wearability is something that comes automatically when one begins to work; it is time and experience that directs you towards the ideal solution for wearability.

*Would you be interested in collaborating with a large jewellery firm?*

GB: I would like to make some pieces that have a connection with the traditions of jewellery. I think that presently Niessing is the only company proposing something innovative that still retains a link with tradition.

I am currently collaborating with a furniture company; however, the relationship is strictly defined along the following lines: I propose furniture designs and they produce and distribute them. There are no adaptations or compromises.

*Are there other interesting aspects to your profession beyond the creative phases?*

GB: Well, working with the furniture company is very interesting. Beyond this, I very much like installing exhibitions. Generally, I curate all my exhibitions. I have my own display cases, and I like to operate under pressure.

*What do you think about the market for jewellery?*

GB: Ever since I began to work, I thought that it might have changed, but it never has. Here in Padua it is a particular situation, where a restricted form of collecting has developed.

*When you work with students, what are the phases you follow when developing a project brief?*

**GB:** I always begin with drawing, even if often it is obsolete – you know students are not in this habit. Then the first approach is not thinking about jewellery. I ask the students to present an object that they find interesting and from there one can begin. From this point of departure, I get them to work with paper. To eliminate the fear of the white page, I ask them to draw or sometimes even to rip the page, and then once I have observed something personal we discuss this. At the end of the project, there must be a tangible object. This is the design method that I follow too.

*What advice would you give to students?*

**GB:** To let go or to suffer. To think not once but a hundred times before working in contemporary jewellery, unless one has the independent means to do so. There are a lot of very capable people who cannot manage to emerge. However, there are certain things that it is important to highlight: be lucky, persevere, and your jewellery must come from within.

**Fig. 29**
Giampaolo Babetto. *Brooch*
2001. Yellow gold.
Photo: Giustino Chemello.

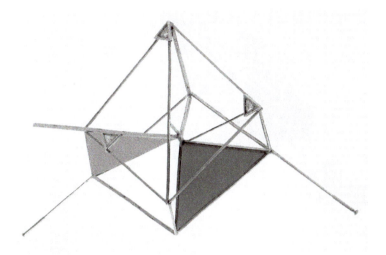

**Fig. 30**
Giampaolo Babetto. *Brooch*
2001. White gold, Plexiglas,
diamonds.
Photo: Giustino Chemello.

# 2

# Gijs Bakker

**Born: 1942, Amersfoort, The Netherlands**

**Fig. 31**
Gijs Bakker. *Porsche Bracelet.*
Series: I Don't Wear Jewels,
I Drive Them. 2002.
Polyurethane. Limited
numbered edition (5) by *Chi ha
paura…?* Executed by Aldo
Bakker, Florian Gottke, Nienke
de Leeuw and Materialise,
Leuven /B.
Photo: Rien Bazen.

*RB: How and why did you decide to go into jewellery?*

**GB:** I don't know! In my whole family, nobody operated culturally; it's all farmers and some small businesses. I had very nice parents, and when I got to the age of study they went – 'Okay, what are we going to do with that guy,' because I was not suited to work in my father's car business, and the only thing I could do was draw. So my father was kind enough to bring me to Amsterdam and to speak to the Rietveld Academy's directors.

*Where you then decided on your final direction…*

**GB:** Yeah, the first year was general techniques and then we had to make our choice, but I had no clue. Furniture was a no because of the measurements – too precise – and fashion too open, whereas the jewellery department had some nice colleagues and good coffee, so it became jewellery. But I mean I was fifteen or sixteen, so it was absolutely without any idea that I did jewellery. It's a very disappointing story, but that's how it was!

*Generally speaking, what are the developmental phases in your making process?*

**GB:** First, it's absolutely the idea and then the idea grows into a concept, because I see the concept as a little wider. I never start with a technique or a material; this is always one of the last decisions. Then the next step is to visualize it, because it has no shape, and thereafter to consider what is the best way to make it tangible, and finally comes the making process.

*Do you have any preferences in terms of materials or techniques?*

**GB:** No, but I am always curious for the newest possibilities. I don't know if I will ever use them, but it's good to know because the bigger my vocabulary is, the better.

*Are you ever afraid that high technology risks eliminating the unexpected error?*

**GB:** I feel nothing for what you are saying, because for me it's just a tool; all those high technologies are great. First, I had the hammer and could chisel, and now I can have an image made by rapid prototyping, but for me they're all simply tools.

*You mentioned that sometimes you might read a newspaper or reflect upon society and then suddenly get an idea. Is this your normal way of harnessing inspiration?*

GB: I think so, more or less. At least all the best works, in my opinion, have always grown like that.

*In your early works, geometry appears to have played a crucial role – for example the circle, ellipse and spiral forms indicative of the Möbius strip. Could you discuss this?*

GB: Apart from mathematics, I would say that throughout my career if I use a form, a measurement, it's never random. If I have measurements, I want those measurements to mean something. They have to have a relation to the wearer, and they have to create a relation amidst the other measurements in the piece.

It was most extreme in the 1970s, where mathematic measurements dominated the complete appearance of a piece. It was a period where we had the absolute belief that we could make society and we could change the world – and one of the ways was to create a universal language. We believed that mathematics could be used to make forms that are as clear and as minimal as possible, and that those objects could help communicate irrespective of whether you were high brow and artistically educated or low class and without any such education. It's a little bit naïve when I think back, but that was the belief we had.

*When did you personally stop making your jewellery?*

GB: Around the end of the 1980s I started to work with two goldsmiths who made my pieces.

*You don't miss handling materials?*

GB: No, not at all. And I am very happy that I can work through hands other than my own, because it means I can continue until very old age. I don't want the sweat and tears present in my jewellery.

*Even though it takes so much.*

GB: Of course! It's a hell of a job! But I had it already with the big aluminium necklace of the 1960s. We were hammering and polishing like you wouldn't believe; it was a hell of a job. In those days nobody knew how to work with aluminium, so we had to do it all by ourselves.

*So, now you don't feel any necessity to make your pieces at all?*

GB: I have learned that the goldsmiths I work with are better than I am. I was okay because of the way I was trained and so was everything I made up until the 1980s, but then new techniques and new possibilities emerged. Nowadays, I have in my head what I want, and I go and I pay them; I don't care how much it costs, but I want to have the result that I want to reach.

*Has delegating the making affected the role chance and accident plays in your practice?*

GB: Yeah, but I don't make mistakes! Of course I make mistakes, but I don't show them, I destroy them. It doesn't make a difference if I make it myself or if another person makes it. It only becomes public when it is manifested according to my ideas.

*The work never changes through the process of making?*

GB: No, not at all.

*Do you make any models?*

GB: Hardly; I draw, make sketches.

*So, when it comes to the making…*

GB: Then I start to make very precise drawings.

*Drawings that delegate?*

GB: Yes, but it's more about communicating with my goldsmiths, so then I have to be very precise.

*Would you say that jewellers should pursue drawing?*

GB: It depends how you work. Maybe some jewellers could work fantastically with photography – taking pictures of what they see, or by taking paper clippings out of magazines, or cutting quotes out of books, I don't care. I mean everybody has their own way of working, but I see everything like drawing, sketches and photography as study material, whatever you do.

*Do you believe then, that all students need to learn traditional techniques?*

GB: I feel sometimes it's a pity when I see students working in jewellery that are so limited. I've thought very often it's because they have not learned all the traditional techniques. However, I am very ambiguous in this matter, because if you look at my career I have never taught in jewellery schools. All my life I have been teaching design; it's just that intuitively I say no – I don't want to teach jewellery. Sometimes it's because I don't want to influence young people towards the jewellery field, which I feel can be such a narrow and limited field, whereas in the design world we have wilder ideas and do much more breathtaking things. I have a strange love/hate relationship with my profession. I love it, making jewellery, but then the whole thing is so nonsensical.

So, if I were to be an old man and say 'yes, young students nowadays should learn all the old techniques', I don't think it would help solve the problem. It's only that later I have admitted to myself that I am very fortunate that I had to do it. I have learned that it has given me a step ahead because I could compare myself with the old-fashioned industrial designers who were only able to draw and to make models in plastic, but never understood what it means to stamp metal or to forge metal into a shape. Whereas by having learned how to hammer and raise a pot and then going back to industrial design, it has been very easy for me to understand how you make three-dimensional shapes, because I have understood firsthand how ductile and malleable metals are – it's unbelievable what you can do with metals.

*What other advice would you give to students?*

GB: I would say during study, the most important thing is to be as open as possible and at least to follow cultural life in the widest sense; including literature, movies and fine art etc.

*As well as your own work, you are well known for* Droog *and also the jewellery collective* Chi ha paura. *Could you summarize the latter?*

GB: It is the idea of craft, design and jewellery slowly coming together. Financially it is difficult, it only sells in some very good shops, but not many shops really dare; for them the pieces are often too difficult despite them being very easy to wear.

*Do you think price is an obstacle to them selling?*

GB: Price plays a role, but also the fact that it is 'special jewellery'. I mean it is not just fancy adornment that is nice to dress up in. It's still designs that demand attention, and it is not everybody who likes that. You still need to have some background in the design world to understand the value of the idea that you are going to buy.

*How do you feel about the gallery system in general?*

GB: Now, life has been so cleaned up that jewellery is completely shifted towards jewellery galleries, and that is a dead-end because it becomes very narrow. I hope that for the younger generation we get galleries again where you have a mixture of attitudes; a sort of philosophy in your work as a jewellery designer that means you can fit in with another artist who is making objects or furniture pieces or making whatever. I think that's much better. Jewellery by jewellery, it's like a ghetto!

*Returning to your work, how do you establish its proportions and scale?*

GB: It's something that is dictated by the concept. I have no intention to be a sculptor, none at all. I know my limits. I know what sculpture means. For me, it is always the human being and the human body that is the drive and the starting point. The way we live, what we are, crazy as we are, that is fascinating for me and that is how I work. That is where ideas come from.

*So, how important is wearability then?*

GB: I used to say you can wear everything. You can even have some wheels underneath yourself and carry them; I mean you can wear anything somehow. There is this crazy thing with jewellery that in a traditional sense it has to be small because then you can easily wear it, but I make a distinction between something that you want to wear as a nothing, and a kind of daily thing that you have more of an emotional connection with, and then you have a piece that you wear because you really want to communicate something. That is a completely different thing from the daily kind of jewellery, which is just something that you forget is even there because it becomes part of your daily habit of dressing. The latter is the kind of jewellery that you feel and maybe you wear once in your lifetime, or twice, and you have a fantastic moment.

Personally speaking, one of my criteria is how does what I do relate to, not only the body, but more importantly to the human being. I feel that is two different things. The body deals with size, the total tangible being of the body, but the intellectual or spiritual part of the human being – well, I want my pieces to do something to the people that wear them. The measurement of the body that's the size of the jewellery, that's very simple, but the more emotional aspect – what my piece does to the wearer – is even more important.

I have noticed that people who buy my work always have their own story with it and that's important for me, because then the work communicates through the wearer and then it is related to the wearer, to the person.

*But obviously you cannot predict what the viewer will think.*

**GB:** No, you are absolutely right. But if the work is rich in meanings, then the wearer can distil their own meanings from the piece, and very often I have noticed that I make something because of such and such, and the buyer sometimes interprets completely different meanings from it.

*So, what if the person doesn't understand what you want to convey?*

**GB:** Well, it's not a matter of not understanding. They give their own interpretation to it. For me it's okay, it means that the piece gives room to the buyer to dream and to think and make their own story.

*Would you say, then, that content is foremost?*

**GB:** For me it's so important to see that jewellery is a medium, as all art media are, that can express something, more than just simply being adornment. I like beautiful things – it is not that I am stupid, but jewellery can be more than just adornment.

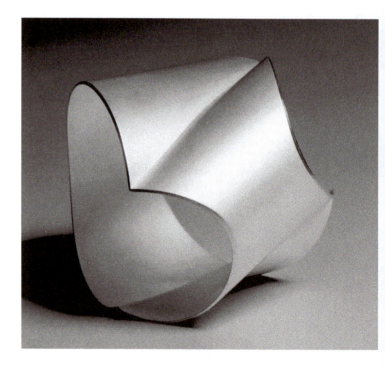

**Fig. 32**
Gijs Bakker. *Shot 6*. Series: Shot 1998. Silver 925, yellow gold 750. Limited numbered edition (10). Executed by Aldo Bakker and Florian Gottke. Photo: Rien Bazen.

*You once said you drive jewellery too.*

GB: Yes, you're right.

*So what is your idea of driving jewellery?*

GB: It's a quote from an advert for Alfa Romeo. You see the picture of a beautiful woman and next to her is a car and the text says, 'I don't wear jewels – I drive them.' I thank you so much. It's a gift, it's a gift! And then I stole it.

**Fig. 33**
Gijs Bakker. *Heavy Lace* 2001.
Yellow gold 585. One-off.
Executed by Pauline Barendse,
Jeroen Brink and Materialise,
Leuven /B.
Photo: Rien Bazen.

# 3

# Manfred Bischoff

**Born: 1947, Schömberg, Germany**

**Fig. 34**
Manfred Bischoff. *Pleh! Pleh!*
2005. Gold. Brooch.
Photo: Aurelio Amendola.

*RB: Why did you start making jewellery?*

**MB:** I didn't choose to make jewellery; I was forced into it by my mother, who decided that I should become a goldsmith because I was a good-for-nothing!

*What inspires your work?*

**MB:** Life and good teachers. My work in the past was always inspired by contemporary times and events, so in 1968 in Berlin it was the student revolts and thereafter punk. My work was never out of synch with time; it was always connected to time. However, nowadays this is not so much the case, because it has developed into a very private language.

*In the 1970s you made some pieces using nonprecious materials such as acrylic; are you saying this was due to the context?*

**MB:** Yes, it was very important to prove which materials worked and which didn't, from acrylic to photographs. So, whilst it was good to work with these nonprecious materials, they didn't do what I wanted because they were too disposable, too throwaway. By working in this poor manner, I realized that the only material capable of translating my thinking was gold, because my ideas were very profound and at the same time superficial. Furthermore, if I started to combine text and drawings with gold, it would then become a real material. In this relationship, every part has its own space: the drawing, the text and the piece.

*Could you discuss the origins of your jewellery?*

**MB:** Most of my pieces come from language, so that's the origin; thereafter I search for some realization in the jewellery world. I do not work with many ideas – mostly two, which means zero and one. I'm not interested in showing the world the plurality of life; I want to only show one, and not more. When I see a thing, I assess whether it's possible to bring it within my ambit, so it's always the same idea, but expressed in different ways. I'm not interested in ornament; I do not make things better with ornament. I am only interested in the purity of my idea and no more.

*During the 1970s and 1980s the pieces were never exhibited with drawings, whereas in the last 15 years they have been displayed directly on their accompanying drawings; why?*

**MB:** I saw that the pieces alone could not hold themselves within a space that is normally not a space. Therefore, I had to frame them, in a certain sense, through language and with drawing so that the viewer could have the possibility to enter from multiple points of view. By this I refer only to the observer; I never think about the eventual wearer. It is my offering, so the drawings combined with the text and the piece is a present to the eventual purchaser. It either helps them or confuses; both states are good. Confusion can be a help. Besides, my input is never immediate or obvious. I don't want the piece to be discovered from the first encounter, but the viewer can interpret how they want.

*If a piece is interpreted in a contrary or unexpected way, does this matter to you?*

**MB:** No. I have collectors who know the title of a piece, but they call it a completely different name. I have no right to force people into my way of thinking. I give them an entrance, possibilities and sometimes confusion. If it's very clear, I like to confuse.

*How is drawing incorporated into your working process?*

**MB:** My drawings are a certain kind of writing, and my writing is also drawing. I was trained to make drawings by very good teachers, so I know what a drawing can be and what is superficial and what is necessary to make drawing work.

In exhibitions, I sometimes change drawings because they do not work in a context, or sometimes I change a drawing if I find a better title. I give the viewer a kind of rhythm; the drawing is the overture to the text, to the *opera,* and the drama which is the piece. The rhythm projected though the drawing should bring the viewer closer to my input. They must not know me personally, but they can construct something from these clues.

*If you buy a brooch, do you automatically receive its drawing?*

**MB:** Yes, I think the drawings are for the people who have the pieces; they cannot put it in a box and compare it with other things, so they become interested in having the piece on the drawing. I have no chance to see what happens to the piece once it is sold, but the drawing protects it a little bit.

*How do you deal with the relationship between a piece and the body of its wearer?*

**MB:** I'm totally uninterested in this. I do my best and others should do theirs. My pieces are not generally worn by younger people because they are only interested in themselves and prefer being looked at. They are not interested in engaging in a conversation with the viewer, and consequently they mostly wear their aunt or mother's jewellery. On the other hand, if a person develops a real personality, which requires a certain age, they are more likely to risk an intellectual exchange.

*Do you have a preference for any specific typology of jewellery?*

**MB:** I nearly always create rings or brooches because the other things are too conventional. The ring is a sculpture and the brooch is a relief. The brooch is very important for me because I want to force the wearer into a discussion with other people. Wearing a brooch is totally confrontational; you cannot hide it behind your back when you meet someone. Therefore, you are guilty; you are responsible for it and for every conversation that arises because of it. Those who do not like this should not wear my jewellery. I like that my ideas are worn as new conversations that I have nothing to do with.

*Why do you contend that the ring is a piece of sculpture?*

**MB:** A ring must be able to survive without the hand or fingers; you can turn it and it must function from all viewpoints like a sculpture. The band is like a pedestal or plinth that supports the sculptural form above, and whilst it usually takes the same form in every ring, only together does it constitute the whole work. Alternatively, a brooch is much more like a picture or relief and it has a definite front and back. Earrings have a pin and fastening, the bracelet has clasps, so the ring is the only sculpture.

*Can you describe your working process once the drawing is finalized? Do you make models or studies?*

**MB:** No, I immediately make the work in gold. In my workshop I only have a few tools, which must suffice for everything. I only use twenty-two carat gold, but I am not anxious with it. This is possible because I buy a lot so that it effectively becomes 'no gold'. If you only buy a small amount, you only think about its value, whereas I am liberated from thinking about its worth and can use it like copper.

*You often counterbalance gold with coral; could you describe how you came to use coral in your work and what it symbolizes?*

**MB:** Having used coral for the first time, I realized that it was applicable to my ideas, if not the perfect material for my thinking. This was the beginning I think of zero and one. I no longer had to search anymore because I had found the right materials: gold and coral. Coral is the *vivace* (vivacious) part, erotic and skinlike, but also capable of making gold more *vivace*. Coral also symbolizes pain for me. It has differing and rich levels, and I like this union of the erotic and pain which results in layered complexities of meaning in a single piece.

*Are there are any tools or techniques that have a particular resonance for you?*

MB: My girlfriend brought me a pitch bowl that used to belong to my teacher Reinhold Reiling. So, this is my most important tool; it is very emotional because I admired him very much. Also, this tool has become very important to my working process, so it's like a soul transformation. Perhaps it's too romantic to say this, but it's a poetic story.

*I know that alongside Reinhold Reiling, you also studied with Hermann Jünger. Was there anything specific you gained from his teaching?*

MB: Reiling opened all doors and said make whatever you want, whereas Jünger was not like that; he thought about each student's future. To those who were capable, he also said make what you want, but he helped other less-capable students because he didn't want anybody to fail. For Reiling this was not important. Jünger gave weaker students the possibility of a future, so this was his great gift. I did not attend the class full time as I was working in Berlin; Jünger allowed me to only attend the school for critical tutorials. Overall, both are very important for me. Well, they were.

*You have stated that you are not a teacher. What do you mean by this?*

MB: I do not teach techniques or prescribe; instead, I give suggestions on how students can progress their work. My experience of making jewellery or art immediately allows me to see where there are some openings. I do not decide for them, but I can say why it could be interesting to pursue a particular course of action. Sometimes, if a student asks whether they should continue in a certain direction, I give no answer because then the responsibility would be mine. I give them trust and I hope I give them courage. I do not limit them and I do not say 'do not make this' unless I can justify why.

*Returning to your interest in language, does it extend beyond content to its means of delivery? For example to an outsider it might seem that the lyrical geometry of the forms you create in certain pieces has a link to calligraphy.*

MB: No, not to calligraphy. Perhaps I am thinking in drawings whilst making jewellery. Perhaps it's a modulated drawing; I have difficulties in writing normally, which may be a psychological defect!

*So you visualize everything in drawings, even if it's a text.*

MB: I remember when I was young I was predisposed to draw well, be it a good ship or car. I always showed it like it was in reality, and I needed a long time to eradicate this perfection. The first form was to go back to drawing, because drawing is the first externalization of the *disegno interno,* which means the inner thinking, the concept, the mind, the mental plan and the construction in language. To bring this into form you need the *disegno esterno,* or external sign, so the first fastening of an idea is very helpful; that's the point where I work and my interest is.

In the past I felt that my external signs were not true, but that nowadays it equates to a much truer external sign, as in the immediacy of speech. So now the first externalization of what I think is what I write down. That is why my drawings have become my handwriting. I write down what I think, but without concentrating on how it will look or exactly what will come out.

I do not draw by holding the pencil in a conventional manner, but invert it at a crooked angle or hold it loosely at the end because I do not want to achieve perfection; I actually want to be a loser in the first external signs. I don't want to be a winner; first, I want to lose.

*You relinquish control to achieve a purer first externalization.*

MB: Yes, that's correct. If you control, then you are fixed. I think human beings can also survive with losing. It's not my intention to give the world a masterpiece; it's more to show that we are losers – but in gold.

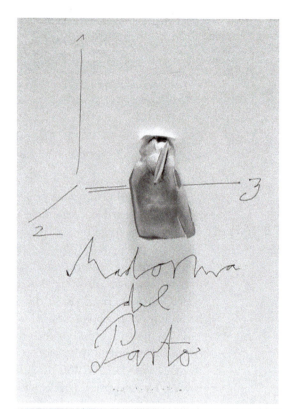

**Fig. 35**
Manfred Bischoff. *Madonna del Parto* 2002. Gold, coral. Brooch.
Photo: Aurelio Amendola.

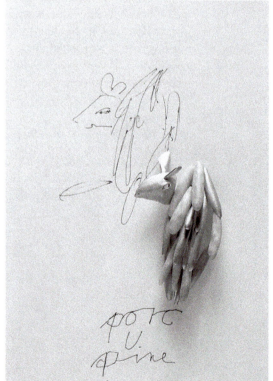

**Fig. 36**
Manfred Bischoff. *Porcupine* 2005. Gold, coral. Brooch.
Photo: Aurelio Amendola.

# 4

# Liv Blåvarp

**Born: 1956, Furnes, Norway**

**Fig. 37**
Liv Blåvarp. *Spirits Talking* 2005.
Dyed birch, whale tooth. Necklace.
Photo: Arild Kristiansen.

*RB: Why did you decide to start making jewellery?*

**LB:** I was more or less forced into it; I really wanted to be a graphic designer, but I wasn't that good at drawing so I had to make another choice.

*What prompted you to use wood as a material?*

**LB:** Originally, I worked with metal during the years I spent at college. However, around the time I was about to graduate, I realized that I didn't have the freedom and the opportunity to create more voluminous forms. So, I decided to combine wood with metal and began by uniting it with stainless steel mesh. I needed a framing device for the steel, so the wood functioned as a picture frame.

*Do you feel that you have reinvigorated the possibilities for wood in contemporary jewellery; a material that might otherwise be seen as traditional or even obsolete?*

**LB:** Yes, I think so. You have to be confident that value is derived not from materials in a traditional sense, but rather from the significance of ideas, aesthetics and movement. It is important to establish within yourself that your planning, process and will to pursue an idea is right; you have to know what you do and why you do it in order to realize your aim.

*Is wood your primary material?*

**LB:** Yes, it gives me such a wonderful freedom; it expresses my need to work with nature. Wood is nature, so it's a perfect synthesis for my ideas. If you look at a beautiful piece of wood, there is a landscape living in it, which can often describe my inner landscape.

*Are you inferring that it couldn't be any other material?*

**LB:** Never say never! However, until now wood has provided more than enough to explore. Wood can be used in so many ways: you can paint it, lacquer it, dye it, and the world has so many different kinds. So this material provides me with an endless range of possibilities to investigate; besides, if something goes wrong, you simply throw it away and start again. Access is endless, so you are not limited by materials and you can also make large voluminous pieces.

*Sometimes you exploit the wood's grain, and at other times you eradicate it. What dictates these choices?*

**LB:** These are more or less conscious decisions. Sometimes when I have an exotic wood with a beautiful or particularly intricate grain, I wait for an idea to emerge through which I can express this fully. Alternatively, there might be other ideas where I decide to paint or dye the wood, so the grain has less relevance. Furthermore, there are pieces that combine painted elements with elements where the grain is visible.

*What inspires your work?*

LB: It depends on the level of consciousness; there are things that I cannot explain, even to myself. Generally speaking, I make connections with nature through materials, expressions and structure. For example, in the 1990s I was working with geometrical plates that you can also find in nature; so how geometry is linked and the specific way things are put together in nature was important. Out of this came the 'spiral' necklaces, made from elements that could stretch and rotate. Subsequently, in 1996 I had an exhibition in Oslo which focused on animals, their movement and muscular anatomy, and then I was using woods such as ebony, palisander and citrus woods in their natural states, so they were not as colourful as before.

I still work with expressions of nature; but I am not able to explain it fully. I recently made a necklace called *Spirits Talking* that typifies the work I have been interested in making for the last five years. These have been much cruder expressions, with big holes edged with whale tooth and white trumpet-like openings. These are dangerous pieces, by which I mean that people experience them as a bit on the edge; you know there are voices from the deep that are a bit scary.

Whilst these pieces clearly present themselves as jewellery, the expression is too strong for most people to wear. This is, therefore, a kind of art object that belongs in a context other than that of the personal intimate relationship ordinarily associated with jewellery. I think they really belong in a museum.

*Is this the kind of relationship you hope to engage in with your audience?*

LB: Yes, because I could make a lot of easily wearable jewellery that is not challenging, but this would be too easy and boring. Just the size or colours alone could be challenging, but without this psychological depth there is no development in artistic direction.

The meeting point between extravagant jewellery and the intimacy of a person adopting it for their personal use is very sparkling; it's an important trigger for me. I have never been interested in making conceptual jewellery. For me it has to be concrete, something that can be handled; a tactile thing so that you can touch it, wear it, meditate with it, take it off and play with it. I've always wanted to fulfill a number of emotional needs, not just one.

*Returning to your pieces, are the necklaces carved as integral sculptures and then divided into segments and threaded as beads?*

LB: Initially, I used to make sketches from which I devised ways of making the elements individually, how to shape them, how to drill the holes and then thread them, and how it would act on the body. So it is more of an engineering process.

*That's interesting because you could start with an element and almost go on forever.*

LB: That's actually quite important because you could go on endlessly building and building. I have had various methods of working during different periods. For example in the 1980s, this way of working was prevalent, meaning that I made a series of elements and could then spend several days looking whilst deciding how to continue; before realizing I could change and continue with elements that contrasted. Then towards the end, when I had what could potentially be a necklace, I could spend another few days staring, deciding how to complete it; at which point I often made radical changes in the shape of the elements to produce greater variety.

Later on, I planned work out before making through precision drafting. Thereafter, I transferred the geometry of the shapes I had designed in paper onto wood, ensuring that all the elements would fit together perfectly.

*So sketches have a different value in the second process?*

LB: Yes, the process of making through impulse is more emotional than when drafting it out. They are two completely different processes, but I don't really have a preference. I really enjoy this spontaneous way of working, but it takes a long time to create a genuinely good piece. On the other hand, when you draft, you have more control.

*At what stage of the developmental process do you establish the material qualities you want, or does this predetermination apply only to the form?*

LB: Well, the drafts are drawn in colour so you have to find some kind of material that suits the drawing, so to some extent this is also preordained.

*I've noted over the years just how surprised many students have been on exposure to the vivid colourfulness of your jewellery.*

**LB:** People expect Scandinavian things to be more moderate, especially if you consider the prevalence of social democracy in politics and also the Scandinavian design movement, which presented the world with these tasteful and understated objects. However, if you look at the cultural history of Norway, we have a strong and vivid culture of folk art that does not exist in Sweden, Finland or Denmark. In fact it's really wild, the way of decorating the interiors of houses in colourful patterns from top to bottom, is actually very surprising. So, in that respect maybe there is some kind of a link that I haven't been conscious of, but that nonetheless exists.

*Could you discuss the series of necklaces that have an internal and an external form, achieved by alternating series of larger, then smaller, concentric discs?*

**LB:** This, like many works, is also an idea that evolved from previous work. I used to do a lot of sketches and have books filled with ideas, some of which I couldn't make, and I think these double pieces had remained as sketches for quite some time. So the idea has been resting until now.

There are three important aspects to this technique: firstly, it's a way of making 'doubleness' – through the inner and outer form; it is also an optical effect; and finally it is very dynamic when worn because as the wearer turns around or moves in relation to you the observer, the outer form casts a shadow onto the inner form. Therefore, you only see the inner form in glimpses. Key to augmenting this effect is ensuring that the inner form is a strong colour that radiates strong light, and that the outer form is a dark wood that acts as a shadow for the inner form. The individual elements are quite refined and thin, meaning the final pieces are really fabulous to wear because they follow the body's form effortlessly.

*How do you go about balancing the relationship between the internal and external form?*

**LB:** The relationship between the internal and the external forms is decided by sketching at first and then a more accurate draft gives a precise picture of the idea. It is important to adjust the sizes of the two forms well, so that the inner part shows in a strong fashion, but still remains somewhat hidden.

*Could you describe the role of movement in your jewellery?*

**LB:** I came from a practical family of carpenters, and this has had an impact on my approach. For jewellery to be wearable, it has to function. I want the pieces to be live things, and movement helps contribute to this, as well as its functionality.

*I note that many of the necklaces' clasps are quite ingenious in that they continue the manifestation of the underlying form, often serving to enhance the visual connections to animals.*

**LB:** This has always been important to me; I want the clasps to be an exciting part of the whole. If for example there is movement in the necklace, I want it to be continued in the clasp; so really the clasp should complement the conception of the necklace.

*Do you title your work?*

**LB:** I didn't used to give titles because I felt it was slightly pretentious, but recently I have increasingly used titles, largely from a practical perspective. I know that a lot of people perceived my work during the 1980s and 1990s to be erotic, strong and wild. But as you get older things quieten down. The first *Double* necklaces were given titles; the first one was *Night,* then there was a series called *Evening,* and then *Shadows Falling.* So you see, the shadow is coming into my life!

*Do you think each piece should be able to survive on its own?*

**LB:** Yes, because a title can only ever touch certain aspects of a work, but never reference all its nuances of meaning. A title is a kind of limitation.

*Is there any intention to communicate anything specific through your work?*

**LB:** It's not possible for me to answer this question, but I can say that I do like the American Indian way of expressing feelings about nature. If that's mythology, then maybe there is something related in my work. I do not, however, want to be linked to Norse mythology. The spiritual feeling that man experiences in nature is innate; no one can enter into nature without having a strong experience. So, this impact that nature provokes is important for me in my expressions; I would like to pass on these strong emotions that nature gives to me by imbuing them into the structures, feelings, and aesthetics of my work.

**Fig. 38**
Liv Blåvarp. *Red Headed Bird*
2007. Dyed cherry, palisander,
whale tooth. Necklace.
Photo: Audbjørn Rønning.

**Fig. 39**
Liv Blåvarp. *Cesaria* 2000.
Stained and lacquered maple.
Necklace.
Photo: Holger Bredesen.

# 5

# Esther Brinkmann

**Born: 1953, Baden, Switzerland**

**Fig. 40**
Esther Brinkmann. *Bell* 1995.
Hammered silver, knitted
textile. Finger vessel.
Photo: Esther Brinkmann.

*RB: How and why did you start making jewellery?*

**EB:** I always liked doing things with my hands, especially building 3D objects. When I was in my twenties, I saw two multiples by Dieter Roth at the Art Fair in Basel – his *Zoo Rings* and the *Huts*. For the first time, I perceived that there was a different way to consider jewellery, and I decided to study jewellery in Geneva, where I was living.

I'm very much involved in creating things which have a relationship to the body. I appreciate the idea that somebody is wearing my piece, reflecting his or her personality.

*Could you describe the main phases in the creation of a piece?*

**EB:** In the beginning there is always an intuition. For example, the desire to carry a stone in my hand and then to translate this feeling to wearing a ring. Next, I start making models with paper or with real materials like metal, trying out different materials and considering the qualities required to support my idea. Then I choose one or more of the ideas, and eventually draw them. Different types of ideas may appear in this phase: like ideas for one-of-a-kind pieces and other ideas that develop as a multiple. Finally I make the piece, most frequently realizing several pieces in parallel.

Through this process of making, I elaborate and develop a concept. I then also get into other ideas which will become a new series, touching a different aspect.

*Do you draw?*

**EB:** Very seldomly. However, I catch ideas or elaborate concepts by means of drawings. Drawing and writing serve further developments or variations.

*Do you make models for pieces in advance of making them?*

**EB:** Yes, often I experiment with materials, and very often I make 3D sketches.

*How do you know when a piece is finished?*

**EB:** A piece is finished when the shape and material correspond with the idea I want to materialize. Or, it is finished when I cannot do better at that time, but then it can happen later that I am not happy anymore, so I deconstruct the piece and transform it into a better result.

*Could you discuss the main ideas behind the recent series:* Last Drop *and* Inside?

EB: The series *Inside* consists of a few pendants which all have the shape of a container. The wearer hangs it around their neck and at any time can bring the hole to their eye and look inside. The only condition is to face a light source, be it daylight or artificial light. *Inside* is about looking through a small hole and discovering a world. In appearance there is not a lot to see, but what you see stimulates the mind, imagination and fantasy. One can look inside a volume and imagine the eye catching a glimpse of the universe. There is a similar series of brooches called *View from Here,* where the focus is on what the wearer can see on their chest through a hole when wearing the piece.

In the *Last Drop* pieces, I try to materialize the idea of the moment before separation. In life, the moment of separation can be quick as lightening, as well as never ending.

*You have an ongoing series of rings called* Finger Vessels; *could you discuss their evolution?*

EB: For over twenty years I have been developing the idea of the finger vessel: like a vase contains and values a flower, a ring contains and values a finger. Through the years, different shapes and types of rings have materialized this idea with a focus on the space between the ring and the finger and incidentally between fingers. In a certain way, one could say the finger vessel concept is the opposite of the ancestral ring concept: whereby a ring symbolizes the appurtenance to a social rank, a community or a spouse.

Of course, the main thing is to experience the weight of the ring and the space around the ring when wearing it – to manipulate it, play with it and feel its presence. Fitting the bell on your ring finger is a very erotic action. The slow gesture of pulling up and down the textile part is reminiscent of gestures associated with wearing stockings.

I have made various typologies of *Finger Vessel*: the first type is a double ring; the first ring is too large, oversize, and the second – inner ring – fits on the finger. The outer is usually made of wood, iron or cast iron and is machine made. The inner ring is made out of a sheet of silver or gold and textured with a hammer. Therefore, the base metal hides the valuable metal. The hard material protects the soft material (pure gold).

The second type is the sphere. A sphere contains the knuckle and the ring fits at its base. This whole is shaped as if you had pushed your finger through the ball.

The third type is the bell. This was partly inspired by beautiful pictures of plants and animals in the sea. I also had the desire to introduce colour into my work. It turned out that knitted silk was the right material which corresponds to the softness and fluidity of the movement in these pieces. The knitted part allows the ring to fit on the finger.

*Is it important that the viewer understands or correctly interprets the meaning of a work?*

EB: Well, before mentioning the viewer, I would like to speak about the wearer to whom I dedicate my work. I contend that wearing jewellery induces a dialogue with the body, with the mind and the emotions. For example, I seek to provoke a different perception of the hand that wears a ring and which spreads the fingers apart. My essential concerns consist in widening perceptions and deepening emotions. So, therefore, yes, it is important that the wearer can experience what I try to materialize in a piece.

*So what kind of relationship do you want them to have with your pieces?*

EB: I maintain that wearing jewellery enables each of us to transmit exterior signs of interior states. In other words, the jewel can bridge between the very personal intimate sphere and the public space.

*The packaging for your work often serves as a jewel box, and it evidently has a significant role in the aesthetics and meaning of a piece. Could you describe how this came about?*

EB: The ideas I just spoke about find their further expression in the jewel box, which have been of great interest to me for many years. A piece that I create is finished only when it has its own box. The box positions the object. It prolongs and reinforces its character. It is a part of a ritual, which consists in arranging, discovering or rediscovering the object. For each piece I invent a package which unveils this never-ending pleasure; this suspense which holds a surprise.

The pleasure also consists in being amazed by the manner in which the object can be taken out of its package and put back there later on. The weight, the texture, the shape and the size of the container widen the perception that one will have of its contents.

The box can also be used as a display unit. The status of an autonomous object that an unworn piece of jewellery acquires is thus emphasized. If a box is used, a priori, as a protective wrapping, it suggests, above all, that its contents are valuable. Valuable not only because of the material the object is made of, but also because of its meaning.

Valuable for the person who buys it.
Valuable for the person who offers it.
Valuable for the person who receives it.

*Is your jewellery like a time capsule, or metaphorically speaking, receptacles for your memories and experiences?*

EB: I guess every artistic expression or work is linked to the author's experiences somehow. Rather than receptacle, I would call it a mirror, because the work reflects what I have experienced even if I do not want it to; because the work has to do with perceptions, and perception includes memory.

*On occasions you have combined gold with non-precious materials such as iron. Why?*

EB: Because of their different physical qualities and cultural background their perception is different. Such combinations underline my ideas like protection, and opposition to the generally recognized views on precious and nonprecious materials. Transforming and working on a material makes it different, so it becomes valuable.

*You moved to Guangzhou in China in 2005. What effect has this had on your practice?*

EB: In the beginning it was very hard to start working. I was under the influence of so many impressions and images. I had so many interesting and intriguing things to understand and/or digest. This introduced many doubts, a lot of hesitation and question marks.

My studio is much smaller. I do not have as many tools as before. This situation provokes new attitudes and new materials. I thought it would be very easy to find collaboration in China. Yet, it is quite difficult to get in touch face to face with the right person who is able to understand my needs and who is able to reach the level of quality I ask for.

*Could you discuss the series* Red Face, *which you have been developing since your arrival in China?*

EB: The series *Red Face* is the direct result of my perception of China: trying to find my position, searching for the original among the copies. These pieces talk about identity, about the singular within the mass. They talk about (my/your/their) different faces which make a personality. Why red? Red is the colour of China.

*How has your work been received in China?*

EB: With a lot of curiosity, fascination and enthusiasm. So-called contemporary jewellery is absolutely unknown in China. During several decades, wearing jewellery was taboo; only minorities were eventually allowed to wear their traditional jewellery for some festivals because these traditions have deep roots and these people live far away from official eyes. For Chinese women, wearing jewellery is a new experience. The traditional mascots and charms are present again, Western commercial and luxury jewellery and its advertisements are omnipresent. Getting in touch with a type of jewellery which focuses on tactile, sensual experiences that convey concepts brought new visions to many of my new friends and to the visitors to my exhibition.

*Should wearing jewellery be a sensual experience?*

EB: Yes. Jewellery enables us, if not requires us on some occasions, to feel and experience parts of our body in a different way. It plays an active role in revitalizing our outer shell, in awakening or revealing an underlying or affirmed eroticism. The ritual of choosing, putting on and taking off our jewellery is further enhanced by the gentle touch of a drop earring against our cheek, the heavy weight of a ring on our finger, a pendant brushing against the stomach.

Jewellery influences our gestures, our way of moving; and it can change our silhouette and our behaviour. Complementing oneself with an object, with a piece of jewellery, causes a change in our attitude, induces a different kind of self-awareness and calls for a more intimate relationship with the body.

*Do you favour a particular typology of jewellery, and if so why?*

EB: My favourite is the ring because it is the most interesting piece to feel for the wearer. Another reason is my interest in exploring the possibilities of shaping pieces for the fingers. Second favourites are the brooch and the pendant for the same reasons just mentioned: exploring possibilities. It seems that these types are the most appropriate to materializing my ideas. The brooch is the only one which is fixed on fabric. As a wearer, I do not feel it, I show it to others. Personally, I love wearing brooches.

*How important is functionality to you?*

EB: As important as possible: a piece must be wearable. However, the notion of functionality is not the same for everybody. For example I try to make the best pin I can to fix a brooch. So when the function follows the concept, then the result is coherent.

*What advice, if any, would you give to students?*

**EB:** Everybody has good ideas; developing and realizing them needs hard work, and only a few will have the energy to persevere. Making jewellery is a passion in life. Choose a partner who is willing to support this passion.

**Fig. 41**
Esther Brinkmann. *Bell* 1994. Electroformed and oxidized gold, knitted textile. Finger vessel.
Photo: Esther Brinkmann.

**Fig. 42**
Esther Brinkmann. *Red Face and One Double* 2008. Red thread, resin, silver or gold setting, one silver-cast piece. Brooches.
Photo: GoGoGo, Guangzhou.

# 6

# Caroline Broadhead

**Born: 1950, Leeds, England**

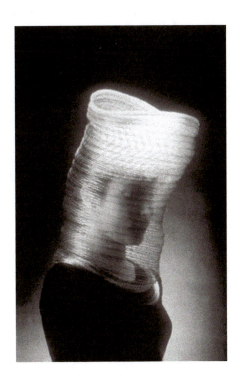

**Fig. 43**
Caroline Broadhead. *Veil*
1983. Nylon. Necklace.
Photo: David Ward.

*RB: How and why did you start making jewellery?*

**CB:** Well, I started making jewellery at the age of sixteen, when I went away to boarding school. I learnt how to solder and how to make three-dimensional things out of metal mainly, some ceramic, but actually what really got my interest was wearing my jewellery and making it for my sisters and friends.

*Could you describe the main phases in the creation of a piece?*

**CB:** I think it's a synthesis of looking, feeling, thinking, drawing, observing, rethinking, starting over, assessing, analysing and it's going back to the beginning – starting all over, following the same path again, but maybe branching off at a different point.

It is actually a very complex process – I think there probably are distinct phases insofar as one is a kind of searching process, and then having arrived at a certain stage, the next part is to consolidate one element of it and then you're still searching for other bits, and then when you are certain of one thing, slowly, as it becomes more and more fixed. Then there is a phase of being the audience; so you start off being a thinker about it and the maker, and then you have to get a distance from it and consider what it would be like for somebody else to use it, view it and wear it.

I think it is also important to let ideas have a bit of space, because sometimes ideas are elusive, can go off track or seem to be not so interesting as you first thought, and you have to persist to get through that phase. Staying with something to find the thread of your interest again is a matter of clarifying the intention or motivation, juggling ideas and possibilities and using your judgement.

*What role does intuition play in your work?*

**CB:** A combination of intuition and reason, and I think sometimes it's more reason than intuition with me. I am analysing at quite an early stage when I am doing things; it is driven intuitively to begin with, and then there is concept and reason that frame it.

*Do you write to analyse your work?*

**CB:** I find it very difficult to write analytically about work when I am doing it. It is fine afterwards, once it's sunk in and been assimilated. Writing can be quite enlightening; I first noticed that when I did an exhibition called *Conceptual Clothing*. Each artist had to write a short statement about his or her work and because the area I was working in had shifted, I had to work really hard to clarify my work with this in mind. I remember spending days on it trying to get the right words and phrases. Then I realized that I had identified an area that I could continue to work on for years to come.

*Do you draw in the design or making process?*

CB: I draw as a method of trying to feel my way around something; it's a long process where I am sort of thinking at the same time, but I probably sketch and write more than I draw.

*Do you make models at all?*

CB: When I made jewellery, yes I always did. When the work gets bigger, it gets tested in different ways.

*Through metal or paper?*

CB: I always tried to use the real materials because they were cheap for the most part. It was to see if it worked in three dimensions, on the body and a practice run to help calculate exactly how to make a piece.

*So, at that point was it important for you to place the work on the body to test its wearability?*

CB: Yes, wearability, but also practical things; proportion and the look of the thing when it was finished.

*I believe your use of plastic emerged whilst still a student at Central St Martins in London.*

CB: There was definitely a hierarchy of materials there, which some of us rebelled against by making out of plastics. But once I had left, I was always looking for different materials to see what they could do. It was exciting coming across a material that offered possibilities, gave something back.

*In Holland there was a quite distinct group of jewellers pursuing these ideas.*

CB: The Dutch were more succinct in rebelling. I remember the exhibition *Revolt in Jewellery* at Electrum with Onno Boekhoudt and Marion Herbst. There was a similar movement in England, but it was not quite so well defined or radical. Nonetheless, there was a big upheaval. People thought it was very brave or misguided to use plastics and other nonprecious materials. This seems ridiculous now as it is much more widely accepted.

*Indeed, in the British context one could discern a certain coura-geousness in the use of materials in your early jewellery.*

CB: I think I was part of a break from traditional jewellery. It was wanting to make jewellery for a wider range of people, it was looking at materials in a more open and investigative way, and it was emphasizing design as the value indicator. It was really about making something lively, thoughtful and exciting.

*Was the use of so-called poor materials anything to with democ-ratizing jewellery?*

CB: It just seemed absolutely appropriate that one should be de-signing things which were available at an affordable price.

*Looking back, could you discuss the evolution of the tufted jewellery?*

CB: It had developed from the cotton jewellery, wanting the tufts to be more structural. Having a sort of a bracelet that did not appear to touch the body, you know the rim of it didn't seem to. Then there was a sort of a play on whether it was held away from the body – maybe something more interesting than some-thing that actually touched it. I had made a very basic model out of wood that kept splitting; I couldn't get it to work. I made this and then I went to Africa for five months. It was very rel-evant to see African jewellery in context as I had been asking myself questions about whether jewellery could be this or that, what was too big, what was wearable. In Africa, massive, bulky, heavy jewellery is wearable; they wear masses of things – all made of nonprecious materials but playing a fundamental and significant role. Jewellery was so embedded into their social structure. That gave me a sort of confidence to come back and follow my ideas.

*These pieces were quite vibrantly coloured. How did this come about?*

CB: I was dyeing something and stirred it with a toothbrush; the tufts of the toothbrush came out blue and I realized this was a good material to use. When I realized I could dye the nylon, it became about making decisions about colour and finding differ-ent types of dyes to produce brilliant colours. I got two colours on one tuft by dip dyeing, and others used a slowly changing dye solution to get a progression of colours. Everything had to be scrupulously clean; it was so easy to get it wrong and have to start all over again.

*Is your work always related to the body in some way?*

CB: The jewellery was made in relation to the body and with the possibility of wearing, but when I started making things that were not intended to be worn, I am still considering the relationship with the body – what scale it is, where it is placed, how you encounter the piece, what you see first etc. At about the same time as the other work stopped being wearable, I started working with dancers, making things for a breathing, moving body, so actually these had to be very practical. The dancers had to have confidence in the garment so that they could move in them, sometimes in an extreme way. The body's measurements change radically when it is active.

*Could you discuss the way you began to use clothing?*

CB: At first, I was not thinking in terms of clothing, but in terms of arm pieces, bracelets and sleeves. I was thinking about the symmetry of clothing and the asymmetry of jewellery; very often you will wear a watch or a bracelet on one hand and not on the other, but clothing at that point tended to be very symmetrical. I was operating in that area between clothing and jewellery. The initial piece was conceived as a bracelet – a long tube of fabric that linked both wrists. I put a bodice on to fix it to the body and it was a surprise that it then became a garment. I realized I had stepped over into a different definition of what the work was.

In Amsterdam in 1982, having two or three shirts with long sleeves, I can remember thinking, well actually, clothing is an area that no one is really working on. This was very exciting; clothing has so many possibilities for communication, it has a familiar form and people have a strong interest in it.

At first, although the pieces were ideas based, I was also concerned with the practicalities – fitting to the body, being able to get the garment on and off – and it was only later that I realized this was not always necessary.

*And how did you then move into making installations?*

CB: I had a break from producing work in the early 1990s, where I gave myself time to reconsider what I was doing, the possibility of starting from scratch, and over that period I became interested in shadows. This led me to make work with shadows that really used the gallery space, the lighting, the walls, and this was where the final decisions about the work were being made. This meant that the first time I saw the pieces was the same time as the audience did.

*You're quite unusual in having moved away from jewellery making when some contemporary jewellers have migrated towards it from other disciplines. Do you miss making jewellery now?*

CB: I teach jewellery, so it means I am thinking about it quite a lot, but I don't miss making jewellery; but I sometimes miss working small in metals.

*Is a piece of jewellery still jewellery when displayed in a museum; or, in other words, does it need to be worn for completion?*

CB: It all depends on what the piece does. There can be pieces which are jewellery and do not need to be worn. I don't have a definite distinction about whether something is a piece of jewellery or not. I quite like that edge – the work that is at the edge of saying it could be this, it could be that, maybe it's something in between and may never be decided. I think there is a sort of enriching tension in hybrid works where they're drawing material from one area and combining it with another.

*I am referring to those pieces that change a lot when you see them interacting with the body.*

CB: I think that's a point for museums or galleries to address, because although it is lovely to see people wearing pieces of jewellery and clothing, it is also good to have pieces in a public collection and you have to use other means to show how things behave on the body. I think we live in a world where things can escape their original role all the time. They are reinterpreted and recontextualized. Even when a piece of jewellery is intended to be worn in a particular way, someone will wear it in a different way.

*How has your career in teaching affected your practice?*

CB: Hugely. I get a lot from teaching because it is a really good exercise in trying to confront all sorts of work and understand it. Sometimes work is quite difficult; maybe it's unexciting or obscure, but you've still got to think of something positive to say. Trying to draw something out, to improve it, is a very good exercise for when I get back in the studio.

*What are the crucial or desirable qualities that you look for when interviewing potential jewellery students?*

CB: A level of energy, curiosity and a sort of adventurous thinking is required; I suppose somebody who has a persistent quality about pursuing things, making things and seeing connections.

**Fig. 44**
Caroline Broadhead. *Shirt with
Long Sleeves* 1982. Nylon.
Shirt.
Photo: John Hilliard.

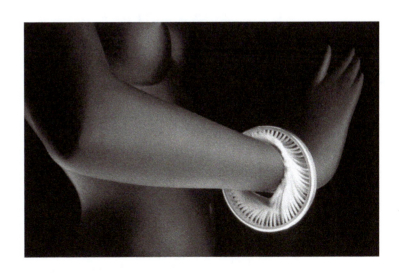

**Fig. 45**
Caroline Broadhead. *Tufty
Bracelet* 1979. Nylon, wood,
silver. Bracelet.
Photo: David Cripps.

# 7

# Iris Eichenberg

**Born: 1965, Göttingen, Germany**

**Fig. 46**
Iris Eichenberg. *Untitled,
Blossom* series 1998. Silver,
wool. Brooch.
Photo: Ron Zijlstra.

*RB: How and why did you start making jewellery?*

IE: In the first place it was the freedom of material in relation to a human size, the ability to handle the objects and the context of the body as subject and object.

*Could you describe the developmental phases of a piece of work?*

IE: If I could define it, it would mean that I had a recipe. Generally, I have a clue, an inkling about a sphere. Then I collect materials and forms, I shift them around and I allow them to talk to each other. I fight with the values and the significance of the materials; I try to push their boundaries and use their stubbornness. I try to overcome their inscribed meaning and value, to boycott the way we are used to identifying them.

*Does your making process incorporate drawing or model making?*

IE: No, never. I work through materials. Very occasionally, I will lay down an object and draw around it, and then the next step has little to do with the drawing, but more with the feeling or the conclusion of the drawing.

*With each new body of work, you often change the primary materials; why?*

IE: I always try to find a challenge in a new material and to tell something in a new voice. I'm interested in the process of developing work, far more than the comfort of knowing how something turns out.

*Do you favour any particular tool or technique?*

IE: I think you need a reason to use a certain tool, just as you need a certain reason to use a material.

*Why have you incorporated a lot of ceramic elements into your jewellery?*

IE: There are certain qualities to the materials I use, which is that they never need a construction and what it becomes is never pre-defined. It is not that I have to make the parts and then assemble them; there is still a lot happening during the process of working porcelain. You can still alter it in so many steps during the making process, so that you directly make decisions about what something will become.

There's also something to ceramics, just as with knitting, which has a domestic quality. It's a material we relate to, it's a material we touch with our hands, we drink out of it; they are the objects of our daily routines and rituals. There are a lot of objects in our daily lives with which we surround ourselves made from porcelain, so you do share a common knowledge with lot of other people that have a bodily response to those materials. It reminds us of bodily functions. The interactions with the objects are what I am actually trying to take, so it's not so much porcelain per se, but more for the quality of porcelain, and the fact that cast porcelain remembers where it has been.

*You've just mentioned knitting; could you describe your attraction to this technique?*

IE: It is something that obviously enables me to address certain things I cannot address in another technique. When I started knitting, I was experimenting, I had a certain idea of what kind of shapes I wanted to make, but whatever I did it would convey so much to its construction. Knitting enabled me to make something step by step. I'd cut something and then I'd add something, so it was a discussion with the form while making, and I could judge whether it was right or not.

I think there's a similarity in the way I work with porcelain and the way I work with knitting; because you create something out of nothing, it's neither taking away nor adding. Whereas my later works have more of a collage quality, and that involves finding materials that have a battle, start a dialogue and inform each other. With porcelain and knitting, they're totally undefined materials; porcelain is fluid and wool is just one long string, which you then start to build something up out of nothing.

*Is there an overall theme that connects all your work?*

IE: The investment in things we handle and for the reasons we keep small-scale objects. The human being and how the things we surround ourselves with talk about us. The care they need, never left on a wall – the neediness of being handled or passed on. The willingness of being in conversation with its surrounding wearer or the table it is placed on or left behind.

The constant dialogue, and the fact that it always makes me see objects and relate to them differently. I guess the way they might serve in that constant dialogue is my biggest fascination. What they say about us and what is value and preciseness. That is the central question of all my work.

*One of the recurring motifs in your work seems to be twigs or bits of trees, as in the series* Baume. *Could you explain their presence?*

IE: I have a fascination with trees, but I probably see something totally different than other people. For me it's a metaphor for so many different systems, whether it's interconnections or a cycle of things that reoccur in your life constantly. I use it as a tool, relying on a subconscious agreement that we all draw from its metaphors.

There are various reasons to what the tree has given me, and it's not so much fixed as one symbol or discourse. For me, they are blood vessels, relations, and systems, but I believe that you cannot work – be – make – think and abstract your thoughts as an artist based on, or starting with, obsessions because nobody else will see them as you do.

*Other frequently present motifs are hands or references to body parts. Could you discuss these?*

IE: The body as a metaphoric tool kit is familiar to me, but in this case you could see them as a representation of keys: keys to houses, keys to the existences of individuals. I could have used other organs or objects, which represent individuals as beings within a system or organization. The making and/or material is what refers to culture, class, taste and folklore.

It has nothing to do with my preferences, because I have used materials and combinations of techniques and materials I dislike, but actually found appropriate to represent a culture or the remnants of a culture or a group of people still represented by a taste or style.

*Is it important for you to give titles?*

IE: I never try to explain work with titles. For example, the names of the different pieces in the series *Heimat* are very normal and do not pretend to be anything that you cannot see. They're archetypal things – the names of my parents, the names of the different fields in the village where I was born. I think by having something that sounds so normal, it leaves far more space for associations.

*How do you feel about people interpreting your work differently to your intentions?*

IE: I am trying to refer to subconscious feelings, whilst trying to stay away from clear messages. I am not telling a story.

*How would you explain the content or narrative of your work?*

IE: What is a narrative? Narration does not always need to explain something, but it can also produce a new realm of emotions. Some of the porcelain works I have done before are not telling a story; rather they enable you to realize something about how you are culturally programmed to interact with the objects that define you. You are part of your surroundings, and without the objects that surround you, you would be a different person.

The discussion I always have with my students is to not illustrate something, but if you have a story or narrative, the work should run parallel. It should not illustrate stories, feelings or concepts, but it should have an existence by itself. It should not retell the narrative, but it should be the consequence of the narrative.

*Often your pieces consist of two or more elements. Could you discuss the dialogue between them?*

IE: How can two objects be placed next to each other and immediately change each other's meaning? By just taking an ordinary object like a cup, a pearl or something out of my studio and placing it next to something else, an undefined form or starting point of work, the significance of the other part is totally changed, and that happens with things that are nearly nothing. They become in relation to each other – give and take meaning.

What is it that we can identify in, say, something found at the curb of a street which might be a leftover piece of plastic that a car's driven over? Why can it be so little, almost nothing, and still be far more than an ornamented, complicated and constructed piece of jewellery?

I'm always interested in how much can you take away to actually say more, instead of piling up stuff and explaining yourself. And how far are you able to actually ever make something? Or do you always depend on the fact that you have to recognize it in something which exists, but you could never actually make. I do not know how to solve this, but I am interested in this process of learning how to recognize beauty in nothing.

*On first glance, your pieces don't look like jewellery. What's your take on this?*

IE: My interest is far more sculptural than a design jeweller's interest. It's far more to do with the object that comments upon the body and relates to the body.

*What relationship do you want your work to establish with the wearer?*

IE: It's a struggle with the wearer, because I don't want the wearer being dominated by a piece. I want the interaction between the wearer and the piece.

*Do you favour a particular jewellery typology?*

IE: I've made a lot of brooches, but actually I hate brooches. I'm constantly trying to find another kind of wearability. The *Timeline* pieces are all chatelaines, and I like that so much more. It is better because if you wear something on your hips or your belt, the piece becomes like a utensil. So, there is a tool-like aspect to them, which I value because it is far more interactive than just using the wearer as a wall to pin something on.

The knitted work sat so naturally on the body, or went through buttonholes, so it didn't need to be changed or altered to be perfectly wearable, but if you took it off the body it did not lose anything. It wasn't dependant on the body, but it was inspired by, and would work with, the body without mechanical additions to make them wearable. Necklaces are always so limited by function. I think I am a strange person in this profession to struggle so much with wearability, but I still search for contact or interaction with the body all the time.

*You have a European cultural background, yet you're presently teaching at the Cranbrook Academy of Art in America. Has your transatlantic move affected your jewellery?*

IE: The recent body of work *New Rooms* is so informed by moving to another country; placing myself in a totally different realm of aesthetics, style and meaning of crafts. Observing it from the outside is such a different thing from being part of it – especially living in Cranbrook and being part of such a strong craft community, where everything I am surrounded by is actually handmade and nothing is alike. No door is alike, no gate is like another door. Everything is handmade. I don't think I can ever produce something which is not influenced by my surroundings; I am a product of the environment I am living in.

I'm constantly making portraits, whether it's a portrait of myself, whether it's a portrait of the society or the context I am in: portraying my life through different bodies of work.

*Do you write about your work?*

IE: If I write about my work it is so cryptic, it's so metaphorical that it's very hard for somebody else to understand. I wonder if when my writing communicates what I think, it becomes a thing by itself. My thoughts about my work are constantly shifting; I've learned I need the outsider observing and writing about my work. However, I want a reaction to the work but, not a description, because everybody can look for themselves. I also think it's fine sometimes to be speechless, and to try not to intellectualize.

*What approach to teaching do you adopt?*

**IE:** I'm trying not to force students to become little copies of myself. I try to find out what they're good at, whether that is art driven jewellery or something that relates more to design and fashion. Whatever they do, I want them to be as original as possible and to develop their own voice.

**Fig. 47**
Iris Eichenberg. *Untitled, Weiss* series 2005. Silver, porcelain. Brooch.
Photo: Francis Willemstijn.

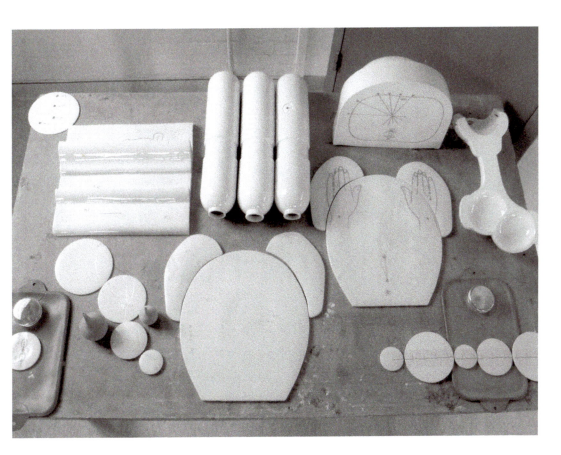

**Fig. 48**
Iris Eichenberg. *Untitled,*
studies EKWC 2000. Mixed
media, rubber, porcelain.
Objects.
Photo: Corne Bastiaansen.

# 8

# Karl Fritsch

**Born: 1963, Sonthofen, Germany**

**Fig. 49**
Karl Fritsch. *Superbia* 2008.
Silver, diamond, crystal,
aquamarine, topaz, zirconia.
Ring (from the series of the
7 deadly sins).
Photo: Karl Fritsch.

*RB: How and why did you start making jewellery?*

**KF:** After school I wanted to work with my hands rather than pursue something academic. My first ambition was to become a wood carver, but I missed the deadline for the course and was due to start national service. Fortunately, I discovered the jewellery school at Pforzheim just in time and ended up there; so you could say jewellery saved me from the army!

*At that early stage, were you fully aware of contemporary jewellery?*

**KF:** Well, I remember seeing Claus Bury's work in the contemporary section of the Schmuck museum in Pforzheim, and this marked a major change in my thinking. I was amazed that anyone would make work like that, so it inspired and encouraged me to make the jewellery that I wanted to see on people, even though at that stage I wasn't sure exactly what that might be.

I started working alone, collecting shapes by making repoussé containers inspired by vegetables and fruits. Then I heard about the academy in Munich without really knowing who Hermann Jünger was. So I arrived from the countryside for my interview with him carrying my collection of mini vegetables and must have made quite a different impression from the norm. It was a good challenge and the right place to exchange ideas, be questioned and get food for the brain! My relationship with Jünger was very important, and we had lots of discussions about jewellery. I had to fight for my ideas in many intense battles. There was a lot of work being done with nice surfaces and arrangements, but I had to challenge this. I made a series of works called *Verschandler,* which were not meant to be aesthetically beautiful and Jünger got very upset about them.

*I believe you made those pieces to challenge notions of beauty.*

**KF:** I was thinking about fractals, unorganized shapes, and whether they can be jewellery. Looking back I now understand that he was upset because he realized the work was actually very aesthetic, but my attitude and understanding were not aligned with the work; rather, they were just provocative. At the academy it was like a statement thrown into the world without proof, and it's taken time to prove that this kind of work can be beautiful. But even just the idea that something reject can be beautiful has a sort of beauty because it requires the observer to look for the beauty rather than having it presented explicitly to them.

*Do you believe that your work can speak alone?*

**KF:** Yes, but I am happy to discuss it as well. I offer something and put things out in the world, but I don't want to fix thoughts or predefine how that something should be received. The viewer can have their ideas and interpretations and they don't have to be identical to mine.

*You don't mind if a work is interpreted differently to that intended?*

**KF:** I think this is actually a quality. I don't consider my work to be finished when I complete it; that is done by the wearer. It's most fulfilling when the right piece finds the right person; it's a pleasure to see how they fit together.

*Do you therefore only work to commission when the person is open to your methods?*

**KF:** Yes, if someone says they want such and such a design, then I point them towards a commercial jeweller. I need an intuitive, spontaneous reaction in my working process, so I can't do an exact drawing of what will happen. The making has its own rules, and then I allow things to happen within these rules.

*Has your approach to technique changed over the years?*

**KF:** I am often catching up with skills and techniques that I learned as far back as my apprenticeship. For example trying to make a basic ordinary solitaire ring that's never been seen before. Reinventing or revitalizing the simplest or most common things, of which hundreds of thousands are already in existence, often presents the biggest challenge.

*Would you say you specifically work with traditional jewellery typologies?*

**KF:** Yes, I ask myself what can I offer to the development of this typology and how can I make a new version of the moment?

*What are the developmental stages in a piece?*

**KF:** I just make. I have to sit down and make, and there aren't really any developmental stages. Occasionally, ideas are developed through writing or models, but mostly it's the concentration of working in the studio. I don't draw; everything is done directly by the hands.

I do make a lot of models with soft wax, because it is so malleable and spontaneous, plus it responds immediately to my fingers.

It can instantaneously translate the touch of the moment into material form.

*How do you decide whether the result is significant or not?*

**KF:** There is a certain excitement that comes with making when things are going well. The rules of the moment are my concentration, the material, my mood and the time of the day, and they all contribute to creating the right conditions for the work to come into existence. Maybe this sounds a bit too mystic.

*How hard do you have to work at creating the sense of spontaneous joy that characterizes much of your work?*

**KF:** I know myself and what I can do at what time. Also, I can put myself into the right state of mind to work. It might take three hours or three days, by which I don't mean that I don't work; I work for three days to get into a state of being close to myself, a state that is in synthesis with my work. Now, I don't have to sit and wait for this to happen, because I can kick-start the process.

*Is it important that traces of the process of hand manufacture, such as fingerprints, remain visible in the final work?*

**KF:** The fact that my fingerprints remain is not important for me; it's not like Gerd Rothmann's work, where the fingerprint means something. Actually, I prefer it when you cannot see exactly how a work is made. I like the look when it seems as though it hasn't been made, so it looks found or even dug up. The technical aspect or making process should not be the first quality that comes through; rather, it should be more an appearance of its shape, or that it looks soft for example.

*How long did it take you to make technique disappear?*

**KF:** It takes much longer than learning it! However, I do think it is important to learn techniques such as casting in the time-honoured fashion. Then it becomes a question of ownership; making it yours rather than making it disappear. It's the same with setting stones, it took me ages to learn how to set stones, and I hated it because it's so labour intensive. Then after years, I learnt how to use it for my means, but you can't learn it like that from scratch; you have to reinvent techniques on your own terms.

*You really appear to have taken on the challenge of reinvigorating the traditional stone setting, for example the recent chewing gum–like ribbon bands or the chunky, almost naïve, cylindrical settings. Could you discuss why this has been so important for you?*

KF: One part of my practice involves the spontaneous work in wax; however, I enjoy juxtaposing it with a contrasting element such as a set stone. The latter is high end, whereas casting soft wax is sometimes prejudicially referred to as a lazy way of working! I like uniting these things; plus the critics shut up as soon as you put a stone in.

*So the stone is a device of elevation.*

KF: Yes, I use it to elevate, or moreover, to contrast this unshaped or spontaneous form. With a stone you can't be that spontaneous, you have to drill a perfect hole and you have to find the right place. Therefore, stones contrast the roughness of the casting and make it a precious piece of pretty jewellery; this changes attitudes and also renders it more sellable.

*Do you ever feel the latter risks compromising the work?*

KF: No. It's just an aspect of my work. I wanted to combine and contrast the high end with what might almost be described as a hobby technique. I think they support one another, and the nice side effect is that people are interested in them. So I don't feel that it diminishes my practice in any way; it's still good work.

*Could you discuss your jewellery that exploits the sprues from the lost wax casting process?*

KF: The sprue has always been important for me. Often, I leave the sprue because it's how the work is born; it's an umbilical cord. When you are applying sprues there are rules, but you can use them in such a way that you retake ownership of the technique.

*Have you ever used non-precious alloys?*

KF: I have, but I prefer precious metals due to my training and they are good at conveying certain ideas. I immediately liked working with precious metals, but it's a little bit uptight because you're taught to be careful so that if you cut something out for example you minimize the remainder. However, one must always remember that even a precious metal is just a material, just stuff. So the challenge was to eliminate this uptightness about using too much for reasons of weight and cost. I wanted to ditch the material preciousness and make gold look like clay or plasticine.

*I believe you recycled a lot of gold to make work in the past. Was it important that these pieces of jewellery had a history of their own?*

KF: I used to buy a lot of gold at pawn shops because it was the cheapest way to get gold to cast. I appreciated the material and its convention of being ordinary common jewellery that had been exchanged for money more than any personal stories it may have carried.

*So, it's not about an echo?*

KF: Correct.

*Melting these pieces together must have produced somewhat unpredictable alloys. Did you attempt to control them when casting?*

KF: Well, as you say, it can be quite unpredictable; the exact colour cannot be foreseen and so on. Then again through experience I know what might come out more or less: knowledge through experience.

*Do you attempt to undermine preconceptions of what jewellery should be?*

KF: This is not my goal or starting point. I offer something, which is a manifestation of the kind of jewellery that I want to see on people. Nowadays, it is a positive offer of a new version and not an attempt to undermine the conventional stuff, which incidentally I believe has every right to be and I really appreciate its existence.

*Would you say then that you reinterpret traditional jewellery typologies through humour?*

KF: Yeah, humour is important. Well no, I mean it's quite a serious business!

*Yet, the work seems to portray a certain sense of joy, enjoyment and fun.*

KF: It's serious, it's not a joke, but it is done with humour. For example with the latest works I am drilling holes into diamonds, which is fun to do. There is humour in devaluing such a precious thing by destroying the status symbol. People think you're crazy because drilling the hole means weight is lost and with it, value. So, effectively the purchaser is paying for the hole and by consequence for something to be ruined. At the same time, the hole is not a joke; it's the shape of the hole that gives value, its sculptural aspect.

A piece is good for me when you not only laugh about it, but when a lot of things come together, its look, its philosophy. So, in other words, strong jewellery facilitates a broad spectrum of interpretations.

**Fig. 50**
Karl Fritsch. *Ring* 2007. Gold oxidized, black diamond with hole.
Photo: Karl Fritsch.

**Fig. 51**
Karl Fritsch. *Models for Rings* 2003–2004. Wax.
Photo: Karl Fritsch.

# 9

# Rian de Jong

**Born: 1951, Zoeterwoude, The
Netherlands**

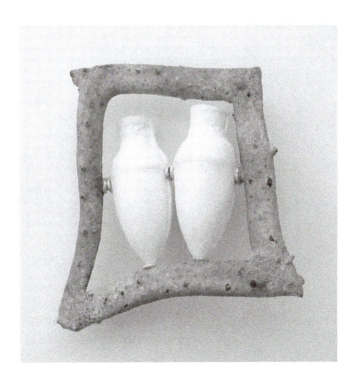

**Fig. 52**
Rian de Jong. *Still* 2003. Black
coral (unpolished), ceramic.
Brooch.
Photo: Rian de Jong.

*RB: How did you realize that you wanted to work with jewellery?*

**RJ:** It was a very long journey. My mum and grandmother were always busy making things, so I suppose they passed this manual dexterity onto me, along with a passion for it. I studied on various courses, including art therapy and a four-year apprenticeship to become a lecturer in textiles. Eventually, I registered with the Rietveld Academy for three years of evening classes in sculpture, during which period I noticed that, in fact, I was more interested in jewellery and then took a three-year class as well. The realization came rather late; I was already over thirty years of age when I graduated from Rietveld and began making jewellery seriously.

*What inspires your jewellery?*

**RJ:** I always find this hard to define. I have travelled extensively and maybe it develops out of that. One takes many impressions back home. I don't mean that they develop directly into the work; however, the impressions do stay with you. Impressions of life you witness and how one lives in different places or countries. In Turkey, where I lived for a long time, life is so simple, so wonderful. If you open a tin of olives, this tin is inevitably used afterwards for another purpose. A functional object often has three or four different lives. I find this beautiful and most precious if life can be like this; that you care for and use the things you have around you.

I use these ideas about life in my work, but not to decorate or make things beautiful. My work always has something rough about it, and therefore reflects life and not beauty. I think ideas like these occupy my mind when I make jewellery. In my head I am not making jewellery, but a form, and this form can then be worn on the body and will communicate while worn.

I think observing and experiencing life is the most inspiring. It does not matter if this is in a third world, second world or first world country; behaviour, attitudes and cultures are always different. After a while this gives the concepts, the forms and the materials to work on.

*What are the developmental phases in your work?*

**RJ:** My practical work is concentrated in the winter. In summer, because of my travelling, I hardly work on jewellery. The advantage is that one's head is emptied in summer, so there is a lot of room for new experiments in autumn.

Most of the time I start by playing around to warm up; then, through working with my hands my brain starts to work as well and the process for new work really gets going. New ideas then often come up in the middle of this process, and those will be developed as well, and sometimes they are better than the previous ones you were working on. The unconscious moments are worth so much; at these moments you can't control, things just happen right in front of your eyes, a gift, and you get better solutions, a new idea or a new piece of work.

*Could you discuss your most recent pieces?*

RJ: The brooch *NYNY* that I made in New York this winter was my last piece in a series of work. If you have a long stay in another country, there are a lot more things you have to remember; where, how, what, whom – sometimes it's confusing or chaotic. Notes will help to structure what you want or have to do, and at which moment.

I had all kind of notes on the wall, in between was the jewellery as well. For me, the jewellery began to look like the notes stuck on the wall. I like it when all of a sudden it projects associations you didn't think of before. That is what I mean with looking very well at the process; during the making process you can enrich the piece by being aware of what happens around it. So for me, it is a kind of note, maybe a very abstract one. I think it has more associations as well, which will occur with time.

*What can you say about the forms and shapes of your jewellery?*

RJ: Sometimes they are forms that everybody can recognize and therefore wear. For example, I made a lot of wearable houses in a naïve style reminiscent of children's drawings, in different materials.

On the way they change into more abstract forms; however, you can always still recognize something of the original house shape within the designs. In fact, this recognition is important; the wearer must be able to identify with it. On the other hand, I also experiment with materials and search for their limitations and qualities, so the form may be dictated by the experiment and might therefore be much more associative.

*Is it important to draw?*

RJ: For me, not really. I draw to keep things in mind while I am working and ideas are coming up, but when I look back to it

I can't work anymore with the drawing; I am already further on at that point.

*Could you specify what role, if any, model making, visual research, photography and writing play in the development of a piece?*

RJ: I do not draw to start a project. I don't know what is going on in my mind. I know this is difficult to understand, but it is for me as well. I have to start working, playing with materials, making models, and after some time ideas and forms occur. Tryouts are around for some time, up to several years, I see them every now and then in the corner of my eye. So I do something with it and put it on the waiting table again to find out if it is not worth working further on, or whether it turns into a concept which works out fine.

Visual research is a sort of everyday awareness – looking at what happens around you and noticing some special things in your mind. And of course exhibitions, libraries – often museum libraries – have information about special subjects, in text and photography, but seeing too much can stop you from doing anything anymore.

*Do you always use natural materials?*

RJ: Of course, after working for more than twenty years things have changed. After graduation, I worked mostly with wood; I could express myself in this material. But after time you want to change, and so I started to experience different materials. I did not love working with metals as much; it is too cold, too shiny and too hard. Finally, for me it lacks emotion. From time to time, I will move away from the material I am working with. I need some fresh input, and a way to achieve this is by using other skills and materials which really can help to get a new angle of incidence. The feeling and emotion I have for natural materials then returns. All you find in nature is so vibrant; it's alive and wonderful to work with.

Now, after years of working, I am able to approach metal in another way; with another technique like electroforming I can handle the form and surface much better. It is the same with stones; I had no admiration for the cuts and facets or means to put them in a small setting. Now, I find stones in nature and use them as I find them. It is fun to realize it's a natural product after all. I discovered a new way of setting the stones and am able to work with any chip, or whatever stony material I find; that is exciting.

*Do you find it difficult to work with materials that are naturally beautiful?*

RJ: When I walk through nature, I think why should we design things ourselves? Nature is perfect, we need a lot of skills, energy, computer technology and raw materials just to create. Yet, how can we reach the perfection of nature? But the urge to develop, the quest, the doing makes us work on it.

I think it depends on whether you consider it as material or as naturally beautiful. With the first, the material, I can work, but with the last, maybe not.

*What role does technique play in your work?*

RJ: Technique is just a medium for me. It does not interest me a lot; you just require it in order to be able to produce work. I am not a technical person, but have gained some technical expertise through time. If I want to do something, I'll just do a short course and then learn the basics. I know how things work and can apply this knowledge. I enjoy working like that. I am working with ceramic by collaborating with a ceramic artist. I don't know much about ceramics; however, I am still able to work with this material in my way and I love that. I am not fond of prescribed techniques because then things all start to look the same.

*Do you mean that you attempt to approach the work like a child discovering something new?*

RJ: Yes, I hope that my work is and looks spontaneous. The experience and emotion the spectator has with the piece is more important than how it is made.

*Which jewellery artists do you like?*

RJ: I admire very much the work of Warwick Freeman, who is from New Zealand, because he is able to show his cultural background through his jewellery. He does work a lot with natural materials and what he does with it, often just a little, makes it so strong.

*Why do you think that over the last four decades or so, there has been a different jewellery culture in northern Europe than in Italy or France?*

RJ: This all depends on the cultural background. In Nordic countries, travel and discovery of the world has always been important. Norway, England, Holland and Portugal have discovered the world and were traders. Holland is very small and for that, needs to look further than its borders. After the Second World War, the country was developing very strongly towards new materials and new systems. All old traditions went overboard and a new way of life was the future. A revolutionary change in social and sexual behaviour took place; it all opened up and freed itself from the Calvinistic boundaries. In the jewellery field, we had a few very strong people in the 1960s who stood up against tradition; they started to work with new, non-precious materials, ready-mades, textiles, which had never taken place. These people were also teaching at the academies, where they influenced the attitude of the students towards a more independent way of working. In Italy and France, there has not been this kind of strong change. I think their rich traditions, as well as using precious materials and craftsmanship, is much more evident in their jewellery.

*How do you see the future of jewellery?*

**RJ:** From the 1990s until now, the work of jewellers has been very individual. The choice of concept, material and techniques is all very personal. I do not know if we can survive with this way of working much longer, because hardly anybody can live from it; only a few manage this feat. I would expect that the more mass products that are produced will affect jewellery makers as well. China produces a kind of jewellery – radiant, celebrity-like, bling-bling – sold for almost nothing. This is a kind of mass-produced jewellery which looks like expensive jewellery and is available to everybody because of the low prices. And who doesn't like to feel like a queen? The majority of people who buy jewellery like to understand it on first sight. For this reason, I do not see a future for mass-produced designer jewellery, because these designs have many more layers to recognize. There are initiatives in producing designer jewellery, but it is all on a very small scale; it needs explanation and is only available in a few places.

I would have imagined that the computer would have had more influence on jewellery makers, but most of the current generation were not brought up with the computer and its possibilities. Maybe the next generations will make more use of computer-produced work.

*How do you feel globalization has affected contemporary jewellery?*

**RJ:** Not long ago, just 100 years back, only a few people travelled. They purchased precious and high-standard art and products, which were a source of inspiration to people back home. Nowadays everybody travels; the products or souvenirs they buy do not have this quality, they are cheap and general products. With the Internet, all our work is accessible to everybody. What does it mean for our work when borders disappear, special cultures can be adopted by everyone? Will it also become cheap and general? As the world continues to globalize, influences come from everywhere. Does that mean that our jewellery will be much more universal, or all more of the same? Or will the work become much more individual? Or will we still find other ways to develop? I think we cannot answer these questions; it is too early. Time will tell!

*To whom would you most like to sell your work?*

**RJ:** I had this exhibition in Germany, Chemnitz, just after the Berlin Wall had come down. The people there still did not have much money, but two young people bought a relatively cheap piece for seventy German marks. For them it was a lot, yet they bought it and loved it so much. That was very rewarding to see and probably my best sale ever. I like to sell to people who really love and appreciate the work, its meaning and the thinking behind it, like some collectors who buy work from almost every series. Several museums all over the world have my work in their collections; this is of course very important, as well as being recognition for your work and highlighting it to other people who buy your work.

*What in your life do you like so much that it could be art?*

**RJ:** To live well is an art form in itself.

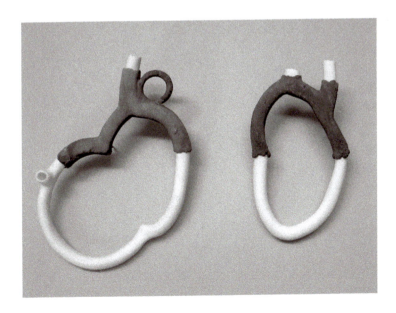

**Fig. 53**
Rian de Jong. *Brooches* 2007.
Bone china, copper.
Photo: Rian de Jong.

*What advice would you give to students or other practitioners working in contemporary jewellery?*

**RJ:** Let your hands dictate the brain and not the other way around; make something with the image already in your head.

**Fig. 54**
Rian de Jong. *2 Takjes* 2005.
Black coral, garnets. Brooches.
Photo: Rian de Jong.

# 10

# Daniel Kruger

## Born: 1951, Cape Town, South Africa

**Fig. 55**
Daniel Kruger. *Necklace* 2001.
Gold, plastic tubing fragments,
linen cord, silver.
Photo: Udo W. Beier.

RB: *How and why did you decide to start making jewellery?*

DK: I grew up on a farm. There were always things being made or repaired – be it baking bread or putting up a fence, darning socks or repairing a windmill. Making things oneself, using manual skills and being inventive were part of farm life then. This may well have had an influence on me.

From early childhood I made things and improvised toys with things I had found. At about the age of fourteen I was sent to a school in Cape Town. In the afternoons I attended an art centre for children where ceramics, painting, textile printing and jewellery were taught. I eventually did art as a school subject.

It was apparent to me that I would choose to do something in this line professionally. Jewellery was the choice in the end but I can't explain why. Perhaps it was because of the intricacy and the small scale and its private nature. Perhaps also because of the fascination gemstones have for me!

*Could you identify what qualities gemstones have that you find so intriguing, and how this filters into your work?*

DK: The light, which is concentrated and reflected when the stones are faceted, or the glow of a cabochon or tumbled stone. The depth, the mysterious inner life of the stones. These are qualities also found in glass and plastic. The difference is that stones are harder and often have a greater brilliance, as in the case of the diamond, or a more interesting inner life. They have a presence and they are found and not made.

Natural stones are supposed to possess certain powers – I would like to believe this. I try to transmit, or refer to these qualities when I use glass. The gemstones I have used are very modest and don't have much more to offer than colour and sparkle.

*What inspires your work?*

DK: The things and objects I have around me or see pictures of, both natural as well as artificial (those things that people make), things from different historical periods and different cultures. Another influence is where I come from: the southern African landscape, the natural environment and the interferences made by people in it. Because the landscape is mostly in a natural state, the interferences are apparent. The European landscape is virtually entirely cultivated.

A farmhouse in the middle of nowhere, the remains of a stone wall or traces of long-since-abandoned irrigation furrows and a well, a simple apparatus like a windmill or sophisticatedly constructed steel pylons carrying electricity across a deserted space.

What I find remarkable is the human effort and ingenuity to make, control and direct and to maintain what he has placed in the natural environment; the temporality of human efforts and nature's ability to reclaim what has been taken from her: Nature as provider of resources and retriever, oblivious of man's efforts. Art and Nature.

*How have you translated these ideas about nature and its cycles into jewellery?*

DK: I don't make jewellery *about* anything. This is the way I see the world and with this view on materials and things I make jewellery.

*What are the phases in the development of a piece after the initial idea?*

DK: The initial idea, its source, is difficult to locate. Ideas come from all over the place, and it could be that I see something that I would like to investigate. This could be a stone or a plant, a constellation of forms or a piece of jewellery in a book or a piece made by someone I admire or an aspect of any of these. There are thoughts in my work, but I do not work with thoughts themselves – there are no intellectual concepts. Sometimes the process of making takes off immediately; sometimes the idea has to ferment and be distilled.

During the making, the aim of what it will be is always present. It will be jewellery in the conventional sense of a ring, a necklace, earrings, a brooch or, seldom, a bracelet. It is important that the piece is sturdy enough for the wearer to enjoy wearing the piece without fearing damage to the piece or damage to him- or herself. This practical side flows into the concept.

Its place is the body, and its intention is to enhance the wearer as well as to be an object of contemplation, to be taken in the hand and looked at from all sides. It is an artefact conceived and made by one person for the enjoyment of another person. It should be more than an amusement or distraction – it should add something to life, be a worthwhile experience and hold its own over time.

*How much importance do you place upon functionality?*

DK: Functionality is when a piece works as jewellery, it then functions as jewellery, which, in my opinion, is why one makes jewellery and not something else.

*What is a piece of jewellery for you?*

DK: Jewellery is an art form in which ideas are expressed in a small format. A microcosm of abstract or figurative forms; a sign on the body, which enriches and elevates, of which the possession in itself gives pleasure, stimulates contemplation, enchants and seduces.

The small scale demands that it is taken in the hand to look at and inspect it from close up. What the jewel feels like, its weight, the material from which it is made, how the piece is crafted, the texture, the surface, the form. What the front and the back look like. It amazes and astonishes.

*Did Hermann Jünger influence you, and, if so, how?*

**DK:** Hermann Jünger was one of the important people in my development. What I admire about his jewellery is that it is jewellery; it is not *about* jewellery. It is the honesty in his work. Jünger gave me the confidence to make the work that was me; he recognized that which was true and that which was affected.

*Could you discuss your experiences of making jewellery in the 1970s and 1980s and say if that differs from your approach now, twenty years later?*

**DK:** In 1974 I came to study with Hermann Jünger. It was a time when we were looking at the natural, the authentic, the honest craftsperson, the origins of ornament in folk art and tradition, avoiding the frivolous and concentrating on the essential while maintaining the expressive.

By the 1980s, a shift had taken place in the idea of what jewellery was about: the craftsperson became less of an honest maker and more of a designer. Jewellery's exclusivity was its innovative appeal, popular and affordable but conceptually sophisticated. Traditional materials were out. It was a stimulating time for me, because many questions were posed about the whys and what-fors and hows in jewellery that I benefited from. I agreed with some of the ideas and assimilated them into my approach. If one looks at what I made in the 1980s and subsequently, it is evident that I did not depart entirely from the approach of the 1970s: the honest craftsman, respect for traditional materials, exclusivity, uniqueness.

*Your work often involves the use of found objects. How do you feel about using materials that already have a history?*

**DK:** It is the history or story that interests me. That which was there before me, which had something to say, had a function, a meaning or in spite of its age or condition, still does. It is a reminder of that which was – it is memory.

I once said in a lecture that I want my work to look old and not new, as if it has always existed. I try to anticipate the aging and wearing of a piece through patination and treatment of the surface.

Something new has not lived, has had no interaction with people and has no history. This does not necessarily mean that an artefact has to show wear to appeal to me. The perfection of something new, its newness, its untouchedness can be exciting in itself. My interest, however, is continuity: the past reaching into the present and extending into the future.

I also once wrote that I aim for imperfection and to show the traces of process, the blemishes incurred by manual manufacture to distinguish what I make from the all-too-predictable perfection that is typical of industrially produced things (this was written in the context of my ceramics).

*Where does your enthusiasm for ceramics come from? Is it simply a medium or something more?*

**DK:** I find ceramics from all periods and cultures exciting; primarily those that are handmade or retain an individual character and are functional or refer to function. Things that are used in the home and enrich life. The small scale, the decorative, the celebratory aspect, whether humble or grand. It is the refinement in civilization.

*Have you or would you ever use ceramics in your jewellery?*

**DK:** Ceramics is about a material and jewellery is about a form. Would I make jewellery with clay instead of metal? No. Would I use a ceramic element in jewellery the way I use plastic or glass? Yes.

*You seem to have developed a language of using materials that speaks about culture and refers to place. Would you agree with this observation?*

**DK:** It seems to be the case.

*If your intention is to communicate to the public through jewellery, what do you want to say?*

**DK:** Communicate to the public – I know what you mean, yet the intention I have is to communicate to a person. That museums buy new pieces feels wrong to me, because this prevents the pieces from being used, of becoming the property of a person or a series of persons, of changing hands and gaining a provenance.

What do I want to communicate? A difficult question…All that which I draw on when conceiving a piece and the skills in making it.

*How important is technique for you? If you have got an idea, would you ever delegate somebody else to make it for you? And, if not, why?*

**DK:** Technique or the acquisition of skills. To be shown or taught a method of doing something or to discover it through contemplation, or by trial and error to find a method and mastering the method is most gratifying and excites me no end. I so thoroughly enjoy the challenges of the making, of solving formal and technical problems, even the repetitive and monotonous, that I would never have someone else make my work for me – it would deny me the satisfaction, and the work would not be entirely mine.

*What role does research play in your work?*

**DK:** I listen to what people have to say and I look at everything. How things are made and how and where they are/were used, interests me. I inform myself about this. Even though I can only seldom say where my ideas come from or what they refer to, I draw on these observations and the artefacts and natural objects I have seen and surround myself with. Does this count as research?

*Have there been any events of specific importance that have changed or influenced your life or work?*

**DK:** What is important and has made a big difference in my life is living in Germany and being in Europe: here I have access to all that which in South Africa, in my social environment there, was admired from afar. I am not a European, I am South African, yet Europe stands for the culture I was brought up in and that which I strive for and identify with. I don't always understand it, I don't always like it, but it is that which I need.

*How do you think the contemporary jewellery market will develop?*

**DK:** An interest in art jewellery does seem to be growing. With the number of schools that exist and what can be seen at jewellery events (Schmuck IHM Munich, SOFA etc), it does look as if it is growing.

*The consequences of globalization can now also be seen in jewellery too. Do you think where you study and live in Europe still determines your chances of being successful in our field?*

**DK:** That seems to be the case. The West – Western Europe, North America – seem to provide the events, schools and the galleries. Australia, Japan in Asia, Israel in the Near East, Stellenbosch in South Africa, South America? Europe and North America seem to decide what jewellery has to look like! The rest of the world follows adding a local flavour here and there.

**Fig. 56**
Daniel Kruger. *Necklace* 2007.
Silver filigree, pigment.
Photo: Udo W. Beier.

**Fig. 57**
Daniel Kruger. *Necklace* 2008.
Silver filigree, pigment.
Photo: Udo W. Beier.

# 11

# Otto Künzli

**Born: 1948, Zurich, Switzerland**

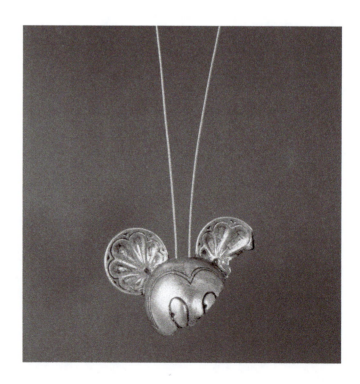

**Fig. 58**
Otto Künzli. *Broken Mickey
Mouse* 1988. Wood, gold leaf,
paint, steel. Necklace.
Photo: Otto Künzli.

*RB: How and why did you start making jewellery?*

**OK:** For a long time, I was unwilling to tell this story because it is so personal and sad. When I was young, my eldest brother Peter went to the Applied Art School in Zurich to become a gold-smith. After various teenage adventures, I eventually ended up at the same art school. In the meantime, Peter had set up a jewellery studio in my father's house. During one summer he was working for a commercial jeweller and tragically had a car accident and subsequently died. So there was this studio left vacant and a close connection to my brother who had lived for this ideal and vision, plus at the time I was unsure of my exact direction, even though I was sure it would be creative. It was a difficult decision to make, and hard to live with. Everybody envied all the tools I had at my disposition, but I felt guilty using them.

*How would you define yourself?*

**OK:** I am a goldsmith, I am a jewellery maker, but am I an art-ist? In my opinion, anyone who honestly tries to create with the attitude of an artist is an artist; whether the result is art or not is another matter. I am not a teacher; rather, I mentor students and encourage them to grow.

*What inspires you to work?*

**OK:** I think everything can be an inspiration. I am consciously aware of some sources of inspiration, whereas others just pop up or fall in my brain, heart or stomach. For example, one day I rec-ognized that I had avoided using colour, ornament and figurative images. So that's why I made the colour brooches, the wallpa-per brooches and the postcard brooches. I titled them a trilogy of overcoming; a kind of aversion therapy for something I didn't want to make. Even something that you don't want to do or that is not part of your personality can be the starting point to try.

*Was this also the impetus for making the pieces related to Mickey Mouse and hearts?*

**OK:** Hearts are bestsellers in jewellery shops around the world, so in contrast I simply tried to make some fat, funny, intelligent, interesting, humble, strange, tiny, noisy, bulky, painful, sharp, and sweet interpretations of the heart.

The first Mickey piece was the *Broken Mickey Mouse*, which I carved from wood and gilded with gold leaf like an antique; its evolution was a very long and complex process. However, in the end I realized it was about fragmenting and destroying some of my childhood idols. I quickly discovered that Mickey Mouse was a universal vehicle for transmitting certain ideas and comments, which can function in many countries with diverse cultural backgrounds. The latest Mickey Mouse piece was created in Japan and is made of two small black pearls and one larger white pearl. It's entitled *Miki Motto* because its inspiration came from a visit to Toba Island, where Mikimoto invented the technique to produce cultured pearls. This piece is the perfect solution to the East-meets-West question and incidentally is a bestseller at Tokyo Disneyland!

*How do you start a piece?*

OK: I never start with a technique or material.

*So, material and technique are subservient to the delivery of content and meaning?*

OK: Exactly.

*Would you say meaning is everything for you?*

OK: No, but without meaning...

Until recently ethnographers and anthropologists believed the earliest signs of human culture dated back 40,000 years, whereas recent discoveries now suggest it's 70,000. Shells were found with little holes in the same place; evidence of threaded jewellery, which the scientists describe as storage of information outside the brain. That's the difference between a tool and an object that's not just been made for functional reasons. When I say *meaning*, I refer to symbolic meaning, and I find this extremely fascinating. I never studied anthropology, but I began asking what is jewellery really about and how did it start? Consider early man or his primate ancestor using their fingers to dig in the mud to find food or whatever, and afterwards they get rid of the dirt somehow, but how? Well, imagine them digging away and then cleaning their dirty hands by wiping them either onto a wall, a stone, their body or someone else's. The wondrous crazy step was them then discovering that you can repeat the act, and also make variations. This was the beginnings of cave painting and body adornment. Therefore, when the painters in the academy say, 'let's get rid of the applied arts', I respond that we've still not proved whether they first wiped their hands on themselves or on the wall! Gaining this awareness of applying pigment onto the body was truly amazing, and that's why I say I am proud to be an applied artist.

You know, some people were afraid that if I got the jewellery professorship at the academy in Munich, I would not support craftsmanship and the art of goldsmithing as Hermann Jünger had, and tradition dictated. My answer was, 'you're right, but you are wrong if you think I am not interested in goldsmithing'. As far as I am concerned, it is a part of something much greater and that is the phenomenon of jewellery, which is much older and has many different branches and roots that have absolutely nothing to do with metal. Therefore, why is it wrong to be interested in the entire phenomena instead of focusing exclusively on goldsmithing?

*What approach to teaching do you adopt?*

OK: I am a partner, a supporter and sometimes a gardener. When I teach, there are no ten commandments; many materials and techniques were discovered by making mistakes, so telling students you have to do this or that would be wrong and counterproductive. I try to avoid the osmosis of my work into that of my students and I never say to them 'follow me' as a leader.

*What do you look for in a potential student?*

OK: Passion, curiosity and a certain openness is necessary for meaningful and fruitful dialogue. Above all, passion; because without it one should not make jewellery or art.

*How would you summarize the aesthetic of your work?*

OK: The aesthetic is the form and proportions, the chosen material with techniques done properly so that my intentions are transmitted. Surface is also incredibly important in jewellery.

*What role does writing play in your practice?*

OK: I'm surprised by how much I have written because I was never good at writing. Sometimes it has helped me understand my work better. If you talk about your work, you may babble or tell a different story each time. However, if you write down and then publish your thoughts, you had better think twice. So that process forces me to be as precise as possible.

*And drawing?*

OK: I think it's a wonderful possibility; I was pretty good at making beautiful drawings that looked like those of artists or architects. Then one day I discovered that this was a lie, so I immediately stopped and subsequently only accepted drawings that either help me to record information, explore proportions or form or to figure out technical problems.

*Do you ever make models once an idea begins to develop?*

OK: It depends. If it helps the project or idea, yes; if it's not necessary, then no. For the wedding ring chain there was no point, but when establishing appropriate size, proportions or form it can be a useful aid.

*Are there developmental phases in each work that are shared?*

OK: They change again and again. I never start from a material; it's much more about the content and whether I can find a form to successfully transmit what I am interested in. Often my work is described as conceptual, but I say what's wrong with stepping back and thinking about your work once in a while? You never really find distance, you are always involved. It's not written in any book that an artist mustn't use their brain, but if you do so you're instantly labeled conceptual. However, I am far from being able to explain everything about my work.

*Really?*

OK: I think so.

*But your work is always so precise and your written texts demonstrate that you have analysed or considered your work from virtually every angle.*

OK: If I write about a piece several years after making it, I am often surprised by what I discover. I don't mind contradictions, but I am disappointed if I notice things that don't fit with the ethos of the piece. Hopefully, there is more to discover once the work is completed; other layers that fit within my vision. Many aspects of my practice operate at a subconscious level; material plays an incredibly important role, and its selection is sometimes open to question for long periods after which my final choice is not entirely rational.

*Your works appear to be characterized by extreme precision, both conceptually and formally. Do you ever worry about being too didactic or not open enough?*

OK: Many people have the desire to be somebody else, but hardly anybody can. You are what you are, but I don't feel trapped. I sometimes envy people who can develop their work from arrangements of coloured stones and materials and make variations of a certain style for decades. I have the feeling they know what to do everyday because they have a whole bunch of drawings of objects they've yet to make. I have experienced this with the wallpaper brooches, I just had to take the Styrofoam, cut a shape and select an appropriately patterned wallpaper from the sample book, or vice versa. I can only do repetition if it is suitable for, and consistent with, a project or idea. I also have certain ideas that I am very insecure about and don't know what they will mean when manifested in my work.

*Some works are self-explanatory, whereas others are more ambiguous. What kind of dialogue do you want with the audience?*

**OK:** I don't have a problem if work needs explaining, but I can also enjoy a glass of wine without reading five books beforehand. I think many of my pieces can be enjoyed by those who just look, touch and wear, but it's naïve to say that all work has to speak entirely for itself. Unfortunately, there is a kind of intellectual writing that simply confuses matters; but for those who want to know more, it's not a crime to read to become more informed. I hope my objects have a magical or poetic appeal that makes people curious.

Hermann Jünger once asked me why the sphere in *Gold Makes You Blind* had to be gold, and I responded by saying that one day it will be opened, either on purpose or through decay, and its title has already projected certain information. There are advantages with a title, namely that you can create an additional layer that supports an idea, contrasts it or even misleads people.

*Are you a subversive artist, perhaps even anti-establishment?*

**OK:** No, but maybe I have done it subconsciously. It's easy to shock, but a simple shock doesn't last long, whereas doing something subversive, ugly or a little bit nasty with a nice wrapping helps balance repulsion and attraction. That's a strategy I have somehow developed, and the used wedding ring chain took this furthest. I showed it to a museum director and on another occasion to Hermann Jünger without commenting, both of them put it on and initially noted how the various sizes of rings with slightly different colours had created an archetypal and beautiful chain. Then this growing awareness that every ring stands for a journey quickly made it pass from being easily wearable to unbearable. The fascination immediately turned into repulsion, and both spontaneously went to the bathroom. Subsequently, they both told me that they had had the strong urge to wash their hands.

*There are some pieces about America that are quite critical.*

OK: Yes, I got e-mail from widows of men who'd died from the malfunction of the M16. I'd made this brooch named *M16,* with two sheets of steel with a hole in the centre matching the diameter of an M16 bullet. The plates sandwiched a fragment of the Stars and Stripes, so there was this vulnerable red dot like a hymen. If you wear this sign, you cover your body with a target.

Some Americans felt *The New Flag* was an insult. It consists of a two-by-three-metre large black flag with a white symbol in its centre. This figure is a combination of several symbols and signs like the Latin cross, the five-pointed star, Mickey Mouse, the broken arrow, which is an American Indian symbol for peace, and a skull. This sinister new flag for the USA clearly recalls the Ku Klux Klan and is reminiscent of a pirate flag. For me, it is the perfect flag for the world police. I grew up believing all the doctrines about America being the land of hope, freedom and democracy etc, but recent events suggest otherwise, so maybe these works are a delayed reaction to the shattered illusion.

*You once said that wallpaper is the most suitable ornament to wear.*

OK: It was an ironic comment; a typical Künzli outburst! The origin of wallpaper is more interesting than how it's used today because walls were originally covered in leather or fabric to reduce humidity, so it was never about the fear of emptiness.

*What you wrote certainly infers a dislike of ornamentation. Do you despise pure ornamentation?*

OK: The pure is problematic because it implies that it's made by somebody not using their brain or feelings. That's the fear of emptiness; and it cannot lead me to form a contemplative relationship with any such piece.

*You also took on the major jewellery typologies in the so-called Wolpertinger or multipurpose jewellery. Could you describe its origins?*

OK: I hate multipurpose objects, and I contend, even as a Swiss national, that the Swiss army knife is not a good tool. The Swiss army knife is no substitute for individual high-quality tools, but it's better than nothing if you're in trouble. The Swiss army knife is particularly beautiful when you open all the tools simultaneously, but that's precisely when it's at its most useless! One morning

I became obsessed with counting the most common jewellery functions and how many sides a cube has, the answer to which is six, hence the multipurpose cubed jewel. The title comes from chimeras – mythical beasts that in reality are the union of parts of disparate animals.

*Do you aspire towards the poetic idea and the iconic?*

**OK:** It really depends on the work and its context. Sometimes it happens and then I am very happy.

Gold Makes You Blind *is surely iconic. What was the intention behind this work?*

**OK:** To put gold back in the dark where it comes from.

**Fig. 59**
Otto Künzli. *Wolpertinger*
1985. Silver, leather, cotton.
Multipurpose jewellery.
Photo: Otto Künzli.

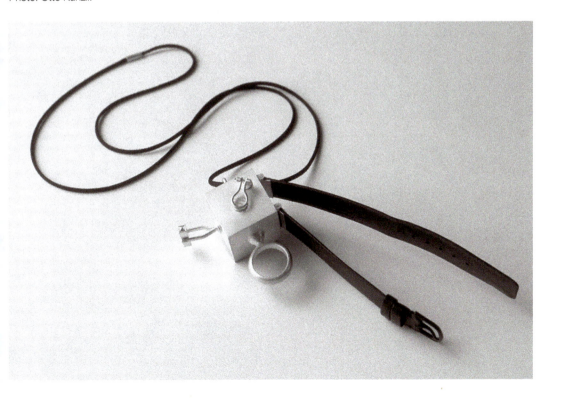

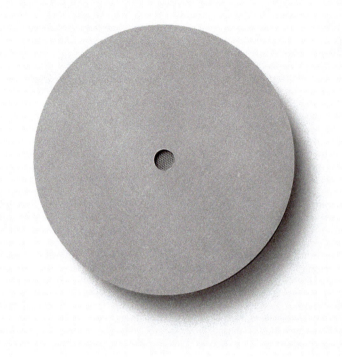

**Fig. 60**
Otto Künzli. *M16* 1991.
Stainless steel, fabric
(American flag). Brooch.
Photo: Otto Künzli.

# 12

# Nel Linssen

**Born: 1935, Mook En Middelaar,
The Netherlands**

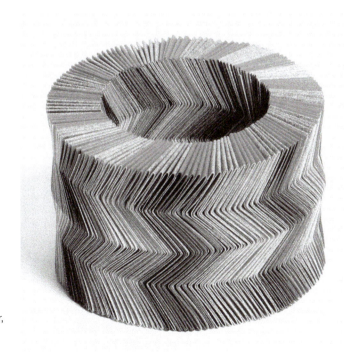

**Fig. 61**
Nel Linssen. *Bracelet* 1986. Paper,
elastic thread.
Photo: Peter Bliek.

*RB: How and why did you start making jewellery?*

**NL:** It just happened to me; I never specifically thought about making jewellery. I had some processed textiles at one point and there was some left over, so I thought I'll look for something new and different to make. I sewed together many pieces of paper in a variety of ways to make this object. Looking at it one way it was flat, but if you twisted it, it turned into a three-dimensional form. That model led to another smaller version, which I thought would be nice as a bracelet. This is how I came to making jewellery. It is a little silly, but oh well. This was the development; it took a long time until I made my first bracelet.

At first, I thought that I could not make jewellery out of paper, but I would just try it anyway as I liked the idea. I started trying to make jewellery in 1985 and produced the first bracelets in 1986.

*So the process of developing your signature paper jewellery was protracted and took many attempts?*

**NL:** Absolutely. First, I made all of my drafts out of paper until I solved the *how* problem, and thereafter I could make bracelets out of materials like crystal or plastic; primarily because I imagined that paper might not be strong enough to be a bracelet. After making the first bracelet out of plastic, I realized that it did not look or feel very nice, it was kind of gravelly. So I made my bracelets out of paper again because I preferred the look of it.

*What inspires your work?*

**NL:** Nature inspires me; my husband's garden inspires me most of all. It is very interesting to watch how flowers and nature grow and how they are constructed. Nature has been my inspiration for all these years.

*Do you draw?*

**NL:** No, but I can draw; I am educated in drawing. I do not use drawings for my work however, because it is not possible to draw my works; you have to produce them step by step. I make a lot of different draft bracelets, and sometimes when I'm not happy with the result I throw it in the corner. The next morning, I pick the draft up again and change something. It is a very long process, and sometimes I dream a solution and have a spontaneous solution for a problematic bracelet.

*So, you do not draw your ideas because they cannot be preconceived.*

NL: That's right. In the beginning, I do not know what I will be making. It's like reading a book: you are very excited about what will happen at the end, and this is exactly the same with my work.

*What are the different stages of the process?*

NL: Well, the ideas and the process are basically the same thing; they belong together in the production – it's an issue of head and hands, thinking and doing.

*How do you decide the colours of the pieces?*

NL: The colours I choose depend on the forms of the jewellery, and this changes with every piece of jewellery I make. The main thing about making jewellery for me is the process of finding an idea and re-alizing this idea; the technical part is an important challenge for me.

*What can you tell me about the form of your jewellery?*

NL: They look very organic and they emerge very intuitively. I somehow have an idea in my head, but I do not know exactly what it is and I really like that. For every single piece of jewellery, I have to look at what materials and what kind of paper I want to use because I use different kinds of papers for different collec-tions. The kind of paper I used in the beginning is very useful and appropriate for my jewellery.

*You tried making jewellery out of plastic too, didn't you?*

NL: Yes, I did. I thought I did not want to use paper anymore. In the beginning, my jewellery was round, colourful and playful, but I was looking for something more mathematic and something more precise, and for that paper is more useful. I also like to make folding in my jewellery, and paper is most appropriate. And paper is still flexible and I did not find any other materials with which I could do all these things.

*Have you ever used other materials, such as metal?*

NL: I made a golden piece once, but I did not have sufficient feel-ing for this material to make others.

*What else could you tell me about your techniques?*

NL: As I said before, I am very intuitive and all the techniques I use, I invented them myself. People tend to think that my jewellery can be related to the Japanese techniques of origami, but this is not true. It emerges step by step. It is very important to me that the technique is perfect and that the jewellery does not fall apart.

*How do you establish the proportions of a piece?*

NL: It originates on intuition during the working process.

*And how important is functionality in your pieces?*

NL: Function comes in first place; the radiation as an object comes next.

*Which jewellers do you admire?*

NL: I admire craftsmanship and originality of ideas as a main quality for (not only) jewellery. Over the years I have seen several examples of Warwick Freeman's work, and it is important I think.

*Do you ever consider future sales?*

NL: Well, the artist makes things because they feel that they have to make it. As an artist I make what I want to make, but the valuation of people gives me satisfaction, yes.

*To whom would you ideally want to sell your work?*

NL: Just to people who like and appreciate my work and definitely to people who are going to wear my jewellery. Some people own one piece of my jewellery, but they are very happy with it. I hear that they really enjoy having it. For instance, there are also people who collect and buy one piece each year. This is interesting, but people who are enthusiastic about it are the best clients.

*Do you wear your own jewellery?*

NL: I wear some of the bracelets and also to test them, but necklaces – well, I myself don't want to get too much attention in that way.

*Do you work alone?*

NL: Yes, but that has been my choice. I want to make things myself. Some people think she makes paper jewellery and this will go on forever, but that is not the case. I have to make the jewellery that feels right. After I made some jewellery, I decided to make some bigger objects. If I had had the chance to start my jewellery career twenty years earlier, I would have created a different future, but nowadays I do not make paper jewellery because people expect me to do it. I make my jewellery because I enjoy making it.

*Are you happy to be where you are now with making your jewellery?*

**NL:** From the day that I had the first piece of jewellery in an exhibition, people started to like my jewellery, and at that point I did not think that I would have made one collection each year for the next twelve years. That was a surprise. I also never had the intention of being well known, and that is not important for me either. But it is nice to know that people like my jewellery; it's like a kick. The most important thing is that I will be able to continue working for a long time.

*Do you have any tips for young and future jewellers?*

**NL:** Try to be original and develop your craftsmanship. Keep looking critically at your own work.

**Fig. 62**
Nel Linssen. *Bracelet* 2009.
Plastic-coated paper, elastic thread.
Photo: Bas Linssen.

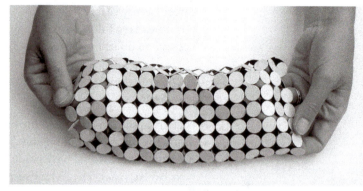

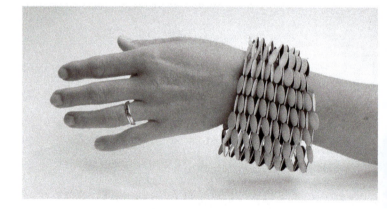

**Fig. 63**
Nel Linssen. *Bracelet* 2006.
Polycarbonate on paper,
polyester thread.
Photo: Bas Linssen.

# 13

# Bruno Martinazzi

**Born: 1923, Turin, Italy**

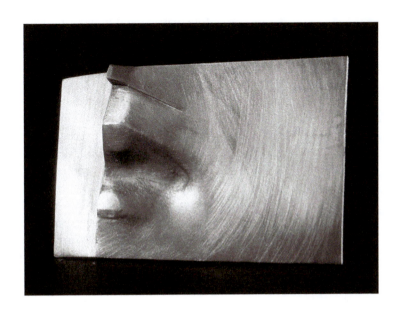

**Fig. 64**
Bruno Martinazzi. *Sibylla* 2006.
Sterling silver. Brooch.
Photo: courtesy of the artist.

*RB: When and why did you decide to express yourself through jewellery?*

**BM:** I started to work relatively late in the artistic field. Firstly, I attended the gymnasium, then I received a degree in chemistry; thereafter I became director of a dye works for four years. I have always been attracted by music, drawings and beauty. Whilst I was director of the Magnoni Tedeschi factory, I was profoundly unsatisfied and was looking for a way to do what I loved; painting, like my grandfather. Vincenzo Capello, a friend and owner of one of the oldest jewellery shops in Turin, was aware of my awkward position and suggested creating jewellery. I figured that being a goldsmith would have allowed me the financial liberty to paint. Consequently, I dedicated myself to a job which I found agreeable because I could create things through manipulating materials. I immediately found joy in what I was doing and discovered the intelligence of our hands.

When I left the factory, I was already thirty. I did a one-year apprenticeship in the workshop of the Mussa brothers in Turin. They were very good goldsmiths, themselves children of goldsmiths with a very strong tradition who worked by appointment for the vice king of Egypt. At that point in time I became familiar with all goldsmith techniques, their possibilities and limits. Sometimes, an old goldsmith sat beside me at the four-place goldsmith bench, and he still used a mouth blowpipe (French torch) to solder. During evening classes I learnt toreutic art with the master Formagnana. Subsequently, I furthered my studies in repoussé and chasing at the Institutes of Art in Rome and Florence. In the latter, I also acquired enamelling techniques. I had a huge hunger to learn. With time passing and without noticing, I had abandoned painting to dedicate myself to sculpture and pieces of work in gold.

*What are the developmental phases of a work?*

**BM:** There is a crowded space in our brain where memories and images live. They are the echo of our lives. The poet and the artist feel the desire to express this sonority, this chaos of thoughts, figures and landscapes that want to live and which clamour to be resurrected. They contradict themselves and wait to become manifest and ordered. Unexpectedly, a moment suddenly arrives, a coincidence, a point in which what seemed to be irreconcilable finds a way to establish some kind of meaningful relationship.

I collect old sketches, reconnect preliminary studies and make a lot of drawings. Then I explore three-dimensionally with cardboard; cutting and gluing the resultant forms. Sometimes, these cutouts are stuck onto a large sheet of paper and left out on an easel. Day after day, the project becomes clearer, and once it has achieved a sufficient level of harmony, I make the piece in gold or stone. Anything unresolved will eventually be suggested by the materials. When I work with my hands, the project is enriched because with our hands we receive the answers asked by the materials; and their questions are invariably good ones.

*Why do you favour gold and stone?*

**BM:** It is a joy to work in gold or stone; both are immune to death or decline. I love their permanence; gold is incorruptible, whereas given time, stone seems to acquire a soul.

*What role does drawing play in your practice?*

**BM:** I always draw a lot: to fix images, to evaluate them or even to study a single line in detail. All diverse, they do not have an autonomous expression and only rarely do they precisely define the object I will make; yet they occupy an indispensable space in the creative process. However, not actually manipulating materials, not transforming them leaves me dissatisfied, as if drawing always has to be a means to an end.

*What significance does the use of parts of the human body have in your sculpture and jewellery?*

**BM:** In 1968 Italy underwent a year of turbulent change. The student protests and workers' struggle was like a huge wave that swept away many things. I had always conserved off-cuts and fragments of gold and discarded works in progress in order to subsequently melt them down for future use. Amongst these pieces was a mouth, a sheet cut in an unusual way that I had been unable to complete. There was, however, something that stopped me from remelting it, so with time it happened that I took that piece and held it in my hands, trying, always without success, to find a solution for it. After a long pause from goldsmithing, I decided to challenge myself by applying myself to that sheet of metal. I began to work on a project, and of course I looked into the small box of fragments. One of them solicited my curiosity; I considered it for long while, and I then put the original mouth onto the fragment and bent that into a ring – it was a revelation. This piece dressed the finger perfectly, and the golden mouth element was put in a new and complete context.

This idea of fragments was in the air because of the 1968 student protests. Once the sea of conflict had calmed, it left a lot of wrecks: utopias, hopes. The fragments that at the beginning

I looked at with irony, silently came to life, no longer wrecks, but minimal points which aspire to wholeness and totality.

Looking to modernity and the past are vital for me, concentrating attention on one point so that the dimensions of what is being considered is relatively important. Therefore, small scale or big scale does not change the substance beyond the chosen object's form.

Those are not fragments that are inserted in a geometrical shape, but it is the cut which creates the shape and describes the geometry. The limit imposed by the form transforms the detail into an entity. Focusing attention on details broadens our outlook; the selection of the small scale draws attention back onto the object. Its central role in art moves away from that culture which often sees art as form of show and art for art's sake. The small object or work obliges us to listen, reflect and think.

*You have spoken about how the dimensions of a work, be they grand or miniscule, do not change its substance. Could you explain how you decide whether a reflection will become wearable or alternatively a sculpture?*

BM: Sometimes an idea is that of a large sculpture, but it is not possible to make it. If the idea is strong enough to live, I search for its essence, or that which can sustain tiny dimensions. Other times it is an idea that takes form and demands to live alongside a body that wears it, such as a bracelet, ring or necklace. Subsequently, and even after many years, that idea can become a sculpture. I only understood these dynamics of osmosis after many years.

*Why have you frequently used fragments of the human body in your work?*

BM: The human experience of the artist, from their consciences extends in time – the language and the form in which it is expressed is the creative act that belongs to us. Parts of the body such as the finger, hand, mouth and eye are a distillate of transformations. They are my personal vocabulary of words that I use to communicate my reflections upon myths, religion and nature. They are foregrounds that render the story alive; Kaos, Narcissus, the happy God, Cain and Abel; interpretations of specific cultural landscapes, symbols in which it seems to be legitimate to contemplate the universal.

*Where does the idea of inscribing an anatomical part of the body into a square or rectangular form originate from? Is this a choice dictated by the concept or the aesthetic?*

BM: They are not fragments inscribed in a geometrical shape; rather, it is a cut which creates the shape that determines the geometry. The limitations imposed by the shape transform the detail into a part. Focusing our attention on a detail expands our vision; the choice of small dimensions returns attention back to the object and gives it a central role in the world of art. It breaks with the culture that frequently considers art to only be for its own sake. Even if we are limited human beings, we feel the fascination of the unlimited and the infinite. However, it would be difficult to satisfy ourselves with fleeting emotions and ephemeral representations which nearly always hide the emptiness. Small-scale objects compel us to listen, reflect and think.

*Could you discuss the evolution of the incorporation of body parts throughout your career?*

BM: Things do not change; it is I who transform and thus see diversely. This process is shown by the transformation of the hands or the mouth or the face – and what emerges is *essential.* They are archetypes that transform in form and meaning according to the context in which they are placed.

*What is the role of the philosophical passages that often accompany your jewellery in exhibitions or catalogues?*

BM: I do not have the academic education to consider myself a philosopher. I do have a preference for those thinkers who unite profound reflections with the beauty of poetry, such as Dante and Plato. I am an orphan, and not having had a father I have always sought one in the greats of literature. I nourished myself with philosophical thoughts that revealed support for my creative endeavours. Sometimes, whilst reading an author I focus on a few sentences, perhaps even a single thought, which would then accompany me for days while I work. That thought establishes itself like an aura, to which I attempt to align my work. My projects are open to solicitations and sometimes they modify the outcomes.

*How do you view the relationship between your work and its wearer?*

BM: Jewellery has been part of culture since prehistoric times. It bears witness to the birth of conscience, sacred feelings, the divine, love, self-awareness and recognition of others. The works I make aspire to communicate these feelings. The person who chooses to wear them shares these feelings – the need to know, to think, to be pleased and to contemplate together.

*Could you compare and contrast the practice of sculpting with goldsmithing?*

**BM:** To sculpt stones makes me free. Arms, hammer and chisel unified happily in the effort of heart, hands and intellect. The sculptor is a bit like Titan; his work grows through subtraction. The goldsmith is a bit like an alchemist; he works with the flame in isolation in a small, closed space. The alchemist is a philosopher who in his research mixes together matter, myths, religion and philosophy. With stones, the process is long and only at the end has the shape been defined; it is as if the stone in itself would say, 'here, I am the hand, the finger or the mouth'. With gold, the shape was born early; however, during the making process the shape is fragile and it needs to be supported by a structure without making it look too heavy or dull. This technical research is rational and it pays attention to the aesthetic and every smallest detail. In small dimensions, the best pieces of work are those in which there is an equilibrium between the art of the sculptor, the art of the architect/goldsmith and the poet.

*Where does the idea of using weights and measures in your work come from?*

**BM:** I was fourteen when I climbed the Gran Paradiso Mountain. 4,061 metres; light, spaces and horizons seemed without boundaries, it seemed that they could touch me. I do not remember another experience which enriched and impressed my wish to go to the infinite.

In 1975 social conflicts were progressively degenerating towards terrorism; I began to read Saint Agostino and Plotino: *Measurement and Beauty*. The order and measurement of Saint Agostino converges on the beauty of form, beauty as an ethical principal, and Plotino became a guide for me. I am now completely occupied by the idea of measurement that sporadically disappeared from my practice in the past. My work concerns measurement, I sculpt weight, metre, pot, thumb. Yet, into my research bursts the temporal dimension.

Whilst sculpting I asked myself: 'Why is stone so heavy?' I re-read books on mineralogy, studied the geological maps, places and formations where the stones came from and discovered that their ages were incommensurable. The measurements that I sculpt, familiar and reassuring, divide their beauty between material and form: 280 million years, a measurement too far from the limits of comprehension. Working blocks of stone that carry millions of years within, I had the sensation of almost touching eternal time. In the forms I sculpted, two measurements converge into a paradox: the reassurance of the human thumb versus the disquieting material. It is a question of equilibrium that in art becomes a harmonic interplay of contrasts.

*What advice would you give to students?*

**BM:** In Florence, I took part in a very interesting conference – Siamo Qui – We Are Here – in which jewellery students from fourteen different nations (from USA, Estonia, Israel to Japan) debated various issues. I thought about Kant's concept of limits and his broader research (*Critique of Pure Reason*) into the understanding of limits and the possibilities of the human mind. I remembered the word *peirata* (limits, boundaries) in the following sentence from Homer's *Odyssey*: '*kalkeia peirata teknes*' (tools hold within what art can give). Limits enable openings. The thrill of passing limits becomes one with a love of limits.

I would say to students: Love limits, treat technique as a bearer of limits, learn a technique not to be dominated by it. I do not possess the truth, but have only the certainty of what the hands know how to do: the need to try to be honest, accommodating, tolerant – to coexist with what descends from reason and what comes from the heart.

**Fig. 65**
Bruno Martinazzi. *Studies* 2004–6.
Cardboard, paper, pencil.
Photo: courtesy of the artist.

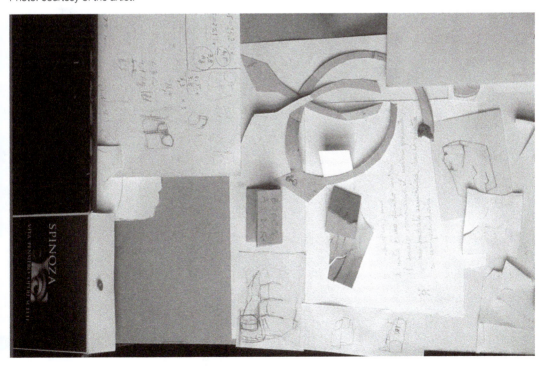

**Fig. 66**
Bruno Martinazzi. *Sibylla* 2006.
Gold. Brooch.
Photo: courtesy of the artist.

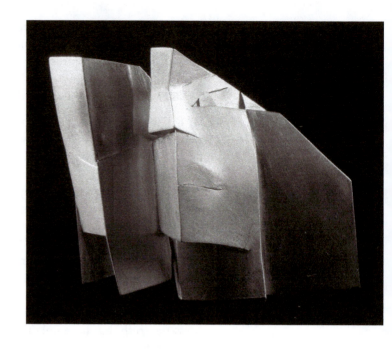

# 14

# Ted Noten

**Born: 1956, Tegelen, The Netherlands**

**Fig. 67**
Ted Noten. *Lady-k4–7* 2007.
Prada bag, heavily gold plated
gun, bullet, acrylic.
Photo: Ted Noten.

*RB: How did you decide to start working with jewellery?*

**TN:** It just happened; I had no idea about jewellery or art when I was twenty. I started out as a bricklayer, then I was a psychiatric nurse for four years, but I was restless and went travelling for three years. Africa, India, and America and so on. I was in Athens and I saw a guy on the street making earrings with shells, beads, and silver wire. I was completely blown away and couldn't go away; he taught me and two days later I was beside him with a piece of blue velvet on the floor selling my things. I immediately had the touch, the feeling for it.

*So, you discovered jewellery by chance?*

**TN:** Yeah. Eventually I returned to Holland and enrolled at the art school in Maastricht at age twenty-seven. They were shocked because most people go in with more artistic vision, whereas I had none. For three years I learnt hammering, soldering and silver-smithing whilst concentrating on aesthetic shapes, and then I saw this book about Otto Künzli and *boom*! I had this shock again – right, so jewellery can also be this. I went to the Rietveld Academy to learn about concepts and meanings with Onno Boekhoudt. However, in the beginning they refused to admit me because I showed them my beautiful silver things and initially they said 'forget it, it's too late, your brain is spoilt'! Fortunately, they gave me a chance and sent me back to Maastricht to paint for three months before returning. That was a great experience as I had to get lost from all that aesthetic work.

*Was that Onno Boekhoudt's suggestion?*

**TN:** Yes, and then afterwards I came back and was accepted.

*Was it especially important to have Onno as a teacher?*

**TN:** Onno and Otto both. Onno taught me to touch materials, to feel the material, to be aware of the material, and Otto Künzli was more the intellectual. So I had to develop my hands and mind in a new way. I had to stop making perfect, scratchless stuff and instead develop a way of thinking how to transform an idea into an object or installation. I was lucky to be able to combine these two influences: my intuition shaped by Onno and my intellectual, critical and analytical skills by Otto. With Onno I never finished, but with Otto I did. I saw a lecture where he described a brooch that he'd drilled with a specially made bit of 1.2567 mm diameter, if I remember correctly, that corresponded exactly to the diameter of a bullet. I freaked out and said, 'why didn't you just buy a gun

and shoot the hole, why are you making this super intellectual?'
He got very angry and I did too, and I realized this was where our
roads would divide. Students are often scared to attach themselves
to a teacher, but I say don't be scared, it's okay to sit on someone's
back for a while and even copy his work or ideas because there
will be a point when you are hammering away and you'll fall
off – it's inevitable.

*Are there any other jewellers you admire?*

TN: Christoph Zellweger for his passion and absolute dedication.
Suska Mackert as well; she's very conceptual, but maybe too intel-
lectually conceptual for me. I am also conceptual, but conceptual
in my intuitions, whereas she's more conceptual in her intellectual
framing. There's a young Spanish guy called Marc Monzó who's
quite intuitive and interesting and I also feel something for Bettina
Speckner because she creates beautiful nostalgic expressions, and
nostalgia is such an important carrier within jewellery. However,
it disappoints me very much when I go to Schmuck in Munich
because so much of the jewellery has the same language and the
same trajectory; it's boring! There are very few people doing new
things. At Schmuck they all speak the same language; it's a pity
given just how much more you can do.

*What else inspires you?*

TN: I like to go the movies, the greyhounds – that gives me more
inspiration than going to a jewellery exhibition.

*How do you start thinking about an idea?*

TN: I'm very primitive, that's what I always say to my students,
you have to make conditions, and that means discipline. It means
that you must focus on jewellery or your work, you have to have a
workspace, but mostly you have to have discipline. Many students
think, 'oh yeah, I can walk in, smoke some marijuana, go to the
movies and then suddenly it comes'. Bullshit! You have to have a
very disciplined way of working and living or nothing comes.

*What do you mean exactly by disciplined?*

TN: You have to read books, go to museums, talk with your colleagues, have good contact with your tools, but mostly discipline
means that every day you are involved in your work. Mostly with
me it's like the conditions are there and then I find things. Like
with the mouse, it's in my mind that I have to make a new interpretation of the pearl necklace, so it's in my system, and then

suddenly I found this dead mouse on the floor and I picked it up and thought 'I've got it'. I gave the dead mouse a miniature pearl necklace and set it within a clear resin form. In fact, that's the only thing I do – I find things, but only because I'm focused on it.

*What other advice would you give to students of jewellery or design?*

TN: First you need to acquire the basics, your own ground, before you can go onto other fields. First, the craftsmanship.

*In other words, the basic skills?*

TN: Yes, but basic skills doesn't just mean knowing how to drill a hole; it's also how to use your hands: feeling. I can touch anything and make it beautiful, but it took me ten years.

*Students are often impatient and want immediate results, and this can mean accepting the easiest solution rather than struggling for the best or most appropriate one.*

TN: This is because they are part of the instant society. Students have it difficult because they get so much information and so many things. They also get stage fright because they think 'how can I ever make an original piece?'

*Could you describe your research method?*

TN: Mostly it's in my mind. If I get an assignment I let it go in my mind, I mull it over, reflect and then I do some historical research. I try to analyse and associate things to it. However, the only way to know if it's a good piece or not is to make it. I'm very quick with my ideas and an idea can come in a day or less – it just happens, but I also like to make something really perfect, well crafted. I make lots of work and often after a month realize it's shit and throw it away.

I'm always reacting to things. For example, with the themed exhibition about pearl necklaces I got angry. This is a contemporary jewellery gallery and they want the most *frigid* jewellery piece ever made. Therefore, this anti-thinking or reactionary thinking is my main device.

*You said your inspiration can come from anywhere…*

TN: Yes, but it also depends on which stage I'm in. I was working for years on my own making very hermetic rings with tunnel vision, and then I became fed up. I didn't want to work only for a few select collectors; instead, I wanted my things to have broader contact. And then I saw the chewing gum on the street and a

Mercedes Benz car and these two pieces just happened in two seconds (*Chew Your Own Brooch*, 2000 and *100 Pieces*, 2001).

*Do you have an ideal customer?*

TN: Certain pieces can only be afforded by the elite, but if they really love it then I feel good. But also if I sell a little piece for twenty pounds for the same reasons, I feel just as good. It's connected to who I am; I have no preferences.

*Some contemporary jewellers would never make something that costs so little.*

TN: I reject that. I do it. I find that an attitude of fear, they're afraid that the real rich collectors will no longer buy their work.

*You don't have any issues about the reproducibility of a work?*

TN: It depends on the work. Some, like the *Cinderella* ring, are unique and there's no sense in producing editions. On the other hand, the *Golden Section* ring is based on the mathematical formulae and it results in a periodical number, the first nine numbers of which were engraved on the first ring, the second nine on the second ring and so on. I make these in batches of twenty as they sell. In this case, I have no problem because the replication is connected with the concept. Another example is the *St. James Cross*; it's a little cross I made in tiny pieces that sells for about seventeen pounds each from a Web site. As well as buying the work, people can upload a picture of themselves wearing the piece, so this adds layers of significance.

*Do people want to classify you in Holland as this or that?*

TN: Yes, people don't trust you if they can't frame you, and in some way I never wanted people to get a grip on me. Most people don't rely on their own feelings when they look at a thing. I can look at a piece and it gives me chicken skin (goose pimples) and I don't have to make it intellectual to understand why it gives me chicken skin. That's what makes me angry about the design, jewellery and art worlds; that so many pieces need so many words to cover them up. It's a switch; the covering up becomes more important than the piece.

*But I have to say that it's important for some people to read about your work to better understand it because otherwise it might sometimes be too difficult.*

TN: I agree, but these words can be more than explanations – perhaps stories because I'm a storyteller. For example, I recently travelled from Tokyo to Holland and made a necklace portrait of each city I visited from the things I had bought or picked up off the street, smells, and my own subjective feelings. People saw the exhibition and said this is exciting, but we want an explanation of each piece. I refused because it's not an educational exhibition – I demand that people use their own imagination, and perhaps sometimes I ask too much of the audience.

*The problem may then be that someone only understands the first few layers of your work, but obviously you try to imbue it with multiple layers of meaning.*

TN: Well, this is a problem for them, not for me. With these city necklaces, I only finished them two months ago, and I'm not sure I fully understand them. Most pieces are made intuitively and then after two years I see how everything came together. I don't want to make a piece and know what it means before I finish.

*How was your experience working with ceramics at the EKWC (European Ceramics Work Centre in 's-Hertogenbosch, the Netherlands)?*

TN: It was very difficult, but I found the perfect way to avoid these problems: there was an open day for the public and I made a clay boxing ball and suspended it so people could come in and hit it. Afterwards, I noticed there were many imprints of rings. So you know, things just come together by themselves.

*How important is function and wearability for you?*

TN: People are so obsessed that you have to wear jewellery; but I always say you don't have to wear it, that it can have meaning by itself. It sometimes makes me tired that jewellery has to be functional. For example, the journey prompted me to make an ice necklace, which you could call anti-jewellery because the moment you hang it around your neck it's gone.

*It's ephemeral.*

TN: Yes, in fact, the first night of the exhibition the caretaker removed the plug from the freezer display cabinet and the piece melted.

*What do you do with all the pieces of work that you don't sell?*

TN: I store them; maybe when I'm sixty-five I'll have a pension auction!

*Are you on a mission through your work?*

**TN:** No, it's mainly that I want to express myself, in that way I'm an artist. It's my medium to shape myself and the world around me, to understand the world. A mission – well, no, I'm not a priest.

Mmm…mission, I find it a big word. Yeah, of course I have a mission, and it's not that I want to make the world better though; I'm not a moralist. My hope is that good jewellery, which is often underestimated by the art establishment, will get the attention and respect that it richly deserves.

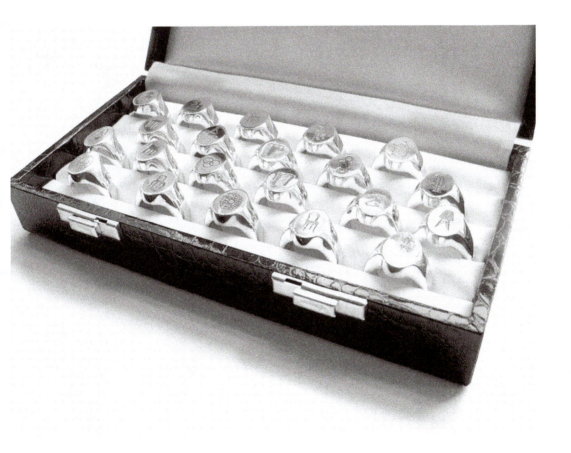

**Fig. 68**
Ted Noten. *Design-Icon Rings* 2006. 21 silver rings engraved with design icons.
Photo: Ted Noten.

custom jewellery

2007 T.N. ©

**Fig. 69**
Ted Noten. *Custom Jewellery*
2007. Cast silver painted
black. Brooches.
Photo: Ted Noten.

# 15

# Ruudt Peters

**Born: 1950, Naaldwijk, The Netherlands**

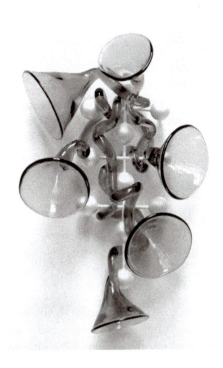

**Fig. 70**
Ruudt Peters. *Chasmalim*
2006. Silver, glass. Brooch.
Photo: Rob Versluys.

*RB: How and why did you decide to make jewellery?*

**RP:** I was nineteen and learning to be a medical instrument maker; they offered me a job and I just knew I wanted to do something else. I had found out that I was very good at making small technical things with fine details. So, I then searched for a school in Holland where they taught jewellery design. I couldn't go to a technical day school because my father didn't want to pay anymore, so I had to go to evening classes at the Rietveld Academy in Amsterdam. When you're nineteen, you don't chose with your mind, but you feel this thing could be a direction for me.

Nowadays, I would say I make jewellery because I can't find another expression for my personal ways and also because people wear jewellery it means it's physically close to them, which is an aspect I really like. Another reason is that it offers the possibility to make something where I can go beyond the boundaries – jewellery has a limitation in that you have to be able to carry it with you. It's nice to have limits and when you don't have any limits you can do anything and there are no borders to challenge. It's not easy. I think it's more difficult to make a good piece of jewellery than a good piece of art because you have to carry it with you afterwards. On the other hand, I don't see so much good jewellery. I feel that a piece of art is good when it has touched me really deeply. However, mostly I don't see pieces of jewellery that really touch me; it's happened a few times when someone has provoked that level of emotion in me.

*How do you feel about your career choice several decades on?*

**RP:** You know, I hate this job! I love it and I hate it. I really hate jewellery. I don't know why I am constantly making it. I'm ambivalent: I want to make it because it suits me to make it, and I like it and even love it. On the other hand, it's such a small, strange, easy world, where everyone reacts to each other. Maybe that's the reason why I find it difficult to name someone doing the best there is.

*So, which artists do you admire?*

**RP:** Jannis Kounellis, Anselm Kiefer, Luciano Fabro, Giovanni Anselmo, Tony Cragg, Rebecca Horn and Anish Kapoor.

*Why are you drawn to Jannis Kounellis?*

**RP:** Because he really works with life and death, and for me the most important thing is that work has a certain kind of romance; and my romance and the only romance of life is that life has an end, and because of this end we try to do all kinds of stupid things. We try to force it, we try to change it, we try to go over the end. When you are young, you don't see the end; we don't know when it will come, happily. And that's the romance of doing something.

*What in life do you consider to be so special it is art?*

RP: Sexual energy – the primary driver of life – and food. So eating, but erotica is also feeding oneself. If you look at the works I make, they often have very erotic connotations. I don't think about doing it consciously, but it emerges in making the work.

*What inspires your work?*

RP: Life and religion. When I was a young boy, I was completely intrigued by the Catholic religion. I had my own church at home; I made my own chasuble, surplice and my own host. I was very serious about it. Everything I do in jewellery has to do with life and death more or less. The religion part is that I made my own religion afterwards. It's not that I'm not a Catholic; I believe in God, but I practice in my own way, not how the Catholic institute wants. The religion part gives me a lot of power, not in the sense of institution, but in the way of the mystic powerful things – in what could be happening; what is life, what is the cosmos, what is the microcosm and the macrocosm? My interest went from Catholicism to the Romans and the Greeks and then backwards to Egypt and then Asia, and now I am studying Buddhism. It's all religion; so I follow the path of what is the most important thing for me – belief – but all together it kind of makes my own religion.

For instance, I am gay, but we got married in church, we found a monastery in Holland who wanted to celebrate us together. So, rituals are important for me in order to commemorate the big steps in life.

*How do you develop a project and what are the stages from the initial idea onwards?*

RP: The idea or starting point can be one word or one line; reading a book and I think 'ah' – I get that word or a certain line grabs my attention, and then I want to know more about it. So I start reading more about it, then I start to make drawings, and then I explore in materials. I often become completely blocked because I am not able to present what I really think and so then it can change completely. I have an idea and I want this, but the final outcome becomes something else. It can be possible that a certain kind of other outcome brings me closer to what I really wanted in the first place.

*Can you foresee the finished work from the drawings, or do you need to make some models to transform the work again and again until it's finished?*

RP: In the beginning, the drawings inspire me to make a piece, so maybe I draw and then make a copy of the drawing, but those pieces are dull; they don't have real guts. So, in the moment that I forget my issue and my drawings and the work is going out of my hands rapidly like whoosh, then I'm not thinking anymore and things start to happen. It's feeling, doing, making, doing, drawing, reading – it's like eating the information and shitting the pieces out. That's how it is; but it can be quite a long period between the research and the final pieces.

At the beginning, I'm searching for something and I don't know, and then once I start working and I get to the stage where I really don't know, then it becomes interesting because I think that's much more interesting than knowing. When you can name art as an art, it's not art anymore, because you don't go beyond the boundaries. So when I can see myself beginning to do something different or something I don't expect from myself, then it could be something. It's not a question of designing because a design can be repeated. My drawings explore how to visualize a source, from which I start with a certain kind of moment of making which can involve searching for the material, laying different things out together, experimenting with colour and so on. And then suddenly something starts happening – maybe someone brought me some material or I found something in the street. Finally, after I've thrown away maybe nine attempts, the tenth piece becomes something of significance that can really be developed.

*What can you say about materials and techniques?*

RP: Nothing, I hate to talk about techniques. However, the materials I use are a certain kind of reflection of the source and they mirror the source. The material follows as a consequence of the idea. I don't have to work in gold, or any other material for that matter – only if it is an expression of what I want to say. That's why it took so long for me to use gold.

*In the series* Sefiroth *you introduced glass to your work; why?*

RP: Well, it's very strange how things happen. I got an invitation from Ursula Neuman from the Museum of Art and Design in New York inviting me to participate in an exhibition of glass jewellery and initially I wrote back, saying 'Dear Ursula, I don't take part in it, it's a pity for you, but it's a freedom for me etc.' And then whilst I was working with *Sefiroth,* which is a Jewish system of the tree of life, my fragility and breakable personality came up. So glass was the material!

The most difficult thing was that I wanted to combine glass and silver, with lead glass blowing out through the silver, and that's impossible because glass melts at 1,250 degrees and silver at 700 degrees. But I did it together with a glass blower in Amsterdam. I would stand behind him saying 'left, to the left, to the right, whoa, whoa, whoa, stop, stop, to the right' until we nailed it.

*Is the colour in your work always symbolic?*

RP: Mostly it's symbolic, yeah, always – because why should you use colour when as a jewellery maker colour is a non-thing because gold has no colour, silver has no colour. Silver and gold have expression and meanings as a symbol in our society. Whenever I use colour and materials, it is always a symbolic and a meaningful choice.

*Your works are always unique and impeccably detailed handmade artefacts; so I therefore wonder if you've ever contemplated using high technology to make or reproduce your work.*

RP: Well, the philosophical answer is you can never make one piece twice.

*Okay, but you could have a small collection of limited editions – for example laser cut or water-jet, or...*

RP: Yeah, yeah, yeah, but you didn't get what I said. The fact is that when I look at you, and I then look again, you have changed. In one second, part of you, particles of your body have already changed. So it is impossible to do the same thing twice. I'm not against this modern high technology, but I'm also not in it. When you make a piece with laser cutting or high technology, you have to know what you want in advance. And I never know what I want when I make a piece. My pieces grow under my hands, so I start and it will go and then maybe I think this or that is interesting and it may change completely.

*Really? Because looking at your work, I think from the 1970s until the early 1990s your work seemed meticulously studied in every detail and chance seems not to have played a major role in its production. Did something happen to change your creative process?*

RP: After I'd finished being a student at the Rietveld Academy in 1974, I started with systematic work, so pieces developed in form from A to Z. Then, when I looked at a piece afterwards, if it was perfect, then I was also perfect and okay. But then, in 1984, came the first break; I wanted to present more emotion in my work and have a more philosophical background. The first piece was a big sculpture called *Breaking the Lanzen,* which was related to the sacrificing of Jesus Christ – a very religious piece. That was really a point when I accepted my Catholic background and realize that it is important and that I can use it in my work too. So from that moment onwards, religion came into my work.

The second big change came in 1994 with the *Ouroboros* series. I had already wanted to work with alchemy for quite a long time. Around that period I spent three months in India, where I saw totally different aesthetics compared with our Western aesthetic, and that changed me a lot. I mean it turned my world upside down, and I thought ugly is more beauty than beautiful and so therefore what is beautiful? So I started to find the shadow of my earlier beautifulness.

Going to India changed my perception of perfectionism a lot: whether a piece has to be perfect or not. In India there are a lot of things that are imperfect, but they have a beauty. So seeing these things taught me to value imperfection as a quality, and you can see this reflected in my work. Before, it was an impossibility to find imperfection in the *Passio* and *Interno* series; they were very straight-laced and perfect – strictly regulated meditations on life. Then afterwards, I let imperfections exist or remain in the works.

*You just mentioned visiting India. Travelling evidently inspires you greatly; could you discuss exactly how?*

RP: The point is this: I believe that when you don't travel you're stable on your own thing and that makes your outlook not so wide – you have a limited view. When you travel you can record a lot of culture, other cultures, but this also makes it clear where you stand in your own culture and that for me is most interesting. I couldn't adapt things from other cultures when I didn't know where I stand in my own culture.

*Do you think creating work in dedicated series is a result of different stages in your life?*

RP: Yep. One of the most important things to me getting older is finding that your work becomes more autobiographical, and I like that very much.

*I have found that particularly in some cultures they have a real issue in dealing with very personal jewellery. Yet sometimes, you have made pieces of work which are very personal. I'm talking about pieces such as* Alexis, *which was engraved with names of your ex-boyfriends. Did you ever worry about how the viewer might feel wearing such a personal piece of work?*

**RP:** It was the most important piece that I've made by myself and for myself. There was a very funny coincidence, because the person that wanted to buy it phoned me and had a discussion with me explaining how she had the same feeling as the expression of the piece – she also had a certain kind of list of all her ex-boyfriends.

*Some of the more recent pieces appear to talk about universal things or about religion; is this so that your audience doesn't feel that outcome belongs only to you, but that they can feel they share it too?*

**RP:** Honestly, I think a good piece must be universal; when it's only your own personal issue, then it's very difficult to communicate with it and you don't find an audience.

*To whom would you like to sell your pieces?*

**RP:** To people who understand it, and ideally to everyone!

*How important is it to find or create the right exhibition space for your work?*

**RP:** Well, after my jewellery studies I worked for ten years as a sculptor, and that made the space and the surroundings very important. I curate each solo exhibition by the millimeter, and the installation has to be more or less a certain kind of finger pointing which directs the audience to the soul behind my work. It's not that it directly gives a clear answer, but rather it prompts them to start thinking in a certain kind of way.

Now with jewellery, the installations have a relationship to the body – not that the body is present, but it is implied in the relation of measurement, physically understandable, that the piece of jewellery is related to the body.

*What advice would you give to students?*

**RP:** The most important thing is that they attempt to understand their own personalities and find out why they are making things. But that's very difficult. It's not given to everyone to find their own source, and it's very painful in that case.

*Which qualities should a good teacher have?*

RP: A good teacher has to be open; they have to be able to listen to what the student wants, but at the same time know what they want and then find the balance between what the student wants and what could be a goal for the student.

*Do you think jewellery must be wearable?*

RP: I am very strict in saying that you have to wear it. When you wear it, then it's jewellery; when you don't, it's an object. Sure, an object can say something about jewellery and even look like jewellery, but it's still an object and not jewellery. Everything that you can carry with you could be a jewel. But then I say, well, carrying an axe doesn't mean the axe is a jewel – it's still an axe, a utensil. There's no use or point in wearing a jewel. There is no need to wear a piece of jewellery, and for that reason it is the most interesting thing to make because it's a kind of art. It's more closely related to art than when compared to glass, pottery or textiles. There isn't any need for it in the applied arts.

*Why do you think contemporary jewellery is more popular in Northern Europe than in Spain or Italy?*

RP: All the people in the South are too elegant and want to express their external outer beauty. Whereas in the Northern countries, I think we are more internal and try to express what our source is. For me, the beauty lies within. Another difference is that northerners are less inclined to show off, whereas in France, Italy and Spain, people are more likely to present themselves, outside, walking on the street.

*How do you feel about the perceived importance of painting and sculpture over jewellery?*

RP: It's a social issue that's happened over time. People forget Benvenuto Cellini was one of the most important jewellery makers. Jewellery makers were always a very important reflection of their time – both ancient and contemporary. That's why I don't want to change the name *jewellery* because you can relate it to older times, to earlier times and the past. When you change the name to *contemporary jewellery,* to body wearing stuff, I don't want it. Jewellery is jewellery.

*So what is contemporary jewellery?*

RP: Contemporary jewellery is just jewellery from nowadays, so you don't have to say contemporary.

*So how should one describe your work?*

**RP:** Jewellery.

*But how do we distinguish it from commercial jewellery?*

**RP:** Yeah, but there are good paintings and bad paintings. I don't have a general definition for good art and bad art; it's just art. Why are we searching for such names?

*Maybe to be more precise.*

**RP:** But for what reason? To label everyone. Anyone can make anything. I love fashion jewellery, I love the jewellery on the street, and I love the jewellery that people make and wear. It's okay.

**Fig. 71**
Ruudt Peters. *Therme* 1990.
Silver. Brooch.
Photo: Rob Versluys.

**Fig. 72**
Ruudt Peters. *Ganesh* 1992.
Silver. Necklace.
Photo: Ruudt Peters.

# 16

# Mario Pinton

### 1919–2008, Padua, Italy

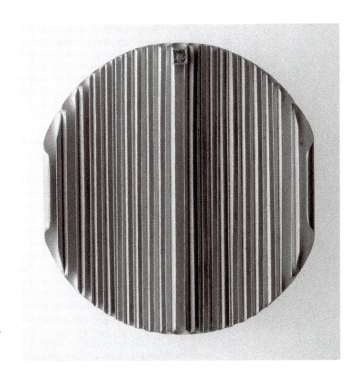

**Fig. 73**
Mario Pinton. *Brooch* 1979. Gold,
ruby.
Photo: courtesy of the artist.

*RB: When you were a student, which teachers and teachings were of fundamental importance?*

**MP:** I had many important teachers; my father was a metal engraver and he was my first teacher of technique. He was an exceptional technician who gave me the initial instruments with which to approach materials. Then, I had other teachers who shaped my conceptual outlook in terms of design method and creativity. Amongst these, the architect Giorgio Wenter Marini was particularly important. He taught me to go beyond traditional approaches that had already become obsolete and too limited. Wenter Marini also suggested other schools that I subsequently attended, where I found teachers including Marino Marini, Umberto Zimelli, Francesco Messina and others, who broadened my way of thinking and seeing, of conceiving objects and considering problems.

*When and why did you decide to make jewellery?*

**MP:** It was a natural evolution. The idea of specializing in jewellery was not originally an absolute intent. When I had occasion to study at the ISIA (Istituto Superiore Industria e Artigianato) in Monza, with various important teachers such as Marino Marini, I realized that through having created various pieces one could risk remaining fixed to a certain theme, technique or way of looking. In painting, I learnt from Pio Semeghini and Raffaele Degrada senior that everything had to be seen from the point of view of looking; and invention became important above all else.

*So, from an invention, you then studied what the material and means might be?*

**MP:** Given a theme, one sought to reinvent the method, to seek new solutions and to contradict the pragmatic; and one sought to invent new functions of the object.

*How do you develop your initial ideas?*

**MP:** I would say that every time they originate from experimentation. I began at school by looking at the world of medieval arts, which we studied at that time, but then I attempted to find my own personal direction, whilst also studying geometry. I gave myself to technical drawing for a long time – a subject which I also taught at school. It was a long process of to-ing and fro-ing between the natural world, examples from art history and geometry, whilst always attentive to serendipitous possibilities.

*What role does the idea, design method, material and technique play?*

MP: They are all important, and they must be intertwined; they cannot be considered singularly. The resolved concept must be solicited from the material, technology and function of the object. When I work practically, I no longer have cognition of how one must commence, be it the formal design of the object or some kind of technological requirement. I always taught my students that first one needs to evaluate a brief by understanding its diversity of meanings, and then developing a mental elaboration before proceeding, attentive to the possibilities offered by traditional methods of making, but above all searching for new interpretations. These are the principle channels of communication that allow the final work to express itself.

*Do you think this process is wholly rational?*

MP: A project is a creative act, it is an invention. However, this invention must not only be a rational act; since it's a work of man, the invention must be enriched by a certain poetic value. The operation must not result from a mere rational process, but moreover a human act with all its gifts.

*Could you describe how a piece generally progresses?*

MP: First comes the idea, which I then coordinate via geometrical elaboration. Then I engrave plaster. At this point I cover the plaster with a very thin layer of wax, and then with hot water I manipulate this sheet of wax to give it expressive form – so that it is not flat, but seems articulated and communicative. My works are often subtle relief. It is a structure of surfaces that is almost drawn without relief, upon which certain areas are drawn upwards into accentuated points. Therefore, the mark is no longer just a broken line but alternates between point and line; an accentuated relief that is pointed, but then continues downwards gently on either side. When one presses down harder, it means one wishes to highlight that detail – in order to better express the idea encapsulated by the mark.

*It appears there might be a link between your marks and those of Medardo Rosso, particularly in terms of their subtlety and delicateness. Do you feel a kinship with his sculptures?*

MP: I don't believe I am connected in any way. From my point of view, the painter and the sculptor, when they work, they must express themselves in personal terms to satisfy their own philosophies, whilst thinking about the observer.

*Generally speaking, what is your view on the role of drawing in the design process?*

**MP:** It represents thought in the expressive phase of the research. This research is generally undertaken according to geometric structures. I maintain that geometry is always important, even in free expression. In fact, geometry reorders, coordinates and establishes the best sense of design.

*Do you make models in card, paper or other materials during the development of an idea or form?*

**MP:** On certain occasions I experiment with thin copper, brass or lead sheets so that I can evaluate the repoussé for the first time; sometimes I commence by engraving plaster directly. Another interesting method is that of drawing on a thin sheet of paper placed directly on clay, thereby creating a line in negative relief. From this negative one can obtain a positive in plaster, which can then be further elaborated. Using a very fine metal point, one can go over the drawing again to obtain filaments that vibrate even more.

*Why do you prefer to work with very thin sheets of gold?*

**MP:** I prefer light jewellery over heavy; it is more airy, it vibrates more.

*Could you explain what you mean by* vibrate?

**MP:** I mean to say that the surface of the object becomes more sensitive and communicative. The object vibrates more when one intervenes by chasing the surface. It is the touch of the chisel that can render the object more interesting and legible. Even in the case of an object cast by the lost wax method, its surface can subsequently be reworked by chasing those parts one wishes to accentuate. The object must speak, and speak the language of the person that creates it.

*This brings to mind the principle of design advocated by some Bauhaus teachings – everything controlled, everything rational.*

**MP:** It was a rational process that I maintain without doubt to be important, but not exclusively so. It is also necessary to have the personal emotional side; and I don't believe that this is only my opinion.

*What makes a piece of work unique?*

**MP:** It is like the brushstroke, its tonality and graphic strength. When something is done by hand, there is a new visual strength every time, more or less intense that constitutes the expressive form of the piece.

*How would you advise students hoping to achieve this feeling for the object?*

MP: It is necessary to educate one's feelings. I don't know if it is possible to teach this, but one can encourage people to think in their own way, using appropriate artistic guidance. The student must submit themselves to this guidance and to their own way of feeling – and in this way everyone is distinguished by their own sensibility, by their own culture and for their own strengths.

*How do you know which jewellery to realize?*

MP: I don't know exactly. When one thinks about a thing and decides to realize it, I believe that it is one's feelings that prompt the choice and elaborate its creation. I don't know if it depends on feelings or the need to experiment with new things; there are things for example that I have never made. Every now and again I discover works published in books and this pleases me, reinvigorates me and induces new experiments.

*I remember that you once wrote about how one should read a work of art; and that is based on the relationship between design method and making.*

MP: When one creates an object, one continues to think and design; in other words, the project is always under control. Every operation has to be lived – meaning the construction of the object should not be a mere execution; the project can be modified in the course of working.

*What role does chance play during the realization of a piece?*

MP: Chance can become part of the process, but it must be controlled. Since the idea is developed during the phases of research and elaboration, it can be useful to have competition from chance.

*When looking at some of your square or circular brooches, it is evident the flashing from their casting has been left on purpose. Was this intended to integrate them into the surrounding space in a more continuous way?*

MP: Yes, these edges are defects from the casting process that I didn't want to remove. In this way, the piece of jewellery inserts itself in space in a more authentic and natural way.

*Other than using small precious stones as touches of colour, is there another reason for incorporating them in your work?*

MP: They are compositional elements. In general, I attempt to accentuate the axes of the object. At the end of the axes I often insert a stone.

*Do you establish the geometry and proportions according to a set method?*

MP: In general, I use the circle or square. However, these forms do not necessarily have to rigorously adhere to pure geometry; it is vital to modulate them to confer an expressive value.

*Is giving titles important for you?*

MP: I never gave many titles, but now I realize that I should have done it more systematically to underline the formal sense of the work and its meaning.

*Do you consider the client when working?*

MP: One thinks about the destination of the jewellery, one imagines the person that might wear the piece. However, when I have to complete, for example, a ring for a specific person, I make a silhouette of the intended hand either by photocopying it or tracing its outline with a pencil on paper – this allows me to individuate the personal characteristics. It is notable that a hand can be slim or short etc. These are variables that one must think about.

*Was there a particular event in your life that marked your artistic practice?*

MP: I would say teaching – because when one teaches, one learns. One not only gives information to one's students, but one studies alongside them – it is an osmotic process of give and take.

*Can teaching ever take over by limiting the time available for practice?*

MP: No, continuing within the limits is possible.

**Fig. 74**
Mario Pinton. *Brooch* date
unknown – ca 1987. Gold,
sapphire.
Photo: courtesy of the artist.

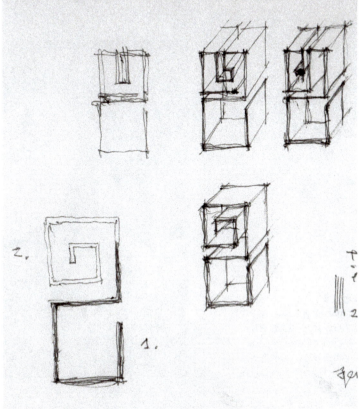

**Fig. 75**
Mario Pinton. Drawing for
*Anello a fascia* (detail) 1979.
Photo: courtesy of the artist.

# 17

# Ramón Puig Cuyás

**Born: 1953, Mataró, Spain**

**Fig. 76**
Ramón Puig Cuyás. *Nº1191,
Utopos* series 2008. Silver,
nickel silver, plastic, paper,
enamel, onyx, pearl. Brooch.
Photo: Ramón Puig Cuyás.

RB: *How and why did you start making jewellery?*

RPC: I need to explain a little about my history. When I was young I used to watch, from my house in front of the sea, how boats passed by and got lost beyond the skyline. I tried to imagine to which possible distant ports and cities they were sailing. I dreamt of being a sailor and discovering new shores, new exotic cities and islands.

Afterwards, I found the infinitude of starry nights. I would have loved to be an astronomer, to spend nights and more nights watching the sky, exploring beyond the universe's deep horizon. I would imagine and discover new worlds and suns; observer of the macrocosms.

Subsequently, I thought about becoming a biologist, penetrating into the mysterious microcosm of life. However, I ended up building my own destiny in order to devote myself to an art which gives you the opportunity to discover, imagine, invent, and transform other kinds of universes: inner universes, which emerge from the depths of our dreams and our desires.

*Could you describe the main phases in the creation of a piece?*

RPC: The last work is always the model for the next. My inspiration comes from my inner feelings. I work inspired by my vital experiences, by my life and by my memories. The thinking almost always arrives with action, with dialogue, with materials and shapes. Making becomes a way of thinking for me. What drives my work is pre-feeling – that is to say, the search for a feeling that I look forward to finding out and which is trapped inside the object I have just made, but which is already in me. At the same time, the making becomes a dialogue, a vain struggle against time and oblivion; it becomes a desire to capture some instant of life, of the present, inside the object that I make, as if it were the place where one keeps relics to project it towards the future.

*What role does intuition play in your practice?*

RPC: The important thing is making, but it is not a making dazzled by a good command of a technique – rather for encountering these magic and disturbing moments in which we realize that we are capable of instilling our enthusiasm in matter and of experiencing the moment when we recognize ourselves in the object that has been produced by our hands.

What really drives my work is intuition, not the thinking.

*Do you draw?*

RPC: Yes, but on most occasions, I like to play directly with materials in three dimensions. I use sketches and drawings to explore new ways and variables in the composition, but I prefer to improvise from the model of the last finished work. Jewellery is a three-dimensional expression, and for me, the best way to approximate to this language is working directly with matter.

*Your pieces can often be quite visually complex, with multiple elements juxtaposed. How do you decide on the final composition?*

RPC: The necessity I have to formally organize my pieces of work according to a strict compositional syntax gives the impression of polyphony. The necessity to look for a sound, some harmonies in the relationship between straight lines and the curved ones, the contrasts of planes, the comparisons of colours and materials. Maybe for this reason most of my works are organized as individual elements, an assembly, creating more virtual spaces than full volumes – taking care not to let the object be seen or perceived in its entirety at first glance. Rather, I intend that one's eyes can wander and travel along a subtle network of visual itineraries, exploring and discovering harmonious and contrasting relationships between the different parts of the object, needing some time in order that the eyes can reach every nook of the composition. I would say my model is to imitate Bach's timeless music, the desire to achieve the perfection and clearness of its structure, but also the depth of its mystery.

*How do you know when a piece is finished?*

RPC: I start new works without a premeditated project or plan. I draw and make schemes exploring the possibilities of the composition, but I have a mental image, nothing defined, but something like a pre-feeling. When I start constructing, I like improvising in contact with the material, in a dialogue between hands and matter, and when it is concluded I want to have a disturbing feeling and to recognize myself in the new piece. I want to see something new and unexpected in the work.

*How do you select the materials and forms of the constituent parts?*

RPC: One can notice in my works a constancy and stability in their shapes and in the symbolic elements used in the composition, which combine one with another, constituting a kind of style which appears spontaneously put together. It is a style which is also directly related to a technique and a way of making. Of course, technique is not an aim in itself, but rather a very important expressive resource. I have always been looking for how to turn technique into a bridge, as short as possible, between ideas, feelings and matter – making the technique facilitate the action and deliberately leaving the lines and marks of the working process.

The work is led at the same time by a desire for precision and fate-driven searching. From the beginning, I like to experiment with the expressive possibilities of varied materials, from natural to industrial origins, but the most present are plastic materials. Also, I like to incorporate fragments of found things.

*It seems that you favour the brooch; why?*

RPC: Because brooches have fewer restrictions in their body functionality, and this gives me more freedom and options in its construction.

*Why do you often use a circle or an ellipse to frame your brooches?*

RPC: It is a metaphor to express the idea that the brooches are closed universes, but at the same time are parts or fragments from bigger universes. Also, it is a means for isolating and protecting my constructed and ordered compositions from the surrounding chaos.

*Many of your pieces appear to be quite planar and do not project outwards into space; is there a specific reason for this?*

RPC: Maybe they don't project outwards physically into space, but rather want to project and magnify the identity of their bearer.

*Your approach to materials shares a lot with that of the Arte Povera movement. Could you discuss why and how you have attempted to imbue so-called poor materials with value and preciousness?*

RPC: I like to use different materials and techniques because I feel freer. It is most important for me that when I am working and composing I feel really alive, playing with materials, colours and shapes without technical restrictions. I want to be sure that when a wearer looks and considers the value of my work, it will only be for artistic considerations, and not for the preciousness of the materials and high craftsmanship.

*Could you discuss the main ideas behind the* Walled Gardens *series?*

RPC: The series of pieces made since the beginning of 2004 grouped under the general title *Walled Gardens* are above all an expression of a desire: The desire to use colour without any limits or inhibitions. They allude to gardens which we imagine or which we only just catch a glimpse of through iron gates or over high walls. These gardens which we cannot enter, which are surrounded and isolated, awaken in us the desire to transgress this forbidden boundary. They invite us to jump over those high walls to discover the universe hidden within. Each piece in this series evokes the microcosms of plants and foliage that grow enclosed behind the walls of these small imaginary paradises.

*And what about* Imago Mundi *and* Corpus Architectae?

RPC: This new group of works with the generic name *Imago Mundi* are based on sentiments that provoke dual and contradictory aspects of our lives and our universe. The dialogue between opposites: there is no light without the contrast of darkness; there is no death without life. This work is based on experience, and on the conflict of feelings.

Colour disappears; this time black and white with some semblance of grey are enough to provoke a denser atmosphere compared to earlier work. Black and white, form and material, microcosms and macrocosms establish a suggestive dialogue, pregnant with significance. Perhaps it is the way to express the darker side of the relationship man has with nature, the conflict between civilization and nature, and the search for primal harmony. In any case, the imaginary background of the pieces in the *Imago Mundi* series is always behind the reality of daily life, like a shadow that can't be caught.

*Corpus Architectae* is the pleasure of playing with lightness. They are like fragments of cosmic weightless architecture, which, worn safely on our body, subtly modify the relations and contrasts between the body and the space that surrounds it, projecting it beyond its everyday limits.

*Is it important that the viewer understands or correctly interprets the meaning of a work?*

RPC: Of course. But at the same time, my work is open to a multiplicity of readings. An artwork with only one interpretation is a dead work. I compare my works to an onion; you can discover something new under each layer. Over time, the work can reveal new states of being, and at the same time make it possible to feel some eternal significance.

*Is your jewellery like time capsules or metaphorically speaking, receptacles for your memories and experiences?*

RPC: Every work of art is a container, a reliquary in which the artist has deposited their ideas, emotions, doubts, experiences, impressions, and definitely a part of themselves, in the intention of reconnecting it all.

*Do you ever wish you could be more of a minimalist?*

RPC: Yes, I'm always training to synthesize my symbolic language. But my models for this are not Bauhaus rationalism, but the archaic and primitive expressions of the Mediterranean culture. The big pleasure for me is not visiting the most famous contemporary art museums in cities, but to visit calm archaeological museums and see little quotidian objects from the past, and discover my connections with them.

*Your work might be described as painterly. Do you think you paint through jewellery?*

RPC: Colour has been a fundamental part of my work for many years. I need to use colour because I want to make enjoyable jewellery. Because in my Mediterranean cultural background light and colour are present in many cultural and quotidian lives. I feel my work is closer to the painting language than the language of sculpture. Colour gives me the possibility to accentuate the expressive contents.

*Outwardly, your work appears to be much more joyful and exuberant than quite a lot of contemporary jewellery from Northern Europe, which appears more typified by dark colours and a certain kind of calm solemnity. Can you identify any causes for this difference?*

RPC: Mediterranean culture is steeped in the conflict between the Greek drama and the Dionysian pleasure – it is in a permanent conflict and fusion between different cultures and religions. The syncretistic attitude of these peoples was the best way for survival in this permanently changing context.

It is a fact that the climate, the light and the sun also have a strong influence on cultural expressions. But maybe the most direct cause in contemporary art languages is that the Bauhaus and its principles were less influential in Southern countries.

*So why do you think contemporary jewellery is more popular in Northern Europe than in Spain or Italy?*

RPC: Spain and Italy have more cultural connections with the old nomadic peoples from North and East Mediterranean cultures, and in the nomadic context, gold and jewellery is the best medium for the accumulation of riches because they can be easily transported and exchanged. These ancestral connections still sustain a prevalent interest in having and wearing conventional gold jewellery – big polished pieces in yellow gold.

*Do you think then that contemporary jewellery or artistic jewellery should be considered a medium that reflects social events?*

RPC: Today, artistic jewellery sits within the realm of fine art debate; however, its position within a history of traditional trade emphasizes the role of its materials. If there is anything that defines contemporary jewellery, it is its connection with material; a connection that resonates with its primitive roots. For centuries, jewellers have experimented with materials in order to understand the ways in which their hands can transform material into physical objects that can be touched and caressed. But the contemporary jeweller doesn't only work in dialogue with physical materials like stone, metal and plastic; instead, they are open to other territories, where the materials are made from doubts and desires, curiosities and fears, uncertainties, and reiterations of unexpected innovations.

*How important is functionality to you?*

RPC: When I am projecting and working on a new work, I am always imagining this piece and its effect on its wearer, and their body and spirit. There needs to be a complementary relationship between the jewellery, the jeweller and the wearer. This relationship needs to be more than one of identification; it needs to be one of sharing and co-participation. It should remain undefined and incomprehensible. Developing these relationships helps humanize our daily lives, and perhaps adds to the feeling of the work. If these relationships are neglected, the object becomes hollow – a simple decoration that contaminates our visual environment.

*Is a piece of jewellery still jewellery when displayed in a museum?*

RPC: No, because it acquires a new function. The jewel is transformed into another thing.

*How has your role as director of the jewellery department in the Escola Massana in Barcelona affected the development of your practice?*

RPC: The effect has been very important in two ways: my periodical contact with students and their needs and questions over thirty years has forced me to acquire a mental agility and sensitivity to feelings, and by involving me in their artistic problems I accumulated more experiences than if working alone in my studio. Being a teacher has also made it easier to be visible and public with my personal work.

*What qualities make a good student?*

RPC: The curiosity to have a feeling of transgression, wanting to feel free and decide over their futures.

*What advice would you give to students?*

RPC: To be honest with themselves. To take risks and be curious. Don't worry; the loneliness is a constituent part of the creative activity. To be enthusiastic in their creative activity.

**Fig. 77**
Ramón Puig Cuyás. *Nº1107, Imago Mundi* series 2006. Silver, nickel silver, plastic, enamel, acrylic paint. Brooch. Photo: Ramón Puig Cuyás.

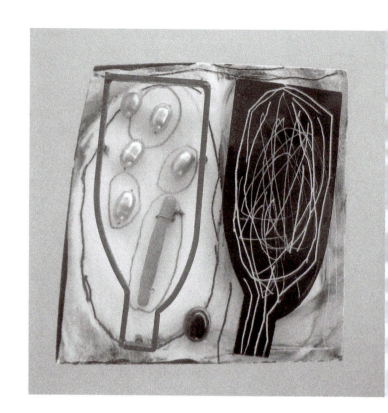

**Fig. 78**
Ramón Puig Cuyás. *Nº1161,*
*Imago Mundi* series 2007.
Niello, silver, nickel silver,
plastic, coral, pearl, onyx,
acrylic paint. Brooch.
Photo: Ramón Puig Cuyás.

**Plate 1**

Jakob Mores, Drawing from *Das Kleinodienbuch
des Jakob Mores* 1593–1608.
Photo: Staats und Universitätsbibliothek,
Hamburg (Cod. in scrin. 1a).

**Plate 2**
Erasmus Hornick (in the style of).
*Pendant* 1551–75
Gold, enamel, ruby, pearl, emerald,
diamond. Germany or Antwerp?
Photo: © Trustees of the British
Museum.

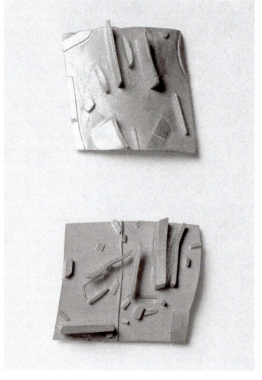

**Plate 3**
Hermann Jünger. *2 Brooches*
1996. Gold, enamel.
Photo: Eva Jünger.

**Plate 4**
Giampaolo Babetto. *Bracelet* 1996.
White gold, pigment.
Photo: Lorenzo Trento.

**Plate 5**
Gijs Bakker. *Lilienfeld*,
Holysport series 1998.
Gold-plated silver,
gold leaf, yellow gold,
computer-manipulated photo,
Plexiglas. Limited numbered
edition (5). Executed by
Pauline Barendse.
Photo: Rien Bazen.

**Plate 6**
Manfred Bischoff. *Kun* 2005.
Gold. Brooch.
Photo: Aurelio Amendola.

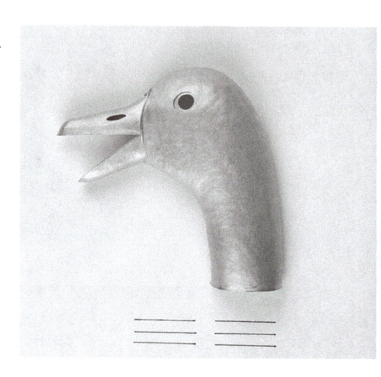

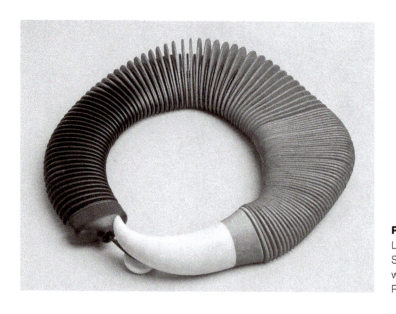

**Plate 7**
Liv Blåvarp. *Wild at Heart* 2007.
Stained maple, ebony, lemonwood,
whale tooth. Necklace.
Photo: Audbjørn Rønning.

**Plate 8**
Esther Brinkmann.
*Inside* 2000.
Hammered gold, green
stone. Pendant.
Photo: XuPei Wu,
Guangzhou.

**Plate 9**
Caroline Broadhead.
*Woolly Necklace* 1977–8.
Cotton.
Photo: Peter Mackertich.

**Plate 10**
Iris Eichenberg. *Untitled, New Rooms*
series 2009. Wood, leather, copper,
enamel. Brooch.
Photo: Tim Thayer.

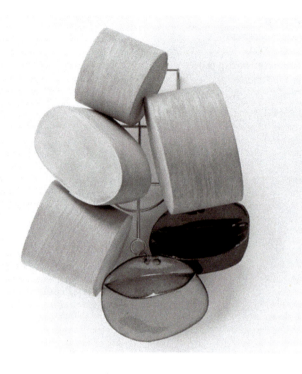

**Plate 11**
Karl Fritsch. *Ring* 2006.
Gold.
Photo: Karl Fritsch.

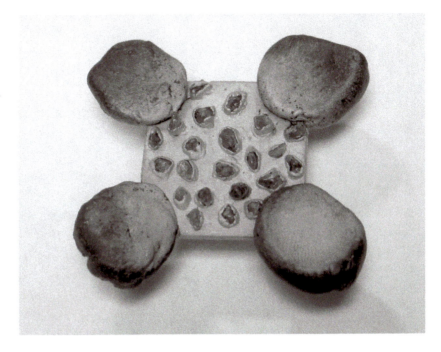

**Plate 12**
Rian de Jong.
*NYNY* 2008. Copper,
gold plate, peridot.
Brooch.
Photo: Rian de Jong.

**Plate 13**
Daniel Kruger. *Necklace*
2001. Gold, glass
beads.
Photo: Udo W. Beier.

**Plate 14**
Otto Künzli. *Wallpaper Brooches* 1983.
Hard foam, wallpaper.
Photo: Otto Künzli.

**Plate 15**
Nel Linssen. *Necklace* 2009.
Plastic-coated paper,
elastic thread.
Photo: Bas Linssen.

**Plate 16**
Bruno Martinazzi.
*Sibylla* 2005. Gold.
Necklace.
Photo: Bruno
Martinazzi.

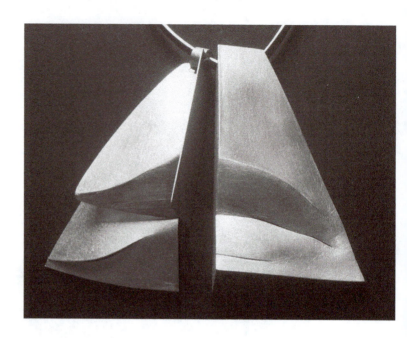

**Plate 17**
Ted Noten. *Erenhot* 2006.
Ceramic sculpture, cut into slices,
gold, yellow thread. Necklace.
Photo: courtesy of the artist.

**Plate 18**
Ruudt Peters.
*Wunstorf* 1994.
Silver, marcasite,
gold leaf. Ring.
Photo: Rob Versluys.

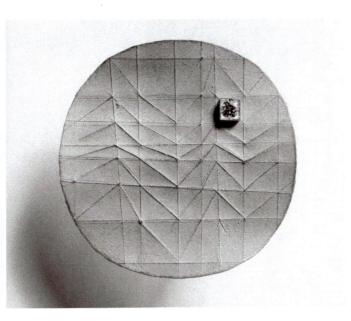

**Plate 19**
Mario Pinton.
*Brooch* date
unknown ca 1988.
Gold, diamond.
Photo: courtesy of
Mario Pinton.

**Plate 20**
Ramón Puig Cuyás.
*Nº1072, Walled Gardens*
series 2005. Silver,
nickel silver, plastic,
acrylic paint. Brooch.
Photo: Ramón Puig Cuyás.

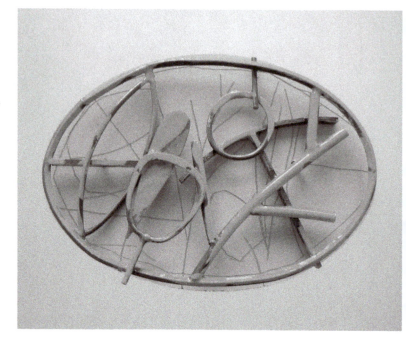

**Plate 21**
Wendy Ramshaw.
*Set of 5 Pillar Rings* 1972.
Silver, semiprecious stones.
Photo: Bob Cramp.

**Plate 22**
Jacqueline Ryan. *Sketches* 1996.
Photo: Jacqueline Ryan.

**Plate 23**
Bernhard Schobinger.
*Mantraring* 1992.
Iron meteorite, gold.
Ring.
Photo: Bernhard
Schobinger.

**Plate 24**
Peter Skubic. *Brooch* 2007.
Reflective stainless steel,
blue and green lacquer.
Photo: Peter Skubic.

**Plate 25**
Tone Vigeland. *Necklace* 1983.
Steel, silver, nickled bronze mesh.
Photo: Hans-Jørgen Abel.

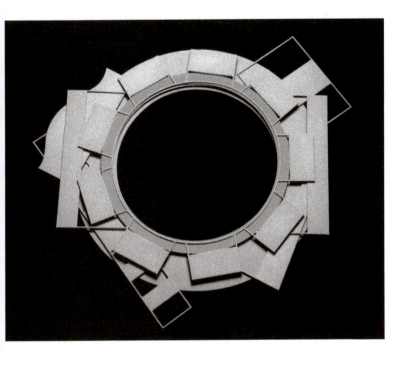

**Plate 26**
David Watkins. *Voyager* 1985.
Neoprene, wood, steel.
Combination neckpiece.
Photo: David Watkins.

**Plate 27**
Annamaria Zanella. *Cellula Blu* 2003.
Papier-mâché, gold, plaster,
acrylic paint, steel. Brooch.
Photo: Ferdinand Neumüller.

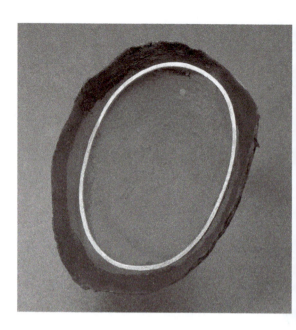

**Plate 28**
Christoph Zellweger.
*Relic Rosé* 2006. Mixed media,
flock, silver chain. Necklace.
Photo: Christoph Zellweger.

# 18

# Wendy Ramshaw

**Born: 1939, Sunderland, England**

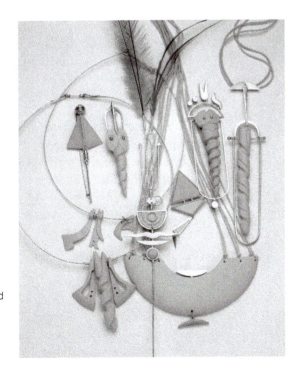

**Fig. 79**
Wendy Ramshaw. *A Collection Made from Australian Porcelain* 1978. Blue-grey porcelain mounted in 18-ct gold, strung on pale blue cotton and embellished with emu feathers.
Photo: David Watkins.

*RB: How and why did you start making jewellery?*

**WR:** I was at art college and I needed some earrings to wear; it was the late 1950s. As you know, I didn't train as a jeweller but as an illustrator and designer of printed textiles. I found bits of metal in the scrap box in the sculpture studio, I drilled and roughly shaped them into one pair for every day of the week. I would have been seventeen or eighteen. Some people were out-raged by these bits of beaten copper and brass swinging from my ears. Those which annoyed people most were not metal, but the torn corners of pound notes suspended from little chains. People addressed me unpleasantly on buses. This was not a promising start to my subsequent career!

*Could you describe the main phases in the creation of a piece?*

**WR:** By the late 1960s I would have made drawings, and then I would attempt to make the pieces; alternatively I would experiment with materials to discover a new possibility. I wasn't trained as a metalsmith, as I said, so when I was buying jewellery tools I'd ask what they were used for, and if I thought a tool sounded useful, I would purchase it. My first rings were made round by using a hammer and the bathroom tap – very very primitive!

When working with a new material, for example the clay in Western Australia in 1978, to discover its potential I pressed it, rolled it, cut it, pierced it, and finally discovered that finishing the clay to a fine surface could be done prior to firing by rubbing tissue paper over the surface. Once I learnt how to handle the clay, I was then able to work from drawings.

*Do you make models?*

**WR:** No. I normally know how a piece is going to look from my drawing. I make first one piece, then the second, the third and the fourth. In the course of making I see there are ideas that I had not thought of and discover different ways of doing things which I can later develop. There are rarely any models unless I am designing to commission, where fit and size are specific.

*Given you had no formal training, where did you want to locate your jewellery initially?*

**WR:** I had studied printmaking as a part of my illustration course in Newcastle; then, at Reading University, I had the chance to expand my skills to include etching. I liked the etched plates very much, especially when inked ready for printing. I made small etched plates from copper and wore them as jewellery – this was the real start of my jewellery making. Very simple, very basic.

In the late 1960s, I decided I wanted to make jewellery which was very contemporary, clearly part of the twentieth century, and this mattered to me. I needed to develop some technical skills, and I began to make some pieces by hand which looked as if they might have been created with the use of a lathe. Eventually David Watkins, my husband, acquired a Myford lathe for me; I also got a small kiln for my enamelling. My aim was to create a collection of jewellery looking space-age and high-tech. This collection was exhibited at the Pace Gallery in 1970.

My intention at this time was to make work which could not have been made at any other period than the mid to late twentieth century. Also, I have always tried to make things that were beautiful.

*What's beautiful for you?*

**WR:** Many things; the world in which we live is extraordinarily and amazingly beautiful. There is no way in which man can excel nature; it is not possible. The natural world is so exquisite and dramatic. My interest lies in beautiful structures and patterns created in the manmade world, predominantly architecture and machines.

*Could you discuss the role geometry plays in your work?*

**WR:** The natural world, our planet, is full of geometry and order. Perhaps sometimes it doesn't look as though it is, but microscopic images show that it is. By 1969, I had discovered the language in which I wanted to work was geometric.

I believe the human body is best embellished or ornamented by patterns and forms which are abstract. An abstract form resting on or encircling a human body can be very beautiful. I think figurative imagery placed upon the body is difficult and can detract from the personality of the wearer.

*Do you see brooches differently because they have a different relationship with the body than most other types of jewellery?*

**WR:** This is a difficult question because it very much depends on the particular brooch. I think most of my brooches are intended to be worn in a central position, like a pendant without a chain or visible support, they relate directly to the face. They are not ornamenting a coat or a garment, but the woman or the man who wears them. Almost all of my brooches have an open frame across which lines and shapes are suspended; the cloth on which they are pinned is the background to the design.

*Does your jewellery have to be wearable?*

**WR:** Yes, it all has to be wearable. I love minimalism, but I also love complexity. I like extremes – some of my work is very basic and wearable, and some of it is more difficult and a strong commitment has to be made to wear it.

*Which were the most successful of the multiple interchangeable rings?*

**WR:** Impossible to say – a ringset that I made in the late 1960s is really important to me. I am still making this design, it is an unlimited multiple. The set consists of four separate rings each with a basic geometric shape: a triangle, a square, an oblong and a circle. I think of it as a classic; it is inspired by, and reminiscent of, the teaching at the Bauhaus.

*Why did you make these pieces with multiple elements?*

**WR:** In the late 1960s, I had a very beautiful friend who became a model. I had made a number of rings for her with large moonstones, and she asked for another. I decided to make the ring in sliver using a number of smaller moonstones each on a separate ring to make her something different. I had made the first ringset. Now, the rings vary from three parts to a very extreme version having forty parts. My idea was to enable people to choose how to wear the rings – taking on and off, they constantly come together in different ways. A set might have a big ring, two narrow bands and a lot of smaller rings; the wearer can make a decision about which pieces to wear and how to arrange them. That seemed to me to be very fascinating.

*How did the ring stands evolve?*

**WR:** The stands arose because when my first sets of rings were displayed by galleries, people tried to buy the rings individually, so the solution was a stand. At first it was a practical concern; then I thought I could develop this concept further. The design of the stand could relate to a specific ring or ring type. As is common in my work, some stands are plain, unadorned cylinders and others very complex in shape, possibly including coloured inlays.

*Could you discuss the* Picasso's Ladies *project?*

**WR:** In 1998, I thought about the idea of working with paintings and making pieces of jewellery for portraits. I knew that Picasso painted in a whole series of different ways, also creating his art with different materials. Initially, I didn't realize that the paintings were of the women who were important to him. The paintings were a way of recording his life. I worked always with postcards from my postcard collection, then acquired many more; I was able to carry the postcards into the studio, which was very important to me.

I tried to work with a whole jewellery gamut – a multiple, a unique piece, a series, a limited edition. Some pieces made with valuable material, others with paper and other non-valuable materials, some pieces costly to acquire, some modestly priced, some difficult to wear, some easy to wear. I tried to think every which way about jewellery within this particular collection using a very wide range of materials.

I related to the women in the paintings – not just their appearance, but also dealing with feelings. Is the image loving, exquisite and beautiful, is it a bit angsty or is it unbelievably, unbearably sad? I began at first to work with the happy images of women loved and loving. Later, I worked with the sad and angry paintings – I had been seriously ill and felt then that I could consider the really difficult images of *The Weeping Woman* and *Guernica*. Before that, I wouldn't have wanted to work on anything so deeply emotional and sad.

I had some criticism from a journalist for the concept of working with the Picasso images, but I never contested it. A comment was made to the effect that jewellery cannot bear heavy emotions. But it has and does – you have both the memento mori and the marriage ring. Jewellery is handed down through generations; we know that it can be much loved, it can acquire personal meaning and become symbolic. This happens when jewellery has become a part of someone's life. The work leaves the hands of the jeweller and becomes part of life beyond the studio. This new life is one of the many aspects of jewellery. Jewellery has many different roles to play – the word itself means joy, but it can also come to symbolize sadness, it can be a solace for people, holding a memory or it can just be beautiful.

*If I understand correctly, each ring was made in response to the sitter in each portrait?*

**WR:** They are made specifically for the image of the woman in the painting, for the woman as Picasso depicted her because that's all

I can see, it's my only information. I don't know her; I can only see what Picasso expresses on the day he paints her. She might be dreaming or very cross. I might work with or against the colours on the canvas, or I may have been inspired by a shape. Working with a painted image was something I had never done before.

*Which jewellers influence you?*

**WR:** My influences in the field of jewellery come, as you may find with many contemporary jewellery artists, from ancient artefacts, ethnic jewellery and body ornamentation as found in parts of the world where jewellery and ornamentation have real meaning. But on the whole, inspiration for my jewellery is not coming from jewellery.

*Where does it come from?*

**WR:** The world around.

*Is it of any importance that the viewer appreciates the sources that inspire your work?*

**WR:** My exact inspiration was clear with the *Picasso's Ladies Collection;* the relationship between Picasso's painting and the jewellery was important. Then the project called *Room of Dreams* in 2002 was inspired by dreams and fairy tales, and *Prospero's Table* in 2004 was inspired by Shakespeare's play *The Tempest.* I create a piece of jewellery which is personal to me and is my own vision; it's interesting if a person wants to know about the inspiration. Even with the three collections I've just mentioned, the jewellery needs to stand alone without words.

*Is a piece kept in a museum still jewellery?*

**WR:** I like to think a piece of jewellery is going to be loved and worn, but it may suffer wear and tear in the process, especially if it is a ring. A piece of jewellery in its second life might have an owner who does not like it, someone who doesn't know what it is or who made it. The only chance most pieces of jewellery have of remaining in perfect order as the artist intended is to go direct from the artist's studio to museums or into cared-for collections, where they are not worn every day.

*Beyond jewellery, you have made large-scale works such as gates for example. How have these projects challenged you?*

**WR:** I am not interested in challenge; challenge is not a word that I care for because it implies difficulty and possible failure so

I don't like it. I draw the gates in the same way I draw the jewellery, though they are much more complex and will be made at a monumental scale compared to jewellery.

If an interesting project is offered to me, I almost invariably say yes. Such is my enthusiasm that I remain to this day working very long hours on each project. I always hope to take a new step forward and add a new dimension. The excitement of developing ideas remains a driving force for me.

*What advice would you give to students who are interested in working in this field?*

**WR:** Don't train to be an artist of any kind, unless you have a real desire, determination and need. My view is very simple: if you really want to do it, and it really matters to you, then do it.

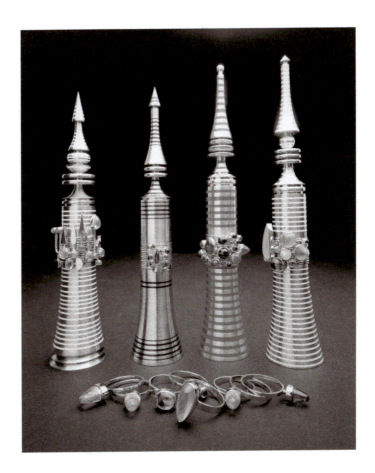

**Fig. 80**
Wendy Ramshaw. *Five Ringsets, One Unmounted* 1989. 18-ct gold, precious and semiprecious stones, on nickel alloy stands inlaid with coloured resin. Photo: Bob Cramp.

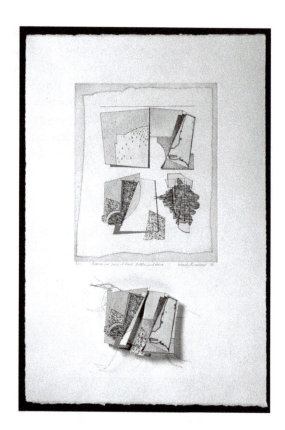

**Fig. 81**
Wendy Ramshaw. *Cubist
Brooch for Fruit Dish, Bottle
and Violin* (Picasso's Ladies
Collection) 1996. Etching,
handmade paper, black
thread, silver gilt. Edition of 10.
Photo: Bob Cramp.

# 19

# Jacqueline Ryan

**Born: 1966, London, England**

**Fig. 82**
Jacqueline Ryan. *Necklace* 2006.
Gold, vitreous enamels,
freshwater pearls.
Photo: Jacqueline Ryan.

*RB: What is the inspiration behind your work?*

JR: I have always loved nature and been fascinated by it as long as I can remember. As a child, I was an avid collector of found natural objects; and still am today. For my work I am inspired by nature, but I am also interested in how ancient civilizations, who had a much more intimate relationship with the natural world than we do today, depicted nature in their art and the way in which these objects remain mysteriously timeless.

*How do you extrapolate details from nature?*

JR: I aim to abstract from nature without imitating, largely by reproducing impressions and sensations that natural objects or growing organisms have transmitted to me. My pieces are intended to narrate impressions from the natural world. No one piece is based on a single natural object or organism, but rather each results from a combination of various aspects I have observed and found inspiring. People naturally want to associate a piece with something that they recognize as familiar, but my work is not meant simply to imitate.

*It might therefore be described as a kind of filtered recording of something you've seen or a sensation experienced.*

JR: Yes, they are memories – of what I've seen or what's inspired me over the years. However, the process is not immediate; it is a much longer distillation that in some cases takes years to be transformed into jewellery. The general process usually involves me working graphically in the first instance from life drawings, which are re-elaborated into very small-scale and intricate paper constructions whose characteristics form the basis for jewellery. Nowadays, I also study microscopic details of insects, plants and other natural structures otherwise invisible to the naked eye using a digital camera and macro lens.

*What are the developmental phases once a starting point has been established?*

JR: I've always worked from making paper models, largely because I didn't learn as many techniques during my studies as I would have liked. My studies at the Royal College of Art were rather more design based than technique oriented; naturally, both are important parts of the development of any work. As my downfall was predominantly technical, paper helped me perceive how things work in three dimensions. In the early days, I started by making paper models and then similar pieces in metal that were very simply curved or forged up from one single sawn-out sheet to avoid any complicated goldsmithing techniques.

*It sounds similar to industrial pattern making, when you construct a solid out of a plane.*

JR: Yes, but then I started to really enjoy the actual qualities of the paper itself and the irregularities and unexpected things that were happening. Consequently, I decided to start making pieces in gold that in some way reflected how I worked with paper. The first pieces looked a little laborious and overworked; they didn't quite match the spontaneity of the paper models. Eventually, I managed to replicate what I'd done with the paper – spiralling and curving the shapes into forms so they took on the qualities of the paper. Replicating the thinness of the paper in metal was, and still is, fundamental.

*How has your working process changed over time?*

JR: Experience has given me much greater technical fluidity, reducing obstacles to fulfilling my ideas and enabling me to more freely express myself than before. Although you can get around technique if you really want to, you are undoubtedly limited when you lack in-depth knowledge. Now, I have the choice and can confidently create technically demanding work.

*Could you discuss the formal aesthetics of your jewellery?*

JR: They are simple and essential organic forms with complex surfaces. I would say the forms are classic and, I hope, timeless. My forms are therefore often based on the most elementary shapes – the circle, square, rectangle and variations thereof. I think if I were to make very complex forms, I might lose some of the freshness I seek, and the rich surfaces I like texturing, fragmenting or decorating would lose their significance. I'd be afraid they might start looking too laborious and overcomplex.

*Which materials do you predominantly use?*

JR: I prefer using gold of at least eighteen carats because it has a beautifully warm colour and a really tactile quality. I've worked in other metals such as steel, copper and aluminium, but no metal has given me the same feeling that working in gold has; it's as though it possesses addictive qualities. Silver is also tactile, but what puts me off it is how quickly it tarnishes. Admittedly, this can be a perfectly valid quality, so that a piece becomes more beautiful as it tarnishes, but I will always see it as detrimental because I would prefer each piece to remain as it was in the moment I finished it.

*So you're not really interested in a piece accruing its own history?*

JR: Again, an ongoing history is a stimulating possibility, but not one that interests me right now. I would like the owner to have a piece that remains pristine for decades or even centuries and which gets passed down as a family heirloom perhaps, if not, then remaining a museum exhibit which contributes as a valuable testimony to our century. In the past, things were made with deliberation and meant to last at least a lifetime and often beyond. In a superficial, throwaway consumer society like today's, this concept has been turned upside down. It is therefore comforting to be able to believe that at least a small quantity of what we produce might last for centuries and much more.

*How much importance do you place upon functionality?*

JR: From a personal point of view, a significant amount. I would like my work not only to be handled and seen, but also to be worn and fully enjoyed in all its aspects. It's one thing to look at a piece or handle it and find that it moves, but quite another to wear it because then it moves in relationship to the body and interacts with the wearer's personality. Wearing a piece also gives it a further dimension in that, as the wearer moves, the light changes around them and shadows creep around the piece and bring it to life. It is at this point that its function is complete.

*How do you achieve the movement that characterizes much of your work?*

JR: I don't solder much, but prefer to fix one part to another with rivets. This allows movement in the first place and gives the work a visual crispness.

*Why has this movement become so important?*

JR: Movement is ever present in nature. Additionally, making jewellery that surrounds curving parts of the body, such as the arm or neck in particular, necessitates a certain degree of movement in two separate directions to make it fully wearable.

*Why do you often incorporate multiple repetitions of a single conic or pyramid unit in one piece?*

JR: Repetition is a very common aspect of nature, as well as an imperfection. Nature repeats itself often in irregular ways. When I construct my pieces, they, too, by consequence, are never quite perfect. The individually formed, hand-pierced and riveted elements collectively make up a single whole that when assembled is irregular and whose construction reflects plant growth. I do not use cutting, pressing or stamping tools, because if all the elements were identical, the result would be monotonous and sterile – closer to much of to-day's industrial mass production whose only quality is anonymity.

*What is the reason for counterbalancing gold with vibrant enamels, such as sky blue or coloured stones?*

**JR:** Much as I love gold's colour, its uniformity can lack expressive qualities. Before working with gold I was using coloured anodized aluminium in quite a painterly fashion. When I started to work with gold, I missed these colour possibilities and wanted to re-introduce them. Subsequently, I have made pieces both with enamels and semiprecious stones such as turquoise and lapis lazuli, or river pearls and corals. All are suitable solutions to negate gold's uniformity, but I am particularly attracted to vitreous enamel. I love its tactility and visual strength.

*What role do titles play in your jewellery?*

**JR:** Names are less important to me than the actual essence of the work. I don't feel I would like to name my pieces, because I would prefer them to be freely interpreted rather than to be approached with preconception.

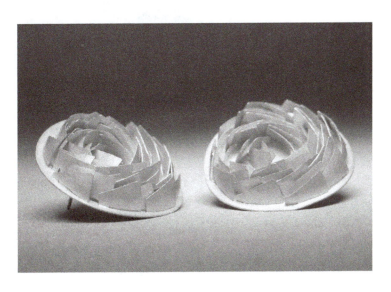

**Fig. 83**
Jacqueline Ryan. *Earrings*
1999. Gold.
Photo: Jacqueline Ryan.

*Which artists do you admire?*

JR: Many past and present. I've always loved the work of Paul Klee and Marc Chagall for their colours, poetic content and aesthetic, but was subsequently much influenced by the photography of Carl Blossfeldt and Ernst Haeckel's illustrations of natural organisms.

*Is there anything in your life you could consider art?*

JR: The answer has to be: Nature.

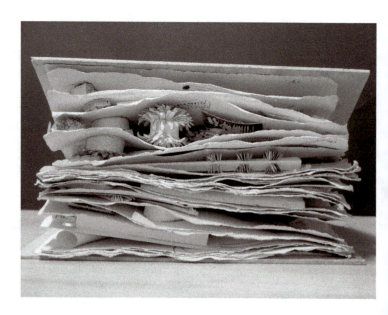

**Fig. 84**
Jacqueline Ryan. *Sketchbook*
1994.
Photo: Jacqueline Ryan.

# 20

# Bernhard Schobinger

**Born: 1946, Zurich, Switzerland**

**Fig. 85**
Bernhard Schobinger.
*Döschenring* 1992. Model paint
tin, gold-bronze pigment, gold,
freshwater pearls, pigment. Ring.
Photo: Bernhard Schobinger.

*RB: How and why did you come to jewellery?*

**BS:** I found some writing in my school work from when I was in primary school, and I had written 'I will learn goldsmithing'; at this time, I would have been about ten years old. Since my early childhood, from the age of five or six, I was fascinated by this kind of material, and I suppose it came from experiences of visiting churches in Switzerland with my parents. So I had contact with relics, the sacred bones from saints and the golden and silver sacred objects, and I was more fascinated by the goldsmith's objects from churches than by other jewellery. Ever since my memory began, I had the desire to make religious precious things.

*Are there any specific developmental phases in your working process?*

**BS:** I don't place any limitations on materials, subject or style. I never draw; I work with the material. If I see something in reality, I have the idea from reality and I never need to design or draw to develop a form; the form is a kind of memory in my head. I see the form in my dreams or fantasies. Maybe I write or make sketches, but only to remember an idea, not to develop it. I have a memory book with drawings and writings so as not to forget those ideas which I think are important.

*So your inspiration can come from your dreams?*

**BS:** The dream is like a mirror; it's a reflection in a mirror of something I encountered in reality. I find or see objects and I also see forms, all of which go into the brain unbeknown to me. So it's like an unbelievable pot with so many possibilities. I always have more ideas than I can realize; therefore, the realization is only ever a very small percentage of the ideas.

*Is intuition important to your approach?*

**BS:** Yes, I am not a thinker; I never use thinking to produce an idea. I never use rational ways to produce an object. That's a big difference to a designer – a design is a construction by rational working, and I am completely different. I'm an intuitive worker.

*Are you interested in tribal jewellery?*

**BS:** Yes, but not as a direct influence on my work. I am fascinated by the spiritual value of ethnic jewellery, because ethnic jewellery is much more than a prestige. It's also prestige, but there's also spiritual values in the piece that are not visible, and that's my interest.

*Is that why you use found objects, because of the residual spirit?*

BS: I find objects, and I discover in the objects an idea or a spirit.

*You have discussed the value of an object having been used; do you try and give your works a sense of history, as though they had already been used?*

BS: They already have signs from daily life, or they may have been destroyed by humans and the destruction is also a kind of design. I discovered there is a big potential in destruction. I have destroyed many pieces through anger.

*Can the destruction involve other people?*

BS: Yes, it's also possible. Maybe a broken glass bottle, it can be from the sea or water too – deformed by nature, by sea waves or an earthquake. For example, I collected glass shards from after the earthquake in Kobe to manifest the destruction – it's like a relic.

*Once you've found something, do you then make the work immediately?*

BS: No, not immediately. I have thousands of found objects. I have so many I cannot use all of them. For example, I am afraid to use these shards from Kobe because the connection with the disaster is too heavy.

*So, when you have an idea you go to your collection and see if something is suitable. Do you then make any models before creating the final piece?*

BS: No, I test the original piece.

*But what about the piece with the iron meteorite inlaid with gold, for example? Inlaying is not easy, so did you try any experiments beforehand?*

BS: No, I try to risk. I didn't make a test before; I will always take the risk.

*Hence, if something unexpected happens when you're working, you try to go with it rather than fighting to overcome it?*

BS: That's a big opportunity because new forms are often made by accident. The most important innovations in science are also discovered by accident, not by design. The discovery of fire, ceramics and glass were all discovered by accident. So I will be open for an accident because there is the chance for a discovery.

*As we have already mentioned, everyday objects have featured in many pieces, and their original function has often been subverted – for example, I'm thinking of the toothbrush bracelet. Could you discuss why you have worked this way?*

BS: It's a kind of challenge to discover new expressions, so it's almost like in times gone by – an expedition to the Far East or the Pacific to discover new islands. I'm on a kind of adventure to discover new expressions.

*Why do it through jewellery?*

BS: The field of jewellery is more interesting than a lot of other fields because jewellery is very conservative and blockaded by conventions. It's more interesting to operate in a conservative field.

*In terms of technique, you have often given considerable attention to how stones are pierced and cut or the formal aspects of jewellery such as settings. Could you discuss this?*

BS: It is done in an unconventional way.

*Do you consciously explore traditional aspects of jewellery such as stones and settings because you want to subvert their normal use?*

BS: I like to work in a wrong way, outside of the conventions. I prefer the forbidden way.

*So it's almost about undermining traditional jewellery?*

BS: Yes, undermine, that's a perfect idea, that's exactly what I mean. I feel like a rebel or guerrilla in the jewellery world.

*You often use a bezel setting rather than claw settings for the stones in your pieces, is there a special reason for this?*

BS: These crown-like claw settings look too conservative, they look like jewellery, like bijouterie. They're bourgeois, and I don't like them – in fact, I hate them.

*Is there a specific kind of jewellery that interests you, for example brooches or necklaces?*

BS: No. I think brooches are the most problematic thing – I don't like brooches. That's a very difficult kind of object, it's a perversion object; brooches are perverted clothes' needles. Brooches are derived from the Roman fibula used to secure a cloak, so brooches nowadays make no sense.

I like rings very much and also the ring as a bangle for the arm, or maybe chains and necklaces. I think the ring is the most interesting, it's an unlimited medium for me – I can work with rings without limitation.

*Why?*

BS: That's difficult to say.

*Well, for example you have chosen not to make cuff links, right?*

BS: That's a bourgeois absurd piece. I maybe made only one pair in my life. That's a good example for only a function; cuff links are only made for a function of closing shirt sleeves. Therefore, there are small possibilities, because if the function is not good enough, it makes no sense. But for a ring, it's the opposite. It can be very big and different – of course there is a limitation, but the materials are unlimited, I can make it out of any material.

*The freedom is because the function doesn't inhibit the selection of materials. I guess you are only really limited by scale, to some extent. Could you discuss the scale of your works, as often they are quite sizeable, with very large individual elements in the necklaces for example?*

BS: The piece must be in relationship to the body. There is for example a bracelet I made from one kilogram of silver and that's borderline; there is a limit in the weight.

*Could it be you prefer rings and necklaces because they touch the body, whereas brooches don't?*

BS: Yes, that's a good idea; this idea's new to me, but it's true. There's contact to the skin, to the body and life and also accumulation. I wrote some texts about the accumulation of irrational values, for example the history in the material, the chain of history is a kind of accumulation. If a piece is from your family, there is heritage, the spirit of your family is inside the piece, it is like a fetish. In a fetish, invisible things are included in the form.

*It is evidently important for you to understand and reference history. Do you undertake research when developing new work?*

BS: No, I don't research, but I am very interested in natural science, astronomy, history, ethnology and anthropology. I know about meteorites, and I think the theories that life on earth was brought by meteorites is unbelievable. I think this is magic – extraterrestrial worlds fallen down on earth and bringing life.

*This otherworldliness is interesting because sometimes your pieces look like they've come from ancient civilizations, almost as if they've been found in caves or archaeological excavations. Is it a quality you deliberately strive for?*

BS: It's by chance; they're not developed to resemble antiques. After completing a work, I may say, 'wow, this looks like an antique object', but it's not a concept to make it look like one.

*Humour seems important too.*

BS: Yes, that's correct; irony as well. Humour and irony are strategies for survival. The social world and the paradoxes of our life are so heavy there's a danger of becoming crazy. Humour is an important tool for not going crazy. I am also a child of Dadaism, which is also a strategy against craziness.

*Should the viewer and wearer understand the ideas behind your work?*

BS: Yes, but the same question can be asked of all objects. For example, in tribal culture each object is important for the society; meaning is not only special to my work.

*Some of your pieces do not seem very practical and perhaps are easily wearable. How important is function and wearability for you?*

BS: I know functionality very well, the function is very important, but the question of comfortable or not is stupid I think. It's a question from those who don't know about the history of jewellery. If you know about comfortableness in tribal art, the question is obsolete. I have a collection of tribal art – pieces from the Naga tribes; one for the chief's head weighs many kilogrammes. It's heavy, so you can ask, is that comfortable? No, of course that's not comfortable, but jewellery doesn't have to be comfortable. In jewellery there are messages that are more important than the function of being comfortable or not.

*Would you say the concept is more important than the form, materials or technique used to make the work?*

BS: No, form and message are one, and not two. If for example you see a piece in a museum from the Greek or pre-Columbian times, you can feel its aesthetic, but you don't have the information about the sense behind it. The sense or meaning has been lost, and if in future times my work survives in museums then maybe the meaning will be lost too.

*Is a piece of jewellery still jewellery when displayed in a museum, where you cannot wear it or touch it?*

BS: Yes, because in spirit it's made for the human and for the body and the function is perfect. It's also sad because it's lost contact with life. I have a collection of old Turkmenian jewellery, heavily worn for generations; they have lost a lot of material and signs, but otherwise they become richer from life on the body. One part is to lose, but the other part is to win from life. A used piece is a more valuable piece than a not-used piece – that's also a paradox. In Buddhist culture, a Buddhist figure that is not used is not strong, whereas the heavily used figure is a very strong one. How long a figure has been used equates to how strong it is because of the accumulation of praying and honouring.

*Are there any jewellers or artists that influence you?*

BS: I don't have a personality of influence, such as a favourite artist. My influence is the sum of all the experience I have had.

*Are you influenced by art at all?*

BS: I think the influence from fine art to jewellery is not as important as you infer. Maybe, you should ask, what is the influence in fine art from jewellery? Why should jewellery be influenced by fine art? That's like the bigger brother influencing the little brother, and I don't feel like a little brother of fine art. I think jewellery art is an independent art and not under the influence of fine art.

I'm against this separation of art – why fine art and applied art? These structures were made in the nineteenth century and before there had been no division. In the art of the Celts or the art of the Greeks, there's no difference between fine art and applied art. All art is a kind of applied art; painting is also made by handicraft, as are sculptures.

*I think it is interesting that you suggest we think about jewellery from the opposite perspective – that jewellery influences fine art.*

BS: Why not, are jewellery people more stupid than other people? Are they less creative? I'm against an applied art department and a fine art department in museums. This is a pyramid structure from the nineteenth-century bourgeois. On top is philosophy – only thinking and no dirty hands. No dirt, only spirit, that's the philosopher. And then comes the composer of music, then the writer, then the painter, then the sculptor and at the very base is the carpenter, the goldsmith and people who work with dirt. So this hierarchy is completely wrong and it's made by the philosophers to place themselves at the top.

*Why do you think contemporary jewellery is more popular in Northern Europe than in Spain or Italy?*

**BS:** I think because Latin people have a different way of thinking than northern Celtic groups. For example, the phenomenon of punk culture is not thinkable in Latin culture; punk is a phenomenon of the north.

*Do you think it could be anything to do with religion?*

**BS:** No, it's a kind of mentality. Latin groups like fashion and an aestheticism based on the antique classical ideal, and not so much provocation or borderline aesthetics.

**Fig. 86**
Bernhard Schobinger. *Plus-Minus* 1994. Bicycle pump valve, gold. Armband.
Photo: Bernhard Schobinger.

*Finally, what advice, if any, would you give to students?*

**BS:** I would say to be an artist it's not necessary to attend an art academy; that's a big mistake. I think it's not possible to learn to be an artist. I never went to an academy; I only did a simple apprenticeship. I'm against academies, I disapprove of them, they are like greenhouses for plants, with air conditioning. You have all the conditions to be an artist, but no real life. I have had other experiences – I am not a greenhouse plant!

**Fig. 87**
Bernhard Schobinger. *Hannya-Shingyô-Kette* 1995. Lignum vitae (wood), cord, lapis lazuli pigment. Necklace. Photo: Bernhard Schobinger.

# 21

# Peter Skubic

**Born: 1935, Gornji-Milanovac, Yugoslavia**

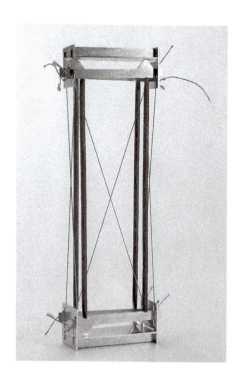

**Fig. 88**
Peter Skubic. *Ferro di Sambruson* 1999. Stainless steel, iron. Brooch. Photo by Petra Zimmermann. Collection of Giampaolo Babetto, Arquà Petrarca.

*RB: How and why did you decide to start making jewellery?*

**PS:** I was interested in making things I could handle, so I decided to make jewellery. All the phases of making my jewellery – from the idea to initial drafts and right through to the final piece occur in, and through, my hands.

My first jewellery was made out of high-quality steel, but their look was very different to the appearance of my jewellery nowadays.

*How would you define jewellery?*

**PS:** Jewellery are signs on the body, but this definition does not indicate quality.

*What inspires your work?*

**PS:** Thinking about life inspires my work.

*How do you go about developing a piece once you have the initial idea or starting point?*

**PS:** After the idea, I start making studies of different proportions as sketches on paper. Then I select. That is what I call thinking on paper.

*Links and movement seem very important in your work; all facilitated through hinges, springs, block and tackle and steel wires. Could you discuss their role in your work?*

**PS:** I didn't learn to be a goldsmith, but rather learned to be an artist during my apprenticeship to be an engraver; this is the reason I developed my own techniques. Some of my works are defined by the theme, such as the tension works.

*Are all the elements in a brooch generally held together under the tension of mechanical force, or is there ever any permanent welding?*

**PS:** The idea behind my tension brooches is that all the pieces are fixed by lever through tension.

*How do you choreograph the tension in your work?*

**PS:** I construct in my drawings and identify how the force path of the tension should be. I do not calculate that, it happens empirically.

*Do you have any interest in exploring flaccidity and materials that sag, such as rubber?*

PS: No, I'm not interested in the flaccidity of materials that sag.

*Do you have any preferences in terms of materials or techniques?*

PS: Yes, I prefer high-quality steel. I saw a lot and drill holes to connect the pieces by tying, riveting or tensioning it in its cold state.

*How do you establish the proportions of a work?*

PS: There are rules for good proportions like the 'golden section'. However, empirically found and felt proportions are more important to me.

*Some might describe the work* Jewellery under the Skin *as an extreme manifestation of jewellery, but nonetheless one that certainly tests the limits. Could you describe how the work came about and what lasting effect it had on your practice, if any?*

PS: *Jewellery under the Skin* was me finding the boundaries of the medium of jewellery, whereby invisible phenomena fascinated me most. In the meantime, I have new 'jewellery under the skin': it is a pacemaker!

*Other examples of testing the boundaries of jewellery and its typologies include the rings with the serrated internal edge,* The Inside of a Ring *project or the* Stand for an Invisible Ring – *could you talk about these a little?*

PS: The visual seen world is just one little way of exploring the world. You can experience so much which is invisible. This is what I try to explore, and if I think it is useful to use it in my jewellery works I do so. I do not just limit myself to making jewellery though.

*I believe that your use of highly polished, and therefore reflective, stainless steel is intended to be a kind of denial of mass and induce the perception of invisibility; is this the case?*

PS: Yes.

*This theme of formlessness was also explored in the mirror works. Could you discuss their evolution and key aspects?*

PS: When I started to take photographs of my jewellery, I noticed that the pieces which I had polished to a mirror finish disappeared in the photos; they actually reflected their environment. Afterwards I worked differently and I made the surface of the jewellery reflectionless and the physicalness of my objects reappeared. After a while this physical effect bothered me. I wanted to eliminate this formalism and therefore used high gloss again, which was seen as depraved at that time.

The mirror is a more complex theme than purely formal; mirrors are often the main themes in sagas and fairy tales. In psychology, the recognition of yourself is critical – and how does this take place? Via reflections – mirroring. I also created a mirror that lets you see yourself how other people see you; that happens via a double reflection.

*What role does drawing play in your practice?*

PS: Drawings are very important for me to be able to get the right proportions. I cannot draw proportions; I can only diagnose them. Above all, drawing is a great way to think.

*Do you always draw on graph paper?*

PS: Yes, I like drawing on millimeter-squared paper.

*How has your jewellery affected your sculpture and vice versa?*

PS: My jewellery is not actually typically decorative. My material choice (high-quality steel) allows me to make bigger objects; my plans are either for jewellery or bigger objects.

*How do you decide whether a work or idea is significant or not?*

PS: I know it.

*How important is functionality in a piece of your jewellery?*

PS: Functionality, certain logic and the functioning of my techniques are very important for me. It is important to me that people can safely and comfortably wear my jewellery. I developed a riffle method for the inside of rings so that they are more comfortable when worn. Furthermore, I developed rings whose size you can change. Double pins for brooches are self-evident, and the cardan joint necklaces work longer than other normal anchor necklaces.

*You have just asserted that the functionality of jewellery is important, but is it essential that your works should be worn for their completion?*

PS: Jewellery does not only have to be worn, but also needs to live long. Most of all jewellery is not worn, but lays around in factories, sits in the showcases of goldsmiths, hangs on walls, lays around in drawers, is locked in security containers, lays in galleries or degenerates in museums. Jewellery is also buried, thrown away, lost and fused again; but jewellery can be worn too.

*Do you think you have to be brave or extroverted to wear your pieces?*

PS: People can easily understand what they are capable of wearing. The way they dress and style their hair and the way they decorate themselves is usually very acceptable. Honestly, I do not really care what people do with my jewellery. There are no rules of how to use my jewellery.

*Do you have an ideal client?*

PS: My perfect client should be open to new and exceptional things, but should also have enough money to be able to afford my jewellery!

*Which artists do you respect or admire?*

PS: My favourite artists are Mark Rothko, Donald Judd, Henri Matisse, Pierre Bonnard, Sean Scully, Richard Serra, Tadao Ando and Michael Rowe.

*Have there been any specific events that have changed your life or work?*

PS: The Second World War strongly changed my life.

*How was the experience of curating the exhibition* Schmuck International *at the Kunstlerhaus in Vienna?*

PS: I was lucky enough to be able to make this event happen and also very happy that the World Congress of Art Councils was in Vienna at the same time. I wanted to demonstrate to people in Austria that jewellery like this exists.

*What approach to teaching did you think one should adopt?*

PS: A teacher should encourage students to think independently and freely, to look behind and beyond things and to question rules.

*What advice would you give to students?*

PS: Learn and train as much as possible. Learn how other artists work and what they think. Go to exhibitions in museums and galleries. Read about art, not only about jewellery, in books, magazines and on the net. Cooperate with other students.

**Fig. 89**
Peter Skubic. *Magnetbrosche*
1980. Stainless steel, magnets.
Brooch.
Photo: Chris Pfaff.

**Fig. 90**
Peter Skubic. *Elisabeth Krause*
2005. Stainless steel, lacquer,
gold leaf. Brooch.
Photo: Petra Zimmermann.

# 22

# Tone Vigeland

## Born: 1938, Oslo, Norway

**Fig. 91**
Tone Vigeland. *Bracelet*
1985. Silver. National Design
Museum – Cooper-Hewitt,
New York.
Photo: Hans-Jørgen Abel.

RB: *How and why did you start making jewellery?*

TV: As a teenager, I made some pieces of jewellery for girlfriends. I was seventeen when I selected the metal department at Statens Håndwerk Og Kunst – Industri skole (art school).

*Could you describe the main phases in the creation of a piece?*

TV: I allow time for play with materials and then evaluate the possibilities.

*Do you draw on paper or make three-dimensional models at all?*

TV: No.

*How do you understand when a piece is finished?*

TV: It is always a question of feeling as to when I can let go of a piece.

*Can you discuss the relationship between the part and whole in your work, and in particular how you establish the relationship between the geometry of the individual unit and the overall form?*

TV: You can easily understand that I, at this stage of my life, have a large production of pieces behind me – made during over fifty years of active work. On this basis it is impossible to give you a general answer. However, very often, an individual unit gave me an idea of the possibilities for the overall form.

*And what about the relationships between the purity of the elemental forms you appear to prefer and the apparent softening of this geometry through the casual falling or hanging of the repeated units?*

TV: It is of importance to me that the repeated units hang in a natural way. In movement, they may go astray, but should always return to original shape.

*Could you describe the consequences on your practice of using what one imagines being an extremely lengthy working process based on continuous acts of repetition?*

TV: I have never had apprentices or people working under my direction making jewellery. The repetitious part of the process has implied an element of rest for me. A curiosity to the final result has kept me going.

*Obviously this repetition has been fundamental to your working process, but how significant a role do accident and chance play?*

TV: They have never played any significant role in my working process. At the same time, I have always allowed myself the time to play with material, to measure its possibilities. For a piece of jewellery it necessitates a more definite plan. Its final form will sometimes only be found after it has been tried out on a body. I may sometimes make a sketch, but never an elaborate one.

*Does that mean you sometimes try a piece of jewellery on somebody to see how it reacts to their geometry and movement whilst you are making it, and then make adjustments to the piece accordingly?*

TV: Yes, that is correct. It is not always so, but sometimes I do it that way.

*Could you describe how movement came to be such an important facet of your work, and how this interest has evolved over the years?*

TV: From the time, in the late 1950s, when I started working, I have been interested in movement and its adjustment to the body. I tried to find my own way to express this. In the mid-1970s, when I started working with chain mail, new possibilities emerged. This has been the basis of most of my works since then.

*It appears as though the response of your work to light is important and how this can enhance the implied or actual sense of movement within a piece. Could you discuss this in more detail?*

TV: Indeed, the response of my work to light is of the greatest importance. Light becomes a third factor, in addition to the form and material.

*Do you feel a particular affinity with silver, and if so, why?*

TV: At the time I started working, it was important to make jewellery for everyday use, for modern women. The cost of silver obviously plays a role here. As for the material itself, I have appreciated that it is easy to work with.

*Could you explain how and why you invariably oxidize silver to varying shades of black?*

TV: I use oxide to give more life to the surface. It varies from black to grey tones, right through to the highly polished parts near the edge.

*Does your work carry a narrative or symbolic meaning, or is it a more formal exercise between geometry, the relationship to the body, light and movement and so on?*

TV: According to my own intentions, there are no narrative or symbolic meanings.

*In 1989, you made a series of bracelets that appear quite different from the norm on first inspection – very elemental simple forms, one in the shape of a cube, or others in hexagonal and triangular cylinders. How did their geometry evolve?*

TV: I am always striving towards simplicity, and this wish may take different shapes.

*In the aforementioned works, the surface is very distinct; it almost looks like old beaten iron. How did you achieve the surface?*

TV: They are made of rusted iron, which has been treated and polished.

*Are you interested in imbuing materials with significance, or spiritual protection, or are you exclusively interested in formal aesthetics?*

TV: I do not believe that material itself is imbued with any possibilities for spiritual protection. However, if the bearer of my jewellery feels that the piece represents an element which strengthens their personality, I would indeed be pleased.

*How do you feel about the associations often made between your work and Viking ornament and the Norwegian landscape?*

TV: I am not comfortable when association is established between my work and Viking ornament. When it comes to the open landscape, I do have my roots in this part of the world.

*How has your jewellery making influenced your sculpture and vice versa? Do you feel that this exchange between the macro and micro has been beneficial?*

TV: When I make sculpture, I do not have to take into consideration the adjustment of the piece to a body, but take into consideration space and air.

*Since the late 1980s, there appears to have been a deliberate intention to remove visible signs of support and functional elements such as clasps. Could you describe how and why this decision was made?*

TV: Their removal was due to a wish to obtain a more simple and sculptural form.

*Have sculptors of primary forms such as Donald Judd, and latterly Martin Puryear and Anish Kapoor, been of any significant influence on your work?*

TV: I cannot say that there has been any direct inspiration from the artists you mention. I do, however, take great pleasure in seeing Puryear's work.

*So, which other artists and/or jewellers do you admire?*

TV: I still think that the early pieces of Torun Bülow-Hübe are very good. Presently there are some I admire, but find it hard to make a selection. Among sculptors, I like Richard Serra.

*Do you feel a particular affinity to the earliest prehistory creators of body adornment in the form of strung shells because of your working method?*

TV: Yes, I do feel great affinity, and I am most interested in the subject.

*Would you say it's fair to suggest that one of the attractions of the morphing neutrality of linked chain mail is because of its universality and democratization of the figure in terms of being able to adapt to any body shape?*

TV: The idea is valid, but, unfortunately, only partly correct. In the best scenario, a piece will find an owner whose personality corresponds.

# 23

# David Watkins

**Born: 1940, Wolverhampton, England**

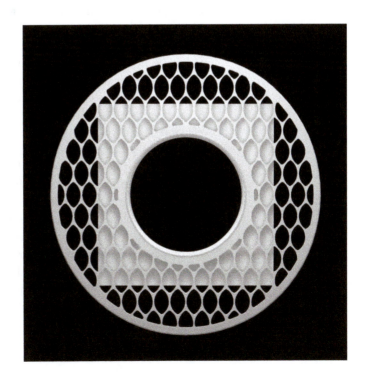

**Fig. 92**
David Watkins. *Taj* 2009. Acrylic,
gold. Bangle.
Photo: David Watkins (CGI).

*RB: You originally started your creative life as a musician and then studied sculpture. How did the latter affect your jewellery?*

**DW:** A lot of the underlying principles and attitudes that guided my ideas in jewellery came through from my work in sculpture. These would have included clarity of form, a minimal approach, the sense of the autonomous object, the use of materials in their natural state or else coloured by painting, and so on.

*Did it influence your understanding of scale?*

**DW:** My received understanding was that one's perception of sculpture is not tied necessarily to its actual physical scale. There was this concept of monumentality – that it was possible to understand a very small sculpture as a monumental piece. On the other hand, I worked through a period when sculpture 'came off the plinth' and confronted the viewer one to one, and I guess this was ultimately more influential.

*Could you describe the main phases in the creation of a piece of jewellery?*

**DW:** The process of thinking an idea through to actually making and completing the work is different according to which materials and techniques you're using. For some materials and processes, I might spend a lot of time sketching many alternatives, whereas for others I might go directly into the material and start shaping it, to judge how it feels or wants to develop the idea. Since the end of the 1980s, however, quite a lot of my ideas have been evaluated in advance through computer drawing and modelling.

I think the expression, the concepts and the forms in my work are always very closely connected with the means of making; the selection of materials and processes are always key. There's a constant feedback between material, method and idea.

I like to layer objects – physical layering seems to chime with layering of meanings – and I'm always open to giving up some element of control, to take advantage of chance. So I often, quite deliberately, make individually complete objects and then offer them up to each other. I let them begin to develop the concept – to tell me what it might become. There is something about designing or arriving at forms which are individually dissimilar but which have some kind of built-in consequence: when you put them together, they might relate to each other but also begin to raise the game in terms of complexity and possibilities. So rather than being completely random outcomes, there is actually already some unconscious predetermined order.

*How do you arrive at this compositional order?*

**DW:** I think it is a combination of knowledge, instinct and intuition. The problem for me, all the time, is that I want to understand things – to be rational, analytical, to know how and why a composition works – but intuitive choices usually turn out to be the most critical. That's not to duck the question, but even intuition is not some kind of unconnected abstract property. It's too easy to talk of it that way. I mean, it's complex, but it comes from somewhere and is fed by one's experiences in some way.

*Do you ever feel that your use of high technology limits chance?*

**DW:** Well, of course it does in one way.

*Because you have to know what you are going to do in advance of starting?*

**DW:** Yes. High technology does tend to drive you to be decisive. But that's simply an aspect of its challenge and not a bad thing in itself. It's possible of course to harness high technology in such a way that one brings in a random element. I have experimented with this idea in the past, when the idea of computer-aided design suggested new possibilities, but it's not relevant to me now. I like to deal with fundamentally simple geometries and am astonished how their interactions can generate more complex resonances. Technology helps. Chance is somewhere else.

*What technical challenges do rapid prototyping or laser cutting entail?*

**DW:** Every technology has its good side and its problematic side; there is no perfect all-round solution. Most of these computer-controlled machines don't actually produce a perfect result; they are good, but there are always compromises. If you had extraordinarily sophisticated machines and used them to the limits, those compromises could, I suppose, be managed to the point where they would be virtually undetectable, but that's not my experience. You are confronted by choices.

What I usually find is that I must at least also hand finish and work things to bring them out. They don't emerge from the machine good to go. I suspect that finishing things one on one, the hard way, is key to the whole process. On a philosophical level, you leave your mark on something even though it may seem ultimately machine-perfect – if that is what you want.

Generally, the same principles apply to all work with tools, whether hand or machine tools: they all have their challenges and limitations, and the evidence of process is there to be expressed and read or to be mediated and concealed – that's simply a choice. Just because pieces are primarily handled by some computer or machine makes no difference.

*You often use the term* clarity; *is it a quality you strive for?*

DW: I think so. Clarity of form and precision are both very important to me. As far as I am concerned, clear form is both un-ambiguous and yet ambiguous, perhaps sonorous. It's something to be aimed for. One does not always achieve precision, and some-times one lets it go for expressive reasons – I can play games with my own rules. I find a kind of sensuality in precision.

*Have you steered away from soft materials such as silicone be-cause you feel they are unlikely to lead to clarity?*

DW: I wouldn't find it very interesting; there's no fight with it.

*So you value the struggle against hard materials?*

DW: On the whole, yes; but not always. I use fairly hard materi-als, or materials that to my mind require precision in order to bring out their voice and beauty.

*Often your pieces seem quite graphic, almost like wearable graf-fiti. Is it a deliberate attempt to create a language of visual signs?*

DW: I think it is. It probably arises from a developing interest in narrative possibilities. Although my work has often seemed fo-cused on strict abstract geometry, I sense it has always carried a certain narrative impulse.

*Why do you define so much of your jewellery through the circle?*

DW: Lots of my work now is based around the idea of circles, and has been for a long time, because I find the circular form fascinat-ing and there is food for me to work with there. And I am not about to change my shape for some arbitrary reasons.

Seriously, the circle is a very fundamental form in jewellery; my interest in it arose from a self-imposed prescription against making things that you couldn't directly put on the body. I do make some pins now, but my practice is essentially about things that push on to the limbs or around the neck – so circles, for example. It's primitive.

*Presumably there's a relationship between necklaces and bangles because they reside close to the body, touching the skin, whereas a brooch is different?*

DW: Absolutely, this is a completely different discipline.

*So why did you decide to make brooches?*

DW: The brooches, or pins, that persuaded me to break the rule were very frontal and very central: you couldn't use them in an informal way; you couldn't simply pin them on a lapel; they had to be situated in the centre of the torso. This put them in an interesting space between the wearer and the observer.

I did quite a lot of jewellery in the 1970s where you could understand the work and its relation to the body in a certain way by looking at both very frontally. The geometry became very clear, but then, when the body moved a little, it became evident how the geometry intersected the body. The work had two lives – as a very frontal symmetrical piece and as an object that surrounded the body, which is the case with the neckpieces that have been my main practice over the years. The key with the neckpieces is that they occupy space around the body, in other words, what happens at the back of the neck, what happens behind you, is as important as what happens in front.

*Is there a specific reason why your works have become planar?*

DW: I think it comes from this perception the body is providing the three-dimensionality, and the jewellery, a kind of single plane, play against the volumes of the body. Again, I think that is rather a primitive thing – which I like: the fact that something I have made – probably putting in a great deal of time, thought, effort and technology – comes out looking as if it might have been made in the Stone Age. I have always thought whoever one day finds it, even a Martian archaeologist, should say, 'Ah, this must have been a piece of jewellery.'

*Is wearability fundamental, too, then?*

DW: Yes, I think so. This doesn't mean to say it has to be easily wearable, just self-evidently so.

I like to make things imagining how they will be when someone walks into a room wearing the object – how will that be? That's in my mind's eye a lot of the time while I work. I mean, that's a kind of touchstone: will it be interesting, will it be exciting, will it make a difference?

*Do you have an ideal customer?*

DW: No, I don't think so, but if someone comes and says – as they often used to – 'I don't know what I want, I just want the next thing you make', it is fascinating because then you are confronted not by some kind of ideal or abstract but by a real person who has colouring, gesture, scale, presence in a room and so on. This produces a series of challenges, so that they don't exactly get the next thing you are going to make; they get the thing that they have provoked you to make. Fortunately, out of these provocations come new ideas, something I might never have thought of in other circumstances. I can almost tie them to a particular person – someone who caused a certain kind of form or piece of vocabulary to enter my working strategies, and that's an amazing thing. That's an experience that I think is very special to jewellery.

*What kind of relationship would you like to establish between the object and the wearer's body?*

DW: I would like the wearer to feel much more special and enhanced by wearing the object. I would like the two to come together in a way which is a little bit extraordinary.

*Do you think a piece of jewellery is decoration for the body or an ornament?*

DW: I'm not sure I know the difference. You asked the question; do you have a point of view?

*I think it is a decoration for the body because etymologically speaking decoration comes from the Latin děcǒro, which means the object has decorum, whereas an ornament implies embellishing the body. Decoration changes the content, changes the body, not just the aesthetics of it. Then again, maybe this is just semantics.*

DW: I think it is semantic and also one of those rather treacherous areas in English. I am always confused because I have this childhood memory of my grandmother's 'ornaments' which stood importantly on her mantelpiece, but when I read sheet music, 'ornaments' were indicated by minimal signs, so the word sits in a very strange position. I rarely use the word *ornament* for jewellery. I prefer the word *decoration* if it comes to it.

*What do you consider jewellery's function to be then?*

DW: I think its principle functions are to do with self-awareness, awareness of persona, awareness of body or awareness of presence;

it's about how one is seen as a total person. It becomes part of the assemblage of a personality.

*Finally, what advice would you give to students?*

**DW:** I would say you have got to be fascinated by the results in order to sustain all the effort and concentration required: you have to be absolutely committed to seeing what comes out the other end, and you have to be prepared for quite a long slog. I wouldn't expect our (RCA postgraduate) students to be finding a genuinely authentic voice with real meaning until maybe ten years after college in most cases.

**Fig. 93**
David Watkins. *Primary Orbits* 1982. Neoprene, steel. Combination neckpiece. Photo: David Ward.

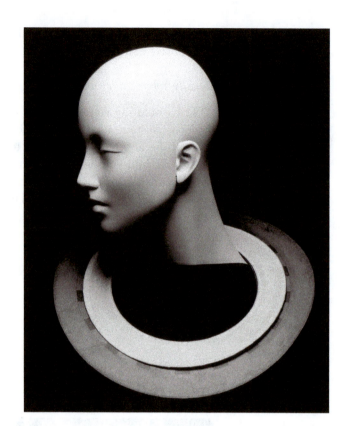

**Fig. 94**
David Watkins. *Blue Dancer*
1983. Paper, inks, steel.
Neckpiece.
Photo: David Watkins.

# 24

# Annamaria Zanella

**Born: 1966, S. Angelo Di Piove, Padua, Italy**

**Fig. 95**
Annamaria Zanella. *Acqua*
1996. Iron, gold, silver, enamel.
Brooch.
Photo: Lorenzo Trento.

*RB: How did you come to make jewellery?*

**AZ:** It all started thanks to the advice of an elementary school teacher, who, having noted my predisposition for drawing and natural sense of colour, suggested a secondary school specializing in art. So, I went to the Istituto d'Arte Pietro Selvatico, a school in Padua where I had originally hoped to enroll in the textiles department. However, because there were no spaces, I joined the jewellery department with a view to changing back after a year. Having begun the first academic year, I slowly fell in love with jewellery and have never changed idea since. I had the huge fortune to be taught by Francesco Pavan, Giampaolo Babetto, Renzo Pasquale and Graziano Visentin, master artists who today constitute the School of Padova.

*Arte Povera seems to have been a profound influence on your work. Who encouraged this interest?*

**AZ:** At the Academy in Venice it was Professor Sprocatti and prior to that, Pavan and Bodini at the Istituto d'Arte in Padova between 1988 and 1993. Pavan, with his immense technical capacity and sensibility, mentored me through my initial research, leaving me free to confront so-called poor materials. He encouraged me to keep experimenting using those non-precious materials which I so loved. Having seen my drawings, sketches, and early prototypes in card and iron, Pavan believed in me and pushed me to continue this research that eventually led to the development of my own personal expressive language.

*Where does the inspiration for your work come from?*

**AZ:** First of all, it is born from my love of sculpture and painting. Out of the two, I prefer sculpture and the strength of its forms, material and light. My own artistic journey originates from a prolonged and detailed research on Arte Povera from the 1960s and 1970s.

In my pieces, I seek to apply this research to re-evaluate the meanings of materials. Gold and precious stones have always carried a huge associative baggage of pain and blood. Indeed many wars were born out of the desire to obtain the power of these materials so it contributes to the history of many civilizations. I find it contemporary and original to be able to create a composition, a jewellery of significance, without using precious metals. This has been, and remains, my primary aim.

*How does the idea for a work come into being and what are the phases in its development?*

**AZ:** A mark, a bit of torn poster on the street, a rusty piece of iron on the ground, a stone, broken glass are the images that arrive in my mind, which I then elaborate until creating some drawings.

I undertake some interventions. Consider for example paper: I use quite heavy paper, therefore I can work with overlaps of colours and wax, then I begin to cut these forms – pieces which already have volume, strength and thickness. Once I have a paper prototype, I can create in iron, but gold is an altogether different matter.

Many times I might destroy the models – seven, eight, nine or even ten times – until I finally attain the solution I have been striving for. Volumes are extremely important; they are what underpin my work. The studies I undertook at the Art Academy in Venice helped me discover and resolve the 'plastic' part of my practice.

*Is time an important factor in your work?*

**AZ:** Extremely. It is the succession of past experiences, knowledge and daily life. This living that is part of each of us – all that happened yesterday and the day before that and so on, all the baggage of memories, situations and emotions.

The concept of time is often strongly present in my works. For example, the enamel I use is never shiny, but left in acid to be eaten away in such a way as to render the surface lived, torn and consumed by time.

*Therefore, one might say that time interacts with, and transforms, the object.*

**AZ:** Yes, even iron when it is willingly corroded by chemical treatment becomes a material where time interacts and transforms, much the same as happens to all of us. Life and the passage of time changes people biologically and also psychologically.

My oxidations are blocked in their consumptive act by applications of a varnish that prevents them from completely destroying the piece. It does not have to be a total degradation of the object because I have not arrived at that conceptual step. It is an interesting notion and might even be a future development for my work.

*Why are there several different ways of considering time in the works?*

**AZ:** Because the patina of time is not a defect. Conceptually speaking, time is an event that passes continually, it is part of existence, so why shouldn't it be part of jewellery?

*Could you discuss the aesthetics of your work?*

**AZ:** The aesthetic is an intersection of things – namely the union between form and material, which for me is all one thing – they exist together and are born together.

*What role does functionality play in your jewellery?*

**AZ:** In my early works I did not pay much attention to its functionality or weight. In fact, they were almost always pieces where the contact with the body became a provocation because they were made of broken glass or sheets of rusty iron. There was always the risk that the piece might stain clothes or that it might cut someone or be dangerous to wear. Many of these pieces made between 1990 and 1993 are part of my private collection because they simply cannot be sold and are in no way functional.

The moment a piece of jewellery comes into contact with the wearer's body, it must confront a series of limits. For example a ring must have a certain measurement, weight or dimension; earrings or necklaces mustn't be sharp and so on. The limits are sometimes enormous barriers for me, because I view a piece of jewellery as though it were a sculpture.

I like the idea that even the movement of the wearer's body becomes a kinetic sculpture. The body challenges contemporary jewellery and jewellery challenges the body in a game of parts. Finding the solution to this conundrum is to unite form and function, and this challenge is always enticing and fascinating for the intellect and soul of the creator.

*So everything must be in equilibrium and neither form nor function should be less valued.*

**AZ:** Yes, it can happen that the front of a brooch is extremely rough and deliberately unrefined because it needs to communicate aggression; but, on the contrary, in order to respect the wearer, the back of the brooch needs to be perfect, with smooth edges and functionally well designed.

*How did the idea for the series which included* Cell, *from 2003, come about?*

**AZ:** It was a meditation on the infinitely small elements from which we humans are composed. It was an invented cell – light, impalpable and precious. Full of a deep blue of the ocean's depths. It is a cell that speaks of dreams and poetry. Otto Künzli defined it as a lake of profound blue which if you look at it for a long time you can find a place of calm and peace.

*The brooch* Leg, *from 2007, belongs to a series of pieces that appear to have a different theme. Could you discuss it?*

**AZ:** Unfortunately during our lifespan our bodies are subject to attack and transformation. Even illness forms part of our lives and marks our existence. For the last ten years I have fought an illness that results in difficulties in walking, and this brooch reflects my daily struggles. It is fragile, vibrating and fixed in its movements like my leg. In effect, I think that my jewellery, and that of many other artists, is always autobiographical; like the pages of a diary written in metal and materials that take form through the consequences of thought and daily reflection.

*Why have you introduced ebony into your work? Does it have a particular meaning for you?*

**AZ:** Ebony is a living material; it is a precious wood with refined nuances of colour varying between black and brown. I have begun to use this material for its intense colour and texture. This piece of ebony for example is very old, and has been seasoning for twenty years; it forms part of my past and contains many secrets, emotions, hopes.

*Could you discuss the pieces that explore the concept of a room?*

**AZ:** The works are dissolving geometries, boxes that are opening, exploding; containers that allow you to catch a glimpse of light, compositions that change according to one's point of view, almost like a worn sculpture.

*What pieces are you currently working on?*

**AZ:** I am experimenting with new plastic materials. The desire to confront new materials, and especially those not generally associated with jewellery, lies deep within me. Throwaway materials are revived through my attention to their textures and chemical composition, alongside transformations achieved through heat and other means.

*Has there been an event in your artistic carrier that has been particularly significant?*

**AZ:** In 1997 I was awarded the Herbert Hoffmann prize in Munich. It was not a moment of arrival, but rather a moment of departure because it gave me enormous strength and repaid many years of struggle and delusions. Winning this prize gave me the joy and desire to continue my research and my experimentations.

*What do you like so much in life that you could consider it art?*

**AZ:** Relationships with people, the nature that surrounds us and events that involve human beings. I believe that before being artists we are all men and women with desires, expectations, delusions, pains, joy, light and shade. It is very difficult to establish a relationship with others; it is difficult to decode the language of fellow human beings and transform them into marks, colours and forms.

Nature is also a strong and ongoing source of inspiration and contamination in my pieces. I love nature because it is an unattainable form of art. We humans are a form of art.

*What are the differences between a designer and someone who creates with their own hands?*

**AZ:** A piece of jewellery created by a designer must be a piece that is studied for industry and must respond to the taste of a huge quantity of people. The research of a designer seeks a form and functional outcome aimed at a wide public audience. On the other hand, the jewellery artist creates projects and makes only a few pieces, each limited in edition for a small group of cultivated people who are sensitive to artistic expressions.

*Who is your ideal client?*

**AZ:** A gallery owner or collector who is in love with the art of contemporary jewellery and follows its every creative development step by step; a person who believes in your work and research.

*What advice would you give to students concluding their studies?*

**AZ:** I would advise them in the first instance to have patience. Great things do not emerge if previously there was not a large amount of study and preparation at the goldsmith's table in school. It is not possible for someone who has just left school, college or university to suddenly become an artist; it is a long, hard road, difficult and full of many sacrifices and deprivations.

Before commencing with this kind of personal research, I would advise students to try a period of professional work as an industrial jewellery designer in order to understand how you work and produce with new technologies and how to make jewellery in series. Before drawing or planning a piece of jewellery, one must know the techniques and technologies available. I would also advise a period of study abroad, ideally in an academic institution with the opportunity to study or improve a second language, preferably German or English.

**Fig. 96**
Annamaria Zanella. *Il Giorno e La Notte* 1998. Gold. Brooch.
Photo: Lorenzo Trento.

**Fig. 97**
Annamaria Zanella. *Leg* 2007.
Silver, ebony, enamel, gold.
Brooch.
Photo: Giulio Rustichelli.

# 25

# Christoph Zellweger

**Born: 1962, Lübeck, Germany**

**Fig. 98**
Christoph Zellweger.
*Commodity Chain K22* 1997.
Expanded polystyrene,
chrome-plated
silver, silicon tube, nylon.
Photo: Christoph Zellweger.

RB: *How and why did you decide to make jewellery?*

CZ: I follow a 170-year-long family tradition of silversmiths, watchmakers, jewellers and goldsmiths. I think I just followed; I had no other idea of what to learn as a profession when I was seventeen. But after almost ten years in the trade, I stopped making jewellery, totally, radically; I had to get away from it. But then after some years I came back to a more contemporary view on the field and I saw its value again and that it is an expressive and, in its complexity, an exciting medium.

*What kind of jewellery did your family used to make?*

CZ: Well, my father is first of all a passionate silversmith and besides that a goldsmith. His work is still interesting and I think it was really cutting edge in the 1960s, 1970s and 1980s. Also my mother ran a very nice fifth-generation jewellery shop; she was never just commercial. My parents were always somehow pushing for the new. My mother for example introduced Scandinavian jewellery design to her customers in Germany, a novelty at the time; she also took on board Niessing jewellery as one of the first retailers, so she was far away from being mainstream at the time. My father trained in Austria, worked in Switzerland and also for the designer Sigurd Person in Sweden; so I think they were quite up to date and I suppose I had a head start when I entered the profession.

*What inspires your work?*

CZ: I have questions and I am curious about what we (I mean people) do, so it is people and politics that inspire me. What makes me want to do the next body of work always comes from a real-life experience, an observation of what happens around me, in society. For years, I have been concerned with fragmentation; people have to adapt increasingly fast to the vast changes we go through. By making my work, I somehow create order from what was less clear to me before.

*So, what is your work concerned with?*

CZ: I think I have been concerned with defining naturalness and authenticity for a long time. Probably, I am also still trying to understand what defines or makes up a person's identity. Nature has been changed by man; now the human body is challenged by aesthetic surgery and other invasive medical techniques. More and more, the human body itself becomes the subject of design, a luxury item, a commodity. There, I continue exploring the tension between nature and artifice and suggest that jewellery may gradually leave behind the stage of being an accessory, in the sense of an appendage or annex, to potentially become an integrated component of man.

*Would you say your work is always driven by ideas?*

**CZ:** Probably, my approach is usually conceptual, in the sense that it is driven by content, and it is speculative because I like to test these ideas and enter new territories. The intuitive and the inexplicable also have a place in the process. A good idea to me is not one I can answer easily; and sometimes the answer lays in the material itself.

*How do you approach the selection of materials?*

**CZ:** I change the material I work with quite a lot. A new body of work is often made out of totally different components than the previous body of work. For me, it is like making a new sentence. For a new sentence with a new meaning, I may have to use different words or even invent a kind of new alphabet. Every material is already loaded with information, so I deliberately choose materials and forms that carry strong cultural and associative references. I have worked for example with polystyrene, because it is of almost no commercial value; it is white and pure and its surface skin-like. I worked with medical steel because of its preciousness and prosthetic use, or with porcelain, because of being a material not dissimilar to the substance bones are made from. I'm not concerned with sticking to a recognizable visual language. I trust in the overall concept I follow and that in the long run people can see the thread that keeps my work together.

*Could you discuss the message behind the polystyrene pieces?*

**CZ:** Well, it was definitely about *not* participating in the world of easy consumption. Working with throwaway materials, especially in jewellery, creates a debate on values. These 'body pieces' in polystyrene referred to human body parts. They were designed as fictitious body implants and prosthesis, which were brought to the outside of the body to become visible. I think I tried to make a statement about my observation that the body itself will become a commodity when the use of invasive medical technologies becomes the norm. My next body of work, *Foreign Bodies,* in medical biocompatible steel, told a similar story, but pointing in a slightly different direction.

*Would you say you want to provoke by using certain materials?*

**CZ:** Not for the sake of provocation. I'm interested in putting forward my issues and of course I am content if there is a debate about the validity of these issues. To create an audience is a main objective, and people are free to aesthetically judge the work. I mean I try hard to work these materials until I find an aesthetic that reflects my own feeling towards my theme, and I am often torn between seduction and repulsion. I think I make work to confront my audience with their own set of values.

*Could you describe how and why you have introduced high-tech manufacturing processes into your practice? I'm thinking specifically of works such as* Data Jewels, Rhizomes *and the interactive light pieces.*

**CZ:** Well, I think I just see opportunities when reading about a new technical process or when I see new materials or products on the market – they inspire me and make me curious. I always aim to visualize how my work could benefit from those techniques, so I just learn about the process and try to finance the experiments, which are often expensive. Over the years I have developed intensive material and technical research, for example in working with biocompatible medical steel for the series *Foreign Bodies,* bought/ built a machine to do 3D-surface flocking (*Relic Rosé*), used water jet cutting (*Rhizomes*), laser engraving (*Body Supports*) and industrial photo etching (*Data Jewels*). I often use these technical processes in combination with traditional craft processes.

The *Light Jewellery* we developed within a team of researchers at Imperial College in London for a venture company. It was a lot about miniaturization of the LED technology, and the vision was to make light become precious and sensual. You have to have a vision of what could be done and then develop the appropriate technologies and material towards these goals. We worked for two and a half years on that project, and I think we made some really wonderful pieces; however, the top-end luxury jewellery market was hesitant and did not take the risk to further invest into this project. I suppose part of the research findings were patented and sold to the mobile phone industry.

*Do you place great importance on functionality and wearability?*

**CZ:** The *Light Jewellery* project was all about wearability, functions and user-friendly handling. In my personal work, I do and sometimes I don't give importance to it. A piece of jewellery can be functional without being wearable or vice versa; a piece of jewellery can be wearable, but its ability to function, to work for the wearer or the viewer, can be limited. The crown jewels for example are worn only for a very very short moment in a queen's or king's life, but its perceived significance to society is enormous. Some crowns were fixed directly over the throne, but were not lowered onto the head. Nobody would argue against calling these crowns jewellery. On the other hand, a very easy to wear jewel may never catch anybody's attention or the wearer's imagination and will finally be forgotten somewhere in the dark. A successful jewel has to work in one way or another; the terms *functionality* and *wearability* can be stretched.

*I see a relic as a religious object, a piece of the body or a personal item of a saint which is not intended to be worn. If your piece* Relic Rosé *has such a distinctive context and is a contemporary relic, how do you see the relationship between this work and the human body when it is worn?*

CZ: A relic, to me, is a significant fragment or leftover of something or someone to be cherished. In some tribal cultures, they chopped off fingers or ears of beloved ones who had died and carried the dried pieces around in little bags or hung the pieces from the ceiling to retain the presence of the loved person. I don't just associate the word *relic* with religious artefacts like we find them in the Catholic Church; for me a relic is a 'loaded object' often connected to the body as well as the mind, but also fragments of cloth from a person's dress for example can be relics. Relics are objects people seem to create because of a necessity; it is more of an intuitive thing to create them, but the Catholic Church for example has formalized this ancient rite perfectly and very cleverly. With this in mind, of course, relics can be worn on the body and in public too, where the object may be differently read than if displayed at home. My *Relic Rosé* pieces, once made functional by adding chains or pins, become wearable. With function or without, they are objects for contemplation and remembrance like all relics. The objects have also been loaded by giving them the title of a relic.

*Do you think a contemporary jeweller can make a successful serial production?*

CZ: Well, I think it needs a certain artistic mindset to do one-off pieces and another to make works for a larger market where success is measured by other criteria. I don't see many jewellery makers or designers who are interested or comfortable working within both mindsets. Maybe this is a pity, as jewellery artists can be rather unaware of how to apply their good thinking to succeeding in the market. Many of us are also relatively unaware of the possibilities technology offers and are slow in developing these skills. So more crossovers between market-led designers and jewellery artists with their ideas would surely lead to exciting jewellery for production: work that could change the perception of jewellery on a wider scale.

With *Data Jewels* and *Rhizomes*, I started thinking in 'wearables' which incorporate technology and are produced using new production methods to potentially compete on the market. It would be nice to do better than Swatch jewellery and company idea-wise, but they are in the lead.

**Fig. 99**
Christoph Zellweger. *Data Jewel* 2001. Stainless steel. Photo: Corne Bastiaansen.

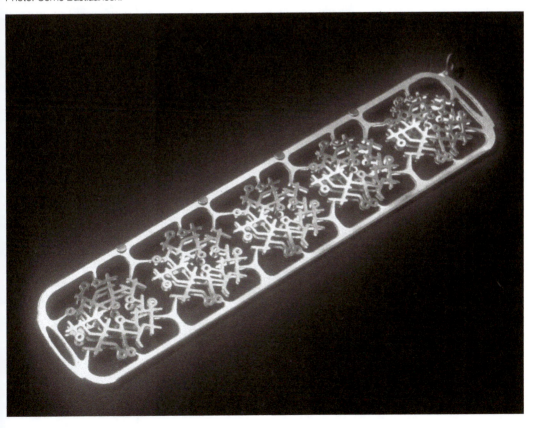

*Who do you consider when making your work?*

**CZ:** It is not only a question of who but also what to consider, and, for me, creating new situations for communication is part of the work. First of all, I like to develop the idea; I want to say something. The work is the vehicle for this. While I'm developing the work, I start to think about a space, an audience, man, woman, a type of person, and I think of the best context for communicating with it, be it choosing the format of a wearable object or an installation. For example, the conceptual departure from displaying jewellery works in specialized galleries into showing them in different historic museum contexts has been a way to test new grounds for the communication of my work.

*Do you think the wearer adds anything?*

**CZ:** I aim to make artefacts that work as autonomous pieces away from the body, but I consider carefully how the functional aspects are incorporated or added to all works. I enjoy when these artefacts age when worn by someone and the pieces show signs of use.

*Finally, to whom would you like to sell your works in an ideal world?*

**CZ:** In an ideal world, we wouldn't make jewellery because we would run around naked as it is nice and warm outside and we would be perfectly happy with nature! But seriously now, the problem began with the fashion of wearing fig leaves, didn't it? And who thought about selling them?

**Fig. 100**
Christoph Zellweger. *Rhizome Chain* 2006. Natural rubber.
Photo: Christoph Zellweger.

# 26

# Conclusion

The twenty-five interviews in this book have provided ample opportunity to hear firsthand the voices of some of the jewellers who have shaped the emergence of contemporary jewellery in Europe over the past five decades. It therefore seems opportune to summarize some of the most salient points from their interviews, with the aim of developing an overview of what contemporary jewellery might be. These annotations will be detailed according to some of the key characteristics of jewellery and its practice as previously identified in the introduction; these include content, technique, preciousness and wearability, as well as a summary of predictions for future developments.

The preceding transcripts have revealed shared beliefs, commonalities in techniques and materials and divergent attitudes, as well as outright oppositions. Consequently, in order to identify the breadth of opinion, both commonly shared and conflicting views will be considered. Perhaps the first step towards defining contemporary jewellery in the words of its protagonists entails speculating on the origins of jewellery. Many of today's jewellers believe the antecedents of recent practice stretch back millennia, even as far as prehistory and the advent of humans. Otto Künzli certainly supports this view, which he relates to the simultaneous origins of cave painting and body decoration:

> Consider early man or his primate ancestor using their fingers to dig in the mud to find food or whatever, and afterwards they get rid of the dirt somehow, but how? Well, imagine them digging away and then cleaning their dirty hands by wiping them either onto a wall, a stone, their body or someone else's.

The next evolutionary link would presumably have been the application of natural objects to the body, which probably would have included shells, bones, feathers and iridescent insects found in our forbears' immediate environment. Thereafter, one hypothesizes a gradual shift to the manmade production of jewellery with the advent of tools and associated accelerations in technology. This chronology centres on the physical manifestation of objects and is therefore strongly influenced by materials. In fact, Ramón Puig Cuyás believes contemporary practice connects to materials in a way that 'resonates with its primitive roots'. However, he then proceeds to differentiate between past and present, suggesting that 'the contemporary jeweller doesn't only work in dialogue with physical materials like stone, metal and plastic; instead, they are open to other territories, where the materials are made from doubts and desires, curiosities and fears, uncertainties, and reiterations of unexpected innovations.'

By contrast, other jewellers such as Ruudt Peters consider that distinctions between the traditional and the contemporary to be unhelpful. He argues against defining hybrids because by not doing so, 'you can relate it to older times, to earlier times and the past. When you change the name to *contemporary jewellery*, to body wearing stuff, I don't want it. Jewellery is jewellery.' Irrespective of the precise term given to the jewellery produced since the late 1960s, various common characteristics persist. The following sections of the conclusion will explore these recurrent qualities.

## Content

One of the factors that distinguishes contemporary jewellery from traditional jewellery is its treatment of content and how materials and aesthetics are frequently manipulated according to an underlying concept. That is not to say jewellery has not previously had meaning or symbolic relevance; far from it. Indeed, Otto Künzli observes how anthropologists think some of the earliest signs of culture were pierced shell beads and described them 'as storage of information outside the brain'. Künzli argues that it is 'the difference between a tool and an object that's not just been made for functional reasons'.

This assertion consequently prompts the question, if jewellery can be considered 'storage of information outside the brain', then what might the message be in our time? The discussions in the introduction suggest it derives from personal expression and is manifested as either content or sensitized materials. Some of the jewellers have also spoken in terms of the self, nostalgia and even invisible spiritual qualities as defining characteristics.

In this context, Esther Brinkmann believes that wearing jewellery enables 'us to transmit exterior signs of interior states'. According to more than one interviewee, the projection of self is a vital source of content, and Annamaria Zanella numbers amongst these. She stated that her 'jewellery, and that of many other artists, is always autobiographical – like the pages of a diary written in metal and materials that take form through the consequences of thought and daily reflection'. Similarly, Ramón Puig Cuyás contends that jewellery is a tiny three-dimensional mnemonic: 'a reliquary in which the artist has deposited their ideas, emotions, doubts, experiences, impressions, and definitely a part of themselves, in the intention of reconnecting it all'. The topic comes full circle, back to the inner perceptions of the wearer, with David Watkins's observation about jewellery's principle functions. He believes these include 'self-awareness, awareness of persona, awareness of body or awareness of presence; it's about how one is seen as a total person. It becomes part of the assemblage of a personality.'

From an etymological perspective, Wendy Ramshaw sagely observes that the word *jewellery* 'itself means joy, but it can also come to symbolize sadness, it can be a solace for people'. She also notes how 'jewellery is handed down through generations', with Ted Noten succinctly summarizing that, as a consequence, 'nostalgia is such an important carrier within jewellery'.

## Extrapolating and Imbuing Content

If contemporary jewellery is to convey content of some kind, then the method of translating this into material form is the 'how'. The diversity of methods discussed range from the methodical to the spontaneous and from the conceptual to the hand driven. The breadth of sources of inspiration was equally divergent; for some – including Jacqueline Ryan, Nel Linssen and Liv Blåvarp – inspiration comes from nature. However, extrapolation from the source is generally not a literal process. Ryan for example attempts to 'abstract from nature without imitating…My pieces are intended to narrate impressions from the natural world.'

Whilst some jewellers seek inspiration in nature, others such as Rian de Jong and Ted Noten find life and everyday events equally rich territory; or, in the cases of Otto Künzli and Christoph Zellweger, this can even include politics. Nonetheless, the question remains of how to extrapolate from the source and how to sensitively filter aspects of significance into the jewellery. The distance of time is de Jong's preferred means, whereas the source is often travelling, because, for her, around the world, 'behaviour, attitudes and cultures are always different. After a while this gives the concepts, the forms and the materials to work on.' Time is also central to Noten's working process, which often incorporates found objects from our everyday lives. He discusses how he will take an object or idea and 'mull it over, reflect and then I do some historical research. I try to analyse and associate things to it. However, the only way to know if it's a good piece or not is to make it.' Nocturnal time can aid other jewellers, one of whom is Bernhard Schobinger. He values the subconscious process of dreaming and describes it as 'a reflection in a mirror of something I encountered in reality. I find or see objects and I also see forms, all of which go into the brain unbeknown to me. So it's like an unbelievable pot with so many possibilities.'

Alongside the external sources of inspiration that usually condition 'jewellery as content', the authors of sensitized jewellery tend to look to the formal relationships in their work. Their methods can appear more rational, as in the case of Mario Pinton and the jewellers from the School of Padua, for whom geometry is both the source and its filter. Pinton believed that 'geometry reorders, coordinates and establishes the best sense of design.' He described how he primarily used 'the circle or square', before explaining that 'these forms do not necessarily have to rigorously adhere to pure geometry; it is vital to modulate them to confer an expressive value.' Geometry is adept at embellishing the body according to Wendy Ramshaw, who believes that 'an abstract form resting on or encircling a human body can be very beautiful. I think figurative imagery placed upon the body is difficult and can detract from the personality of the wearer.' Irrespective of the inspirational source and the content to be imbued into any piece of jewellery, all jewellers are obliged to engage with making techniques in order to shape the dialogue between the object, the wearer and observers.

## Technique

The role of technique and manual dexterity elicited much consensus from the jewellers. Whilst no doubt still valued, technique is not regarded as the common denominator of quality, as perhaps it might once have been. In contrast, it is more likely to be considered a means to an end, which can therefore be subject to manipulation, refinement or even distortion. Technique appears to have become a servant of content and sensitization; nonetheless, the acquisition of technique is still considered to be a pressing need by several of the jewellers.

Karl Fritsch, for example, feels that comprehensive technical skills must still be learnt and honed in the time-honoured fashion, after which it then 'becomes a question of ownership; making it yours…you have to reinvent techniques on your own terms.' This contention is shared by Ramón Puig Cuyás, who strives to refine technique 'into a bridge, as short as possible, between ideas, feelings and matter'. Perhaps the middle ground is staked out by Ted Noten, who not only advocates the traditional acquisition of skills but believes this also entails a sensitizing element. 'First you need to acquire the basics…the craftsmanship…but basic skills doesn't just mean knowing how to drill a hole; it's also how to use your hands: feeling.'

Technique can also include those actions that precede making, such as the methods of research, preparation and form generation. Many of the jewellers share the opinion that this can include writing, drawing, model making or even taking photographs. Perhaps the use of writing and analytical thought to progress work can be considered indicative of conceptual practice, but, as Künzli humorously underlines, this is hardly a crime: 'I say what's wrong with stepping back and thinking about your work once in a while?…It's not written in any book that an artist mustn't use their brain.' Whilst Künzli might be considered methodical in his approach, a jeweller like Schobinger situates himself at the other end of the scale, open to intuition and the solicitations of dreams. Indeed, he even welcomes unexpected accidents in the making process, believing them to be 'a big opportunity because new forms are often made by accident'.

As might be expected, the jewellers' responses to questions about their technique cover most eventualities. However, it is perhaps Gijs Bakker who most stridently challenged traditional outlooks, when he chose to stop making his work around 1980. Instead, he delegated its manufacture to highly skilled craftspeople, according to his designs and instructions. It was a decision that categorically distinguished mind from hand and design from practice. It appears to have given preeminence, or at least equal footing, to the mind and the design process. Intriguingly, Bakker does not consider this relinquishment as disadvantageous; on the contrary, he believes it to have been entirely beneficial, 'because it means I can continue till very old age', and also because he does not 'want the sweat and tears present in my jewellery'. Notwithstanding the sometimes contrasting responses from the jewellers, it seems commonly accepted that technique, or the 'how', is considered subservient to the 'what'. The realignment of views on technique has also been allied to changing perceptions of value; both in terms of preciousness, commodity, craftsmanship and how materials can be sensitized and imbued with content.

## Preciousness

The notion of value in recent jewellery has questioned traditional markers, as witnessed by the frequent attempts to imbue common materials with qualities previously associated with gold and gemstones, or moreover a rejection of these values. In contrast to the past, value can be accrued through the jeweller's actions and thoughts rather than simply being inherent in materials. Consider for example gold, where three concomitant approaches have emerged: firstly, where gold is used so liberally that its fiscal value is subverted; secondly, where it is eliminated in favour of poor materials; and thirdly, where its value becomes the content of the work.

Two jewellers whose practices typify the first approach to gold are Manfred Bischoff and Karl Fritsch. The vast majority of Bischoff's works are made wholly or partly in gold, it therefore comes as no surprise that he buys a lot so, 'it effectively becomes "no gold". If you only buy a small amount, you only think about its value, whereas I am liberated from thinking about its worth and can use it like copper.' Fritsch shares Bischoff's fascination for gold but cautions that 'even a precious metal is just a material, just stuff...I wanted to ditch the material preciousness and make gold look like clay or plasticine.'

Several jewellers have eliminated gold completely, including Caroline Broadhead, who confirmed that, even during the early 1980s, 'there was definitely a hierarchy of materials there, which some of us rebelled against by making out of plastics.' Rather than using plastic, Liv Blåvarp creates in wood, a choice even she has found somewhat intimidating, because 'you have to be confident that value is derived not from materials in a traditional sense, but rather from the significance of ideas, aesthetics and movement'.

A final realignment entails gold's judicious and deliberate use as a signifier rather than a de facto means to guarantee values of commodity and status. In these pieces, the value of gold, or its symbolic metaphors, become the content, with humour often underpinning the transgression. The brooch *Swiss Gold*, 1984, by Otto Künzli exemplifies this wit and consists of a gold foil chocolate wrapper fixed around a box in the form of a large ingot of gold. However, perhaps one of the most iconic and revolutionary gestures against the perceived excesses of gold was Künzli's *Gold Makes You Blind*, 1980. The piece encapsulates a sphere of gold within an opaque black rubber bracelet, and, according to its maker, it was an attempt to 'put gold back in the dark where it comes from'.

## Wearability

The advent of contemporary jewellery appears to have charged the relationship between the wearer and the jewel, an outcome invariably conditioned by the extents of the latter's functionality. As might be expected, divergent views have been expressed on the need for jewellery to be worn. However, within this broad spectrum, Christoph Zellweger saliently observes that 'A piece of jewellery can be functional without being wearable or vice versa...The crown jewels for example are worn only for a very very short moment in a queen's or king's life, but its perceived significance to society is enormous.' Yet there is a certain irony in jewellery's predicament that Peter Skubic wryly savours. Despite being wearable, jewellery spends so much of its time not being worn; rather, it:

> lays around in factories, sits in the showcases of goldsmiths, hangs on walls, lays around in drawers, is locked in security containers, lays in galleries or degenerates in museums. Jewellery is also buried, thrown away, lost and fused again; but jewellery can be worn too.

Even traditional jewellery can place extreme burdens on the wearer, so the idea that contemporary jewellery breaks new ground by testing the body or psyche is misguided. To dispel this notion, one only has to imagine the endurance required to wear tribal neckpieces or labrets that physically distort the body over time. As Bernhard Schobinger notes, 'in jewellery there are messages that are more important than the function of being comfortable or not'.

Wearable or not, there are subtle differences in how contemporary jewellery relates itself to the body, and in the main these derive from the conceptual shift to self-expression. As a consequence, the wearer may increasingly be expected to do more than just physically wear jewellery. For example when discussing what some of the jewellery from his collective *Chi ha Paura...?* demands of the customer, Gijs Baker acknowledges that 'you still need to have some background in the design world to understand what is the value of the idea that you are going to buy'. He continues to explain how he wants his jewellery 'to do something to the people that wear them'. With other pieces of jewellery, the challenges provoked can be quite extreme, either physically, mentally or emotionally. Examples of the latter include Ruudt Peter's silver pendant *Alexis,* 1992, which bears the names of his ex-boyfriends engraved into its outer surfaces, or the seemingly physically threatening nature of wearing Schobinger's necklace of broken bottles: *Flaschenhalskette (Bottle-Neck Necklace),* 1998.

Whatever the dynamic between maker, wearer and object, Ramón Puig Cuyás argues that if their interrelationships 'are neglected, the object becomes hollow – a simple decoration that contaminates our visual environment'. It is a contention that appears central to a new approach to jewellery that prioritizes content and self-expression over more decorative concerns.

## Northern and Southern Europe

If jewellery can influence the relationship the wearers have with themselves and their perceptions of their body, cultural habits and conditions must in turn charge and temper this dynamic. Accordingly, certain differences inevitably exist between Mediterranean countries and those in Northern Europe. Likewise, similar variance exists in the reception contemporary jewellery has generally garnered in these differing regions of the continent: with greater acceptance in the north and a reticence, perhaps tantamount even to suspicion, in the south. Some of the complex reasons for this diversity have been addressed by Ramón Puig Cuyás and Bernhard Schobinger, who both incisively analysed the reluctant relationship with Southern Europe. Puig Cuyás sees causation in the connection to nomadic peoples: 'in the nomadic context, gold and jewellery is the best medium for the accumulation of riches because they can be easily transported and exchanged. These ancestral connections still sustain a prevalent interest in having and wearing conventional gold jewellery.' Beyond the consequences of wealth protection, Schobinger suggests that adherence to Classical ideals is also a contributory factor. He believes that, in contrast to Celtic tendencies, 'Latin groups like fashion and an aestheticism based on the antique classical ideal, and not so much provocation or borderline aesthetics.' According to the opinions of these two jewellers, it therefore follows that the contemporary jewellery that subverts fiscal values and traditional aesthetics is far less likely to be received enthusiastically in Southern Europe.

Another jeweller, Rian de Jong, provided insightful analysis of the more open attitudes prevalent in Northern Europe, which she believes originate from the colonial pasts of nations such as Norway, Holland and England, where travel, discovery and trade were central to their historical development. I contend, too, that the Industrial Revolution must have played a role in shaping the antecedents of taste for contemporary jewellery. Citizens of those countries subject to the proliferation of advancements in mechanization would in general have been more aware of, and perhaps more accustomed to experiencing, a continuing evolution of design styles and machine-made tools, artefacts and objects. Generally, the latter exhibited cleaner expressions of shape, form and surface than handmade objects.

After the Industrial Revolution, the next major shift in thinking was inevitably provoked by the Second World War and its aftermath. In this context, the Dutch jeweller de Jong continues her analysis of her own culture, which 'was developing very strongly towards new materials and new systems. All old traditions went overboard and a new way of life was the future. A revolutionary change in social and sexual behaviour took place; it all opened up and freed itself from the Calvinistic boundaries.' She equates the opening of society with the emergence of jewellers, who, as we know, broke down the traditional precepts of jewellery practice. However, she also underlines the importance of how 'These people were also teaching at the academies, where they influenced the attitude of the students towards a more independent way of working.' In other words, they were spreading the word and championing the new ideals that enhanced the dissemination of contemporary jewellery.

If the speed and willingness to accept contemporary jewellery has been conditioned by differing geography, cultures and mindsets within Europe, it is probable that the latter will also affect the rate of future developments and the particular paths it will take in each country or region.

## Future Developments

It seems appropriate to end the conclusion by considering the jewellers' predictions of how the language of jewellery might evolve. It is entirely conceivable that significant developments will derive from the holistic incorporation of computer-aided design and manufacture (CAD/CAM). Indeed, its relatively slow uptake to date is surprising, despite exceptions such as Gijs Bakker, Christoph Zellweger and David Watkins. Rian de Jong suggests this may be because 'most of the current generation were not brought up with the computer and its possibilities.'

As amazing as all these new technologies may seem, Bakker sounds a resonant warning note against considering digital manufacturing to be a utopian panacea, arguing, 'it's just a tool; all those high technologies are great. First, I had the hammer and could chisel, and now I can have an image made by rapid prototyping, but for me they're all simply tools.' Bakker infers that the means is not paramount, no matter how wondrous it may be. Even if the hand is replaced by a machine, it is still subservient to, and has to be driven by, the mind and soul. It is a discourse reminiscent of the advent of mechanization during the Industrial Revolution, as discussed in the introduction.

Ruudt Peters also notes that the making process tends to be less intuitive, because 'when you make a piece with laser cutting or high technology, you have to know what you want in advance.' One jeweller with considerable experience of using these technologies is David Watkins, and he counters this argument whilst acknowledging that it 'does tend to drive you to be decisive. But that's simply an aspect of its challenge and not a bad thing in itself.' Computers and new digital technologies simply appear to offer additional ways of creating, each with their own parameters, vocabulary, advantages and disadvantages. Watkins agrees, maintaining that 'generally, the same principles apply to all work with tools, whether hand or machine tools: they all have their challenges and limitations…Just because pieces are primarily handled by some computer or machine makes no difference.' Given its fairly recent intervention in the world of contemporary jewellery and the relative cost of technologies such as rapid prototyping, a broader diffusion and the culmination of its influence will take time. The duration of this gestation is likely to be linked to the artistic maturing of jewellers who have grown up in synthesis with the digital realm.

Allied to the computer, one envisages that the Internet will also assert greater influence on contemporary jewellery, in part through Web sites that facilitate sales and bypass the traditional gallery system. In fact, Bakker believes the status quo of that system to be creatively stifling, hoping instead for 'a sort of philosophy…that means you can fit in with another artist who is making objects or furniture pieces or making whatever…Jewellery by jewellery, it's like a ghetto!'

Contemporary jewellery is inevitably influenced by globalization, and Daniel Kruger's view is that 'Europe and North America seem to decide what jewellery has to look like! The rest of the world follows adding a local flavour here and there.' Esther Brinkmann has exported the medium beyond these Western confines by practicing in China since 2005. She reported how 'so-called contemporary jewellery is absolutely unknown in China. During several decades, wearing jewellery was taboo…For Chinese women, wearing jewellery is a new experience.' Yet, if the economies of the Indo-China region continue their long-term expansion, surely it is inconceivable that they will not in some way shape contemporary jewellery in the future. Overall, globalization and the Internet have no doubt enriched the field by enabling cross-pollination between continents and cultures through international exhibitions, educational institutions and master classes, both in the real world and online.

## Summary

The conversations with the twenty-five jewellers have revealed both common and divergent approaches, a great deal of consensus, but equally as much disagreement in philosophy. On the whole, they seem to agree that contemporary jewellery is driven by ideas. This conceptual underpinning elevates materials through design, thought and action and results in objects imbued with self-expressive meanings, which in turn individuate authorship. They also concur that contemporary jewellery's significance means it cannot, and should not, just be a purely decorative ornament; nor should the old values of commodity and status symbol hold sway. Thus, the sensitization of material, irrespective of whether to instil content or for more formal reasons, is accorded considerable significance. Penultimately, the need for this jewellery to be worn is generally considered vital. Through the ensuing relationship with the human body, each piece of jewellery comes alive to shape the perceptions of the wearer and those who observe it. Perhaps the final tribute should come from Daniel Kruger, who persuasively and evocatively describes jewellery as 'a microcosm of abstract or figurative forms; a sign on the body, which enriches and elevates, of which the possession in itself gives pleasure, stimulates contemplation, enchants and seduces'.

Finally, as the reader has no doubt already discerned, all the jewellers interviewed have a great deal of passion, respect and excitement for the medium. Above and beyond the personal expression that defines contemporary jewellery, I contend that a passion for the subject is another determining characteristic. Once the first shoots of these sentiments have appeared, they need to be nurtured, followed and fortified. This precious and indispensible passion nourishes and supports the jeweller during every phase of his or her life. Personally, I believe that this passion is a gift that makes our lives a joy – or, in other words, a jewel.

# Resource Appendix

Please note, the author and publisher take no responsibility for any changes to the following listings, which by their nature can be subject to change and discontinuation.

## Contemporary Jewellery Artists' Web Sites

www.babetto.com
www.gijsbakker.com
www.ralphbakker.nl
www.artfree.de (Peter Bauhuis)
www.robertabernabei.com
www.estherbrinkmann.com
www.calder.org
www.cepka.sk
www.peterchang.org
www.lincheung.co.uk
www.giovanni-corvaja.com
www.iriseichenberg.nl
www.hibernate.fi
www.leonorhipolito.com
www.mari-ishikawa.de
www.riandejong.nl
www.machteldvanjoolingen.nl
www.nellinssen.nl
www.fritz-maierhofer.com
www.marcmonzo.net
www.tednoten.com
www.ruudtpeters.nl
www.ramshaw-watkins.com
www.mahrana.com

www.n-e-r-v-o-u-s.com
www.jacqueline-ryan.com
www.auquai.com (Philip Sajet)
www.schobinger.ch
www.karinseufert.de
www.peterskubic.at
www.robertsmit.eu
www.bettina-speckner.com
www.monikastrasser.ch
www.toresvensson.com
www.luziavogt.ch
www.digitaljewellery.com (Jayne Wallace)
www.schmuck-zahn-helga.de
www.christophzellweger.com

## Contemporary Jewellery Repositories

www.klimt02.net
www.metalcyberspace.com
www.artjewelryforum.org
www.ganoksin.com
www.noovoeditions.com

## Associations

www.acj.org.uk
www.agc-it.org
www.artjewelryforum.org
www.craftscouncil.org.uk
www.craftscotland.org
www.designforum.fi
www.german-crafts.org
www.konsthantverkscentrum.se
www.snagmetalsmith.org
www.wcc-europe.org

## Contemporary Jewellery Galleries

### Asia and Oceania

| | | |
|---|---|---|
| Gallery Funaki | Australia | www.galleryfunaki.com.au |
| Fingers | New Zealand | www.fingers.co.nz |
| Deux Poissons | Tokyo | www.deuxpoissons.com |

## Austria and Switzerland

| | | |
|---|---|---|
| Beatrice Lang | Bern | www.beatricelang.ch |
| Vice Versa | Lausanne | www.viceversa.ch |
| Galerie S O | Solothurn | www.galerieso.com |
| Galerie Slavik | Vienna | www.galerie-slavik.com |

## Belgium and Luxembourg

| | | |
|---|---|---|
| Villa De Bondt | Gent | www.villadebondt.be |
| Galerie Sofie Lachaert | Gent | www.lachaert.com |
| Galerie Orfèo | Luxembourg | www.galerie-orfeo.com |

## Eastern Europe

| | | |
|---|---|---|
| Galeria Bielak | Kraków | www.galeriabielak.pl |

## France and Germany

| | | |
|---|---|---|
| Oona Galerie | Berlin | www.oona-galerie.de |
| Galerie Stühler | Berlin | www.galerie-stuehler.de |
| Gallerie Pilartz | Cologne | www.pilartz.com |
| Hilde Leiss | Hamburg | www.hilde-leiss.de |
| Galerie Rosemarie Jäger | Hochheim | www.rosemarie-jaeger.de |
| Galerie BIRÓ | Munich | www.galerie-biro.de |
| Galerie Spektrum | Munich | www.galerie-spektrum.de |
| Galerie Hélène Porée | Paris | www.galerie-helene-poree.com |

## Italy

| | | |
|---|---|---|
| Le Arti Orafe Art Gallery | Lucca | www.leartiorafeartgallery.it |
| Marijke Studio | Padova | www.marijkestudio.com |
| Alternatives | Rome | www.alternatives.it |
| Galleria Maurer Zilioli | Brescia | www.maurerzilioli.com |

## The Netherlands

| | | |
|---|---|---|
| Galerie Rob Koudijs | Amsterdam | www.galerierobkoudijs.nl |
| Galerie Louise Smit | Amsterdam | www.louisesmit.nl |
| Galerie Ra | Amsterdam | www.galerie-ra.nl |
| Galerie Lous Martin | Delft | www.galerielousmartin.nl |
| Galerie Marzee | Nijmegen | www.marzee.nl |

## Scandinavia

| | | |
|---|---|---|
| Galerie Metal | Copenhagen | www.galeriemetal.dk |
| Galerie Hnoss | Gothenberg | www.konstepidemin.se/hnoss/ |
| Platina | Stockholm | www.platina.se |
| Gallerie Metallum | Stockholm | www.metallum.com |
| Nutida Svenskt Silver | Stockholm | www.nutida.nu |
| LOD | Stockholm | www.lod.nu |
| Konsthantverkarna | Stockholm | www.konsthantverkarna.se |

## Spain and Portugal

| | | |
|---|---|---|
| Klimt02 \| Gallery | Barcelona | www.klimt02.net |
| Shibuichi | Leça da Palmeira | www.shibuichi.com |
| Galeria Reverso | Lisbon | www.reversodasbernardas.com |

## United Kingdom

| | | |
|---|---|---|
| Scottish Gallery | Edinburgh | www.scottish-gallery.co.uk |
| CCA | London | www.caa.org.uk |
| Electrum | London | www.electrumgallery.co.uk |
| Flow Gallery | London | www.flowgallery.co.uk |
| Lesley Craze | London | www.lesleycrazegallery.co.uk |

## United States

| | | |
|---|---|---|
| Mobila Gallery | Cambridge, Massachusetts | www.mobilia-gallery.com |
| Sofa | Chicago / New York | www.sofaexpo.com |
| Ornamentum Gallery | Hudson, New York | www.ornamentumgallery. com |
| Sienna Gallery | Lenox, Massachusetts | www.siennagallery.com |
| Gallery Loupe | Montclair, New Jersey | www.galleryloupe.com |
| Charon Kransen Arts | New York | www.charonkransenarts.com |
| Velvet da Vinci | San Francisco | www.velvetdavinci.com |
| Sculpture to Wear | Santa Monica | www.sculpturetowear.com |
| Patina Gallery | Santa Fe | www.patina-gallery.com |

# Miscellaneous

www.afsoun.com
www.fvandenbosch.nl
www.chihapaura.com
www.droogdesign.nl
www.etsy.com
www.objectfetish.com
www.sharedutchdesign.nl

## Museums of Interest

| | | |
|---|---|---|
| CODA | Apeldoorn (Netherlands) | www.coda-apeldoorn.nl |
| Ilias Lalaounis Jewellery Museum | Athens | www.lalaounis-jewelry museum.gr |
| Museum of Decorative Arts | Berlin | www.smb.spk-berlin.de |

| | | |
|---|---|---|
| Pergamon Museum | Berlin | www.smb.spk-berlin.de |
| Fuller Craft Museum | Brockton (United States) | www.fullercraft.org |
| Museum of Applied Art | Cologne | www.museenkoeln.de |
| Silver Museum | Florence | www.firenzemusei.it/ argenti/index.html |
| Museum of Applied Art | Frankfurt | www.angewandtekunst-frankfurt.de |
| Groninger Museum | Groninger (Netherlands) | www.groninger museum.nl |
| Museum für Kunst und Gewerbe | Hamburg | www.mkg-hamburg.de |
| Grassi Museum of Applied Art | Leipzig | www.grassimesse.de |
| Victoria and Albert Museum | London | www.vam.ac.uk |
| British Museum | London | www.britishmuseum.org |
| Design Museum | London | www.designmuseum.org |
| Poldi Pezzoli Museum | Milan | www.museopoldipezzoli.it |
| Museum of Arts and Design | New York | www. madmuseum.org |
| Sainsbury Centre for Visual Art | Norwich | www.scva.org.uk |
| The Louvre | Paris | www.louvre.fr |
| Schmuckmuseum | Pforzheim | www.schmuckmuseum-pforzheim.de |
| Museum of Decorative Arts | Turin | www.fondazioneaccorsi.it |
| Egyptian Museum | Turin | www.museoegizio.org |
| Museum of Oriental Arts | Venice | www.arteorientale.org |
| MAK Austrian Museum of Applied Arts | Vienna | www.mak.at |
| Metropolitan Museum of Art | New York | www.metmuseum.org |

## Sources of Inspiration

Students of contemporary jewellery and three-dimensional design are encouraged to seek inspiration from the broadest range of objects that characterize the primary syntax, grammar and vocabulary of the three-dimensional language of form. Consequently, the following section details the Web sites of a selection of modern exemplars that will hopefully provide starting points for further investigation. Also included are broader sources of inspiration such as art, science and nature. This is followed by a brief bibliography of books that students of the 3D language may find useful in their visual and theoretical research.

## Architecture

www.alvaraalto.fi
www.archrecord.construction.com
www.arcspace.com
www.arup.com
www.shigerubanarchitects.com
www.barragan-foundation.org
www.calatrava.com
www.fondationlecorbusier.asso.fr
www.domusweb.it
www.foga.com
www.fosterandpartners.com
www.future-systems.com
www.greatbuildings.com
www.zaha-hadid.com
www.toyo-ito.com
www.kkaa.co.jp
www.daniel-libeskind.com
www.glform.com
www.niemeyer.org.br
www.jeannouvel.com
www.freiotto.com
www.pcfandp.com
www.pricemyers.com
www.fondazionealdorossi.org
www.rpbw.com
www.pritzkerprize.com
www.richardrogers.co.uk
www.rvapc.com

## Art

www.anishkapoor.com
www.artnet.com
www.anthonycaro.org
www.fondation.cartier.com
www.eduardo-chillida.com
www.chinati.org
www.christojeanneclaude.net
www.cittadellarte.it

www.tony-cragg.com
www.diacenter.org
www.richarddeacon.net
www.flashartonline.com
www.gagosian.com
www.antonygormley.com
www.guggenheim.org
www.garyhill.com
www.damienhirst.com
www.shirazehhoushiary.com
www.juddfoundation.org
www.lissongallery.com
www.richardlong.org
www.fondazionemerz.org
www.noguchi.org
www.olafureliasson.net
www.jorgepardosculpture.com
www.beverlypepper.net
www.jaumeplensa.com
www.fondazionearnaldopomodoro.it
www.fondazioneprada.org
www.caiguoqiang.com
http://archaeologydataservice.ac.uk/era/
www.pipilottirist.net
www.musee-rodin.fr
www.medardorosso.org
www.saatchi-gallery.co.uk
www.sculpture.org
www.sculpture.org.uk
www.davidsmithestate.org
www.fondazionenicolatrussardi.com
www.centerforvisualmusic.org
www.bernarvenet.com
www.billviola.com
www.whitecube.com
www.ubu.com


## Craft

www.bamboocraft.net
www.galeriebesson.co.uk
www.bmgallery.co.uk
www.ceramicstoday.com
www.craftscouncil.org.uk
www.ekwc.nl
www.glassartists.org
www.rupertspira.com
www.edmunddewaal.com

## Design

www.alessi.com
www.ronarad.com
www.bengtssondesign.com
www.tordboontje.com
www.campanas.com.br
www.achillecastiglioni.it
www.thecoolhunter.co.uk
www.demakersvan.com
www.designboom.com
www.design-conscious.co.uk
www.designspotter.com
www.dezeen.com
www.tomdixon.net
www.freedomofcreation.com
www.michaelgraves.com
www.industreal.it
www.patrickjouin.com
www.materialise-mgx.com
www.isseymiyake.co.jp
www.carlosmotta.com.br
www.marc-newson.com
www.notesondesign.net
www.oktavius.co.uk/resource.html
www.karimrashid.com
www.scandinaviandesign.com
www.shift.jp.org
www.philippe-starck.com
www.stylepark.com
www.ted.com
www.tjep.com
www.todayandtomorrow.net
www.kenjitoki.com
www.philiptreacy.co.uk
www.wallpaper.com
www.viviennewestwood.com
www.we-make-money-not-art.com

## Film and Multimedia

www.aardman.com
www.aniboom.com
www.atom.com
www.awntv.com
www.bfi.org.uk
www.centerforvisualmusic.org
www.coldhardflash.com

www.dam.org
www.dataisnature.com
www.expcinema.com
www.fastuk.org.uk
www.oskarfischinger.org
www.ilm.com
www.lux.org.uk
www.nausicaa.net
www.pixar.com
www.rhizome.org
www.submarinechannel.com
www.youtube.com

## Information Technology, Computer-Aided Design, Computer-Aided Manufacturing, and Three-Dimensional Design

www.3dlapidary.com
www.3dlinks.com
www.autodesk.com
www.blender.org
www.cgsociety.org
www.creativecrash.com
www.digitaltutors.com
www.luxology.com
www.processing.org
www.rhino3d.com
www.simplymaya.com
www.shapeways.com
www.techjewel.com

## Science and Nature

www.anatomyatlases.org
www.arkive.org
www.bgci.org
www.exploretheabyss.com
www.extremescience.net
http://portal.onegeology.org
www.geology.com
www.hubblesite.org
www.kew.org
www.nasa.gov
www.nationalgeographic.com
www.newscientist.com
www.weatherscapes.com

## Inspiration Bibliography

Antonelli, P. (2003) *Objects of Design from the Museum of Modern Art*. New York, Museum of Modern Art.

Blossfeldt, K. (1986) *Art Forms in the Plant World*. New York, Dover Publications.

Blossfeldt, K. (1998) *Natural Art Forms*. New York, Dover Publications.

Brownell, B. (2006) *Transmaterial: A Catalog of Materials That Redefine Our Physical Environment*. New York, Princeton Architectural Press.

Brownell, B. (2008) *Transmaterial 2: A Catalog of Materials That Redefine Our Physical Environment*. New York, Princeton Architectural Press.

Byars, M. (2004) *Design Encyclopedia: The Museum of Modern Art*. New York, Museum of Modern Art.

Ekiguchi, K. & McCreery, R. (2001) *Japanese Crafts: A Complete Guide to Today's Traditional Handmade Objects*. Tokyo, Kodansha International Ltd.

Fiell, C. (2005) *1000 Chairs*. Cologne, Taschen.

Haeckel, E. (1974) *Art Forms in Nature*. New York, Dover Publications.

Hagiwara, S. & Kuma, M. (2007) *Origins: The Creative Spark behind Japan's Best Product Designs*. Tokyo, Kodansha International Ltd.

Hudson, J. (2006) *1000 New Designs and Where To Find Them: A 21st-Century Sourcebook*. London, Laurence King Publishing.

Jones, O. (2008) *The Grammar of Ornament*. London, A & C Black Publishers Ltd.

Kasson Sloan, S. (2009) *500 Plastic Jewelry Designs: A Groundbreaking Survey of a Modern Material*. New York, Lark Books.

Kowalski Dougherty, C. (2008) *Jewelry Design*. Cologne, Daab.

Koyama, O. (2005) *Inspired Shapes: Contemporary Designs for Japan's Ancient Crafts*. Tokyo, Kodansha International Ltd.

Leighton, J. (1995) *1,100 Design and Motifs from Historic Sources*. New York, Dover Publications.

Le Van, M. (2004) *1000 Rings: Inspiring Adornments for the Hand*. New York, Lark Books.

Le Van, M. (2005) *500 Brooches: Inspiring Adornments for the Body*. New York, Lark Books.

Le Van, M. (2006) *500 Bracelets: An Inspiring Collection of Extraordinary Designs*. New York, Lark Books.

Le Van, M. (2007) *500 Necklaces: Contemporary Interpretations of a Timeless Form*. New York, Lark Books.

Mollerop, C. (2006) *Collapsibles: A Design Album of Space-Saving Objects*. London, Thames and Hudson.

Munari, B. (1965) *Discovery of the Circle*. London, Alec Tiranti Ltd.

Munari, B. (1965) *Discovery of the Square*. London, Alec Tiranti Ltd.

Munari, B. (1971) *Design as Art*. London, Penguin.

Munari, B. (2007) *The Triangle*. Mantova, Corraini Editore. (reprint)

Nerdinger, W., Ed. (2005) *Frei Otto, Complete Works: Lightweight Construction – Natural Design*. Basel, Birkhäuser.

Pipe, A. (2007) *Drawing for Designers*. London, Laurence King Publishing.

Rudofsky, R. (1964) *Architecture without Architects: A Short Introduction to Non-Pedigreed Architecture.* New York, Hacker Art Books.

Rudofsky, R. (1977) *The Prodigious Builders.* New York, Harcourt Brace Jovanovich.

Speltz, A. (1959) *The Styles of Ornament.* New York, Dover Publications.

Takeji, I. (1999) *Katachi: Classic Japanese Design.* San Francisco, Chronicle Books.

Untracht, O. (1985) *Metal Techniques for Craftsmen: A Basic Manual on the Methods of Forming and Decorating Metals.* London, Robert Hale Ltd.

# Notes

## Preface

1. Exceptions that focus on interviews with jewellers, or that detail some jewellers' statements include: Radice, B. (1987) *Jewellery by Architects*. New York, Rizzoli International Publications. Turner, R. (1976) *Contemporary Jewellery: A Critical Assessment 1945–1975*. London, Studio Vista. West, J. (1998) *Made to Wear: Creativity in Contemporary Jewellery*. London, Lund Humphries.

## Introduction

1. Vanhaeren, M. et al., (2006) Middle Paleolithic Shell Beads in Israel and Algeria. *Science*. 23 June 2006, 312. pp. 1785–8.
2. 'Towards the end of the Republic, the gold ring was bestowed on civilians.' Higgins, R. A. (1961) *Greek and Roman Jewellery*. London, Methuen. p. 179.
3. Hughes, G. (1972) *The Art of Jewelry*. London, Studio Vista. p. 23.
4. 'At the formal betrothal ceremony at which the father or guardian of the bride made a solemn pledge of marriage, the prospective husband gave his bride a ring (annulus pronubis) as his own form of warranty.' Bury, S. (1984) *Rings*. London, Victoria and Albert Museum. p. 15.
5. Hughes, G. (1972) *The Art of Jewelry*. London, Studio Vista. p. 19.
6. Pliny noted, 'the emperor Claudius gave permission for people to wear his portrait engraved on a gold ring.' Higgins, R. A. (1961) *Greek and Roman Jewellery*. London, Methuen. p. 189.
7. See Voillot, P. (1998) *Diamonds and Precious Stones*. London, Thames and Hudson. pp. 20–7. Other items also incorporated into settings were believed to have special properties; for example 'the

power to counteract epilepsy and dropsy were attributed to ass's hoof and toadstone', respectively. Scarisbrick, D. (2003) *Finger Rings: Ancient to Modern*. Oxford, Ashmolean Museum. p. 44.

8. Coral was also used to symbolize the passion of Christ and also rebirth through association with the mythological Greek character Medusa, whose gushing blood is said to have become coral on contact with the sea. The protective qualities of coral were believed to derive from its form, which often resembles multiple lances. Balboni Brizza, M. T. (1986) *Gioielli: moda, magia, sentimento*. Milan, Museo Poldi-Pezzoli. p. 98.

9. Christianity was adopted as the official religion of the Roman Empire in 313 AD during the reign of Constantine. This slowly led to an open manifestation of personal faith through jewellery, and particularly the ring. See Lambert, S. (1998) *The Ring*. Hove, RotoVision. pp. 49–51.

10. Many drawings were executed through engraving, and the hatching used to define form in two dimensions influenced pieces of jewellery, such as the tabernacle possibly attributed to Erasmus Hornick, late sixteenth century. Several of the architectural details on the rear of the item were hatched using parallel lines, curves or symbols. These engraved lines and marks often served the dual purpose of giving purchase to the applied enamels and providing hints of stylistic flourish. Hughes, G. (1972) *The Art of Jewelry*. London, Studio Vista. p. 95.

11. Pattern books can also bear historical testament to pieces of jewellery that were subsequently broken up for their constituent stones. Also, the fact that various custodians went to the trouble of conserving these books gives weight to the perceived value of the thinking constituted by the drawn jewellery designs.

12. See Somers Cocks, A. G. (1980) *Princely Magnificence: Court Jewels of the Renaissance, 1500–1630*. London, Victoria and Albert Museum and Debrett's Peerage Ltd. pp. 113–41. And Scarisbrick, D. (1979) *Pierre Woeiriot: Livre d'Aneaux d'Orfevrerie*. Oxford, Ashmolean Museum.

13. Hackenbroch, Y. (1979) *Renaissance Jewellery*. London, Sotheby Parke Bernet. p. 272.

14. Holbein's documentation of existing jewellery was an activity also undertaken by other artists including Hans Mielich. See Foister, S. (2006) *Holbein and England*. London, Tate Publishing. p. 83. Also Hackenbroch, Y. (1979) *Renaissance Jewellery*. London, Sotheby Parke Bernet, p. 272.

15. Hackenbroch, Y. (1979) *Renaissance Jewellery*. London, Sotheby Parke Bernet. p. 157.

16. Digital scans of Hornick's designs for vessels and large hollowware can be viewed at http://codicon.digitale-sammlungen.de/Blatt_bsb00012873,00001.html?prozent=1 (accessed 5 May 2011.) See also Hayward, J. F. (1976) *Virtuoso Goldsmiths and the Triumph of Mannerism: 1540–1620*. London, Sotheby Parke Bernet. pp. 243–51.

17. Hackenbroch, Y. (1979) *Renaissance Jewellery*. London, Sotheby Parke Bernet. p. 160.

18. Hornick was by no means unique in his use of lead patterns, it being a method in fairly broad usage at the time. See also Hackenbroch, Y. (1979) *Renaissance Jewellery.* London, Sotheby Parke Bernet. p. 159.

19. Hackenbroch, Y. (1979) *Renaissance Jewellery.* London, Sotheby Parke Bernet. pp. 178–81.

20. Stettiner, R. (1916) *Das Kleinodienbuch des Jakob Mores in der Hamburgischen Stadtbibliothek.* Hamburg, Staats und Universitäts-bibliothek. See also Hackenbroch, Y. (1979) *Renaissance Jewellery.* London, Sotheby Parke Bernet. pp. 209–10.

21. Somers Cocks, A. G. (1980) *Princely Magnificence: Court Jewels of the Renaissance, 1500–1630.* London, Victoria and Albert Museum and Debrett's Peerage Ltd. p. 128.

22. A strong parallel already existed between engraved jewellery designs and jewellery, because the latter would often feature engraved surfaces that heightened surface decoration. In these cases, the tools and marks used to produce both were often virtually identical. However, the same cannot be said for the inked and watercolour drawings for which Mores became known.

23. Cellini, B. (1949) *The Life of Benvenuto Cellini.* London, Phaidon. p. 80.

24. Cellini, B. (1967) *The Treatises of Benvenuto Cellini on Goldsmithing and Sculpture.* New York, Dover Publications. p. 2.

25. Hackenbroch, Y. (1979) *Renaissance Jewellery.* London, Sotheby Parke Bernet. p. 151.

26. For detailed analysis on the guilds, see Hayward, J. F. (1976) *Virtuoso Goldsmiths and the Triumph of Mannerism: 1540–1620.* London, Sotheby Parke Bernet. pp. 38–44.

27. Similar ideas were also elaborated by Cennino d'Andrea Cennini in his *Book of the Arts.* Cennini, C. A. and Thompson, D. V. Jr. (1954) *The Craftsman's Handbook: 'Il Libro dell' Arte'.* New York, Dover Publications.

28. Cellini, B. (1967) *The Treatises of Benvenuto Cellini on Goldsmithing and Sculpture.* New York, Dover Publications. The third volume of Theophilus Presbyter's *De diversibus artibus,* ca 1100–20, also focused extensively on goldsmithing.

29. Hayward, J. F. (1976) *Virtuoso Goldsmiths and the Triumph of Mannerism: 1540–1620.* London, Sotheby Parke Bernet. p. 146.

30. Steingraber, E. (1965) *L'Arte del Gioiello in Europa.* Florence, Editrice Edam. p. 117.

31. Steingraber, E. (1965) *L'Arte del Gioiello in Europa.* Florence, Editrice Edam. p. 121.

32. Phillips, C. (2008) *Jewels and Jewellery.* London, Victoria and Albert Museum. p. 64.

33. Mason, S. (2009) *Matthew Boulton: Selling What All the World Desires.* London and New Haven, CT Birmingham City Council and Yale University Press. Mason, S. (1998) *Jewellery Making in Birmingham: 1750–1995.* Chichester, Phillimore and Co. Ltd. pp. 20–6.

34. Matthew Boulton archive, Birmingham Central Library, United Kingdom. The original pattern books of the Boulton and Fothergill firm

(1762–90) were eventually sold to manufacturers Elkingtons. They subsequently cut up the originals and reorganized them according to their needs, which has meant some of the contextual information and keys to the objects have been lost.

35. The pattern book concerning jewellery and sword hilts (see Fig. 10) was eventually purchased from the Boulton Soho Manufactury in 1895 by Samuel Timmins and given to Messers Tangye in 1896. Given the dislocation of contextual information, it is difficult to say with any certainty whether the designs for brooches, buckles, buttons, swords and chatelaines were used by Boulton, or whether they had been acquired from another firm. Matthew Boulton archive, Birmingham Central Library, UK – reference MS 3782/21/11 Image 5418 B+W Vol 168a p62.

36. Bradford, E. (1953) *Four Centuries of European Jewellery*. London, Country Life Ltd. p. 169.

37. According to Judith Miller, Stras 'explored the potential of a glass developed by an Englishman, George Ravenscroft'. Miller, J. (2003) *Costume Jewellery*. London, Dorling Kindersley. p. 20. Miller goes on to describe how paste stones, as well as precious ones, were often foil backed to force the reflection of light back through the gemstones to enhance their luminosity and sparkle. Stras was no exception in undertaking this operation, but he became so adept at working the substitute glass that his jewellery was valued in its own right, not simply perceived as a cheaper substitute for the real thing. So valued were his works that he was eventually appointed a court jeweller to the French king in 1734.

38. Miller, J. (2003) *Costume Jewellery*. London, Dorling Kindersley. p. 20.

39. Clifford, A. (1971) *Cut-Steel and Berlin Iron Jewellery*. Bath, Adams & Dart. p. 31.

40. The distinctive colour of Berlin iron jewellery was achieved by applying linseed cakes to the piping hot parts upon their removal from the sand mould during the casting process. Phillips, C. (2008) *Jewels and Jewellery*. London, Victoria and Albert Museum. p. 72.

41. Pinchbeck was invented by watchmaker Christopher Pinchbeck in 1732. An alloy of copper and zinc, it was initially used to simulate gold in circumstances where theft might be a problem, such as stagecoaches. It eventually became valued in its own right. See Bradford, E. (1953) *Four Centuries of European Jewellery*. London, Country Life Ltd. p. 169.

42. Perhaps the most famous objectors were John Ruskin and then William Morris, who, along with the wider Arts and Crafts movement, operated in parallel to the continuing production of costume jewellery. They rejected the anonymous look of repetitious forms to champion the role of the individual designer/maker in producing handmade artefacts. Many of the arguments central to their analytical debates were precipitated by the Great Exhibition in 1851, which showcased amongst other things, artefacts resulting from industrial mechanised production.

43. Gregorietti, G. (1970) *Jewellery through the Ages*. London, Hamlyn. p. 289.

44. The third volume of Theophilus Presbyter's *De diversibus artibus*, ca 1100–20, focused on goldsmithing, reprinted in Hawthorne, J. G. and Smith, C. S. (1963) *Theophilus: On Divers Arts*. Chicago, University of Chicago Press. And Cellini, B. (1967) *The Treatises of Benvenuto Cellini on Goldsmithing and Sculpture*. New York, Dover Publications.

45. Raulet, S. (2002) *Art Deco Jewellery*. London, Thames and Hudson. p. 173.

46. Raulet, S. (2002) *Art Deco Jewellery*. London, Thames and Hudson. p. 255.

47. Weiss-Weingart, E. (2006) *Ebbe Weiss-Weingart 1947–1998*. Hanau, Sammlung Deutsches Goldschmiedehaus. pp. 22, 23.

48. van Leersum, E. (1979) *Emmy van Leersum*. Amsterdam, Stedelijk Museum. Unpaginated (p. 5).

49. van Leersum, E. (1979) *Emmy van Leersum*. Amsterdam, Stedelijk Museum. Unpaginated (pp. 2–3).

50. Turner, R. (1976) *Contemporary Jewellery: A Critical Assessment 1945–1975*. London, Studio Vista. p. 160.

51. van Leersum, E. (1979) *Emmy van Leersum*. Amsterdam, Stedelijk Museum. Unpaginated (p. 5).

52. van Leersum particularly valued stainless steel because of its resistance and its capacity to be bent whilst retaining the shape without solder. Turner, R. (1976) *Contemporary Jewellery: A Critical Assessment 1945–1975*. London, Studio Vista. p. 160.

53. Turner, R. (1976) *Contemporary Jewellery: A Critical Assessment 1945–1975*. London, Studio Vista. p. 160.

54. On removal, the implant was inserted into the casket-shaped bezel of a ring.

55. Drutt, H. W. and Florian Hufnagl, F. (2001) *Peter Skubic: Between*. Stuttgart, Arnoldsche. p. 133.

56. Around this time, another jeweller had begun to extend the potential for jewellery to flow seamlessly around the body. Tone Vigeland constructed neckpieces and collars similar to chain mail. Consequently, her linked works adapt to and move around the body's complex geometry, making light work of the complex joints that simultaneously move in multiple directions. It follows that the wearer can modify the work by moving their body, thereby creating a symbiotic relationship between the work and any wearer. Therefore, Vigeland's pieces often seem a universal response to the body as a paradigm rather than being designed for a specific individual. The same cannot be said of Gerd Rothmann, who, in contrast, appears fascinated by the characteristics and geometry of the individual. His early works, such as the *Ear Pieces* of 1983, fill the inner ear cavity or extend the earlobe with prosthetic-like appendages. The site of display and the content of the work therefore become one. Subsequent works systematically mapped body parts synonymous with identification such as fingers and hands, often cast directly from the commissioner.

Eventually, signature works emerged where fingerprint impressions are cast from the client and translated into jewellery, albeit of a more conventional type.

57. Giuseppe Uncini noted how 'my pieces of jewellery remain distinct from the imagery of my sculpture…However, this is not the rule for artists wishing to make jewellery. The works of major artists like…the Pomodoro brothers demonstrates this; the techniques and imagery of their sculptures is found in all the techniques and imagery of their jewellery' (my translation). Cerritelli, C. and Somaini, L. (1995) *Gioielli d'Artista in Italia 1945–1995*. Milan, Electa. p. 163.

58. Joris, Y. and van Zijl, I. (2006) *Gijs Bakker and Jewelry*. Stuttgart, Arnoldsche. p. 160.

59. Künzli's work has echoes of Yves Klein's performance work *Zone of Immaterial Pictorial Sensibility*, 1962. Klein sold a specially designed certificate to the buyer; he then bought gold with the money before finally throwing the flakes of gold back into the river Seine. It was a symbolic ritual, intended to return gold back to the earth from whence it came.

60. Künzli, O. (1991) *The Third Eye*. Amsterdam, Stedelijk Museum. p. 20.

61. The founder members of *Bond van Ontevreden Edlesmeden* (BOE) included Marion Herbst, Onno Boekhoudt, Francoise van den Bosch, Karel Niehorster and sculptor Berend Peter Hogen Esch.

62. Joris, Y. (2000) *Jewels of Mind and Mentality: Dutch Jewellery Design 1950–2000*. Rotterdam, 010 Publishers. p. 32.

63. Becker, F. (1997) *Friedrich Becker: Jewellery – Kinetics Objects*. Stuttgart, Arnoldsche. p. 89.

64. See Jünger, H. (1996) *Hermann Jünger: Uber Den Schmuck Und Das Machen Neue Goldschmiedearbeiten*. Munich, Anabas-Verlag.

65. Jünger, H. (1996) *Hermann Jünger: Uber Den Schmuck Und Das Machen Neue Goldschmiedearbeiten*. Munich, Anabas-Verlag. pp. 136–7.

66. Jünger, H. (1996) *Hermann Jünger: Uber Den Schmuck Und Das Machen Neue Goldschmiedearbeiten*. Munich, Anabas-Verlag. p. 125. In the same statement, Jünger goes on to castigate the technical doctrines of Cellini's treatise on goldsmithing and Theopilus Presbyter's *Schedula Diversarium Atrium* because they both imply, 'making is reduced to the technical application necessary to give body to the artefact'. p. 126.

67. Jünger, H. (1996) *Hermann Jünger: Uber Den Schmuck Und Das Machen Neue Goldschmiedearbeiten*. Munich, Anabas-Verlag. p. 127.

68. Grassetto, G. F. (2007) *The Padua School: Modern Jewellery from Three Generations of Goldsmiths*. Stuttgart, Arnoldsche.

# Bibliography

## Jewellery

Adamson, G. (2007) *Thinking through Craft*. Oxford, Berg Publishers.

Anderson, P. (1998) *Contemporary Jewellery in Australia and New Zealand*. North Ryde, New South Wales, Craftsman House.

Andrews, C. & Tait, H. (Eds) (2007 revised edition) *7000 Years of Jewellery*. London, British Museum Press.

Astfalck, J., Broadhead, C. & Derrez, P. (2005) *New Directions in Jewellery*. London, Black Dog Publishing.

Bakker, G. & Ramekers, R. (1998) *Droog Design – Spirit of the Nineties*. Rotterdam, 010 Publishers.

Balboni Brizza, M. T. (1986) *Gioielli: moda, magia, sentimento*. Milan, Museo Poldi-Pezzoli.

Barros, A. (1997) *Ornament and Object: Canadian Jewellery and Metal Art*. Ontario, Boston Mill Press.

Becker, F. (1997) *Friedrich Becker: Jewellery – Kinetics Objects*. Stuttgart, Arnoldsche.

Becker, V. (1998) *Art Nouveau Jewelry*. London, Thames and Hudson.

den Besten, L. (2009) *Designers on Jewellery: Twelve Years of Jewellery Production by Chi ha paura…?* Stuttgart, Arnoldsche.

Bradford, E. (1953) *Four Centuries of European Jewellery*. London, Country Life.

Bury, S. (1984) *Rings*. London, Victoria and Albert Museum.

Cellini, B. (1949) *The Life of Benvenuto Cellini*. London, Phaidon.

Cellini, B. (1967) *The Treatises of Benvenuto Cellini on Goldsmithing and Sculpture*. New York, Dover Publications.

Cennini, C. A. & Thompson, D. V. Jr. (1954) *The Craftsman's Handbook: 'Il Libro dell' Arte'*. New York, Dover Publications.

Cerritelli, C. & Somaini, L. (1995) *Gioielli d'Artista in Italia 1945–1995*. Milan, Electa.

Cheung, L., Clarke, B. & Clarke, I. (2006) *New Directions in Jewellery II*. London, Black Dog Publishing.

Clarke, B. & Clarke, I. (2006) *New Directions in Jewellery II*. London, Black Dog Publishing.

Clifford, A. (1971) *Cut-Steel and Berlin Iron Jewellery*. Bath, Adams and Dart.

Dormer, P. & Turner, R. (1994) *The New Jewelry: Trends and Traditions*. London, Thames and Hudson.

Dormer, P. (1997) *The Culture of Craft: Status and Future*. Manchester, Manchester University Press.

Drutt, H. W. & Dormer, P. (1995) *Jewellery of Our Time: Art, Ornament, and Obsession*. London, Thames and Hudson.

Drutt, H. (1998) *Brooching It Diplomatically*. Stuttgart, Arnoldsche.

Evans, J. (1970) 2nd Ed. *A History of Jewellery 1180–1870*. London, Faber and Faber.

Falk, F. & Holzach, C. (1998) *Modern Jewellery 1960–1998*. Stutt-gart, Arnoldsche.

Foister, S. (2006) *Holbein and England*. London, Tate Publishing.

Fraser, F. & Hida, T. (2001) *Contemporary Japanese Jewellery*. London, Merrell.

Gabardi, M. (2009) *Jean Després: Jeweler, Maker and Designer of the Machine Age*. London, Thames and Hudson.

Game, A. & Goring, E. (1999) *Jewellery Moves: Ornament for the 21st Century*. Edinburgh, NMS Publishing.

Gilhooley, D. & Costin, S. (2001) *Unclasped-Contemporary British Jewellery*. London, Black Dog Publishing.

Grant-Lewin, S. (1994) *American Art Jewellery Today*. London, Thames and Hudson.

Grassetto, G. F. (2007) *The Padua School: Modern Jewellery from Three Generations of Goldsmiths*. Stuttgart, Arnoldsche.

Gregorietti, G. (1970) *Jewellery Through the Ages*. London, Hamlyn.

Hackenbroch, Y. (1979) *Renaissance Jewellery*. London, Sotheby Parke Bernet.

Hayward, J. F. (1976) *Virtuoso Goldsmiths and the Triumph of Mannerism: 1540–1620*. London, Sotheby Parke Bernet.

Higgins, R. A. (1961) *Greek and Roman Jewellery*. London, Methuen.

Hufnagl, F., Ed. (2003) *Found Treasures: Hermann Jünger and the Art of Jewellery*. London, Thames and Hudson.

Hughes, G. (1972) *The Art of Jewelry*. London, Studio Vista.

Joris, Y. (1994) *Broken Lines – Emmy van Leersum, 1930–1984*. 's-Hertogenbosch, Museum Het Kruithuis & Gent, Snoeck-Ducaju & Zoon.

Joris, Y. (2000) *Jewels of Mind and Mentality: Dutch Jewellery Design 1950–2000*. Rotterdam, 010 Publishers.

Jünger, H. (1996) *Hermann Jünger: Uber Den Schmuck Und Das Machen Neue Goldschmiedearbeiten*. Munich, Anabas-Verlag.

Jünger, H. (2002) *Hermann Jünger: Schmuckstucke – Fundstucke*. Mainz, Hermann Schmidt.

Jünger, J. (2006) *Hermann Jünger, Goldschmied: Zeichnungen*. Mainz, Hermann Schmidt.

Königer, M. & Künzli, O. (2007) *The Fat Booty of Madness: The Goldsmithing Class at Munich Art Academy*. Stuttgart, Arnoldsche.

Koschatzky-Elias, G. (2006) *Fritz Maierhofer: Jewellery and More*. Stuttgart, Arnoldsche.

Lambert, S. (1998) *The Ring*. Hove, RotoVision.

Lange, C. (2009) *Gerd Rothmann: Catalog Raisonné 1967–2008*. Stuttgart, Arnoldsche.

van Leersum, E. (1979) *Emmy van Leersum*. Amsterdam, Stedelijk Museum.

Mason, S. (1998) *Jewellery Making in Birmingham: 1750–1995*. Chichester, Phillimore and Co.

Mason, S. (2009) *Matthew Boulton: Selling What All the World Desires*. London and New Haven, CT, Birmingham City Council and Yale University Press.

Miller, J. (2003) *Costume Jewellery*. London, Dorling Kindersley.

Mouillefarine, L. & Possémé, E. (2009) *Art Deco Jewelry: Modernist Masterworks and Their Makers*. London, Thames and Hudson.

Newman, H. (1981) *An Illustrated Dictionary of Jewellery*. London, Thames and Hudson.

Phillips, C. (1996) *Jewelry: From Antiquity to the Present*. London, Thames and Hudson.

Phillips, C. (2008) *Jewels and Jewellery*. London, Victoria and Albert Museum.

Pomodoro, G. (1997) *Giò Pomodoro: Ornamenti*. Florence, Artificio.

Radice, B. (1987) *Jewellery by Architects*. New York, Rizzoli International Publications.

Risatti, H. (2007) *A Theory of Craft: Function and Aesthetic Expression*. Chapel Hill, NC, University of North Carolina Press.

Rower, A.S.C. (2007) *Calder Jewelry*. New Haven, CT, and London, Yale University Press.

Sautot, D. (2007) *Rene Lalique: Exceptional Jewellery, 1890–1912*. Milan, Skira.

Scarisbrick, D. Ed. (1978) *Livre D'Aneaux D'Orfevrerie par Pierre Woeiriot*. Oxford, Ashmolean Museum.

Scarisbrick, D. (2003) *Finger Rings: Ancient to Modern*. Oxford, Ashmolean Museum.

Schmuttermeir, E. (1995) *Cast Iron from Central Europe, 1800–1850*. New York, Bard Graduate Center.

Seymour, S. (2008) *Fashionable Technology: The Intersection of Design, Fashion, Science, and Technology*. New York, Springer Wien.

Somers Cocks, A. G. (1980) *Princely Magnificence: Court Jewels of the Renaissance, 1500–1630*. London, Victoria and Albert Museum and Debrett's Peerage Ltd.

Steingräber, E. (1965) *L'Arte del Gioiello in Europa*. Florence, Editrice Edam.

Strauss, C. (2007) *Ornament as Art: Avant-garde Jewelry from the Helen Williams Drutt Collection*. Stuttgart, Arnoldsche.

Turner, R. (1976) *Contemporary Jewellery: A Critical Assessment 1945–1975*. London, Studio Vista.

Turner, R. (1996) *Jewellery in Europe and America: New Times New Thinking*. London, Thames and Hudson.

Untracht, O. (1998) *Jewelry Concepts and Technology*. London, Robert Hale Ltd.

Voillot, P. (1998) *Diamonds and Precious Stones*. London, Thames and Hudson.

Watkins, D. (1993) *The Best in Contemporary Jewellery*. London, Quarto Publishing.

Watkins, D. (2002) *Jewellery: Design Sourcebook*. London, New Holland Publishers.

Watkins, D. & van Zomeren, K. (1997) *Onno Boekhoudt: Why Not Jewelry?* Groningen, Groninger Museum.

Weber, C. (2007) *Art Déco Jewelry: Jakob Bengel, Idar-Oberstein/Germany*. Stuttgart, Arnoldsche.

Weiss-Weingart, E. (2006) *Ebbe Weiss-Weingart 1947–1998*. Hanau, Sammlung Deutsches Goldschmiedehaus.

West, J. (1998) *Made to Wear: Creativity in Contemporary Jewellery*. London, Lund Humphries.

## Interviewees

Babetto, G. (1991) *The Jewels by Giampaolo Babetto at the Peggy Guggenhiem Collection*. Zurich, Aurum.

Babetto, G. (1991) *Giampaolo Babetto: I Vuoti d'Oro*. Zurich, Aurum.

Babetto, G. (1996) *Babetto*. Milan, Skira.

Barbisio, G. (1997) *Bruno Martinazzi: Schmuck/Gioielli/Jewellery 1958–1997*. Stuttgart, Arnoldsche.

van Berkum, A. (2002) *Nel Linssen: Papieren Sieraden – Paper Jewellery*. Nijmegen, Nel Linssen.

den Besten, L. (2002) *Ruudt Peters: Change*. Amsterdam, Voetnoot.

Bischoff, M. (2002) *Manfred Bischoff*. Boston, Isabella Stewart Gardner Museum and Schlebrugge Editor.

Bischoff, M. (2002) *Personale: Manfred Bischoff – Schmuck und Zeichnung*. Pforzheim, Schmuckmuseum Pforzheim.

Bollmann, K. & Maurer, E. (2007) *Bruno Martinazzi: Jewellery and Myth*. Stuttgart, Arnoldsche.

Brinkmann, E. (2008) *Not For Your Body Only*. Guangzhou, China, Fei Gallery.

Cartlidge, B., Gaspar, M. & Watkins, D. (2004) *David Watkins: Encounters*. Barcelona, Edicions-Hipòtesi.

Chadour-Sampson, B. (2008) *David Watkins: Artist in Jewellery*. Stuttgart, Arnoldsche.

Corvaja, G. & Ryan, J. (1999) *Jacqueline Ryan, Giovanni Corvaja – Art Jewellery*. Treviso, Canova.

Drutt, H. W. & Florian Hufnagl, F. (2001) *Peter Skubic: Between*. Stuttgart, Arnoldsche.

Eichenberg, I. (2004) *Iris Eichenberg: Heimat*. Amsterdam, Galerie Louise Smit.

Fayet, R. & Florian Hufnagl, F. (2003) *Bernhard Schobinger: Jewels Now!* Stuttgart, Arnoldsche.

Fritsch, K. (2001) *The Jewellery of Karl Fritsch*. Amsterdam, O Book Publisher.

Hoogland, C. R. (2005) *Iris Eichenberg: Weiss*. Amsterdam, Galerie Louise Smit.

Hughes, G. (2009) *David Watkins, Wendy Ramshaw: A Life's Partnership*. London, Starcity Ltd.

de Jong, R. (2005) *Rian de Jong: Wanderungen*. Munich and Vienna, Galerie Spektrum and Gallery V&V.

Joris, Y. & van Zijl, I. (2006) *Gijs Bakker and Jewelry*. Stuttgart, Arnoldsche.

Kruger, D. (1994) *Daniel Kruger: beldende kunst*. 's-Hertogenbosch, Museum Het Kruithuis.

Künzli, O. (1991) *Otto Künzli: The Third Eye*. Amsterdam, Stedelijk Museum.

Malm-Brundtland, C. (2004) *Tone Vigeland: Jewellery + Sculpture*. Stuttgart, Arnoldsche.

Noten, T. (2000) *Ted Noten*. Amsterdam, Galerie Louise Smit.

Noten, T. (2003) *Ted Noten: Vorschläge*. Munich, Galerie Spektrum.

Noten, T. (2006) *CH2=C(CH3)C(=O)OCH3 Enclosures and Other TN's*. Rotterdam, 010 Publishers.

Peters, R. (2002) *Ruudt Peters: Azoth*. Munich, Galerie Spektrum.

Phillips, C. & Vaizey, M. (2004) *Wendy Ramshaw: Jewellery*. Kendal, Abbot Hall Art Gallery.

Pinton, M. (1995) *Mario Pinton: L'oreficeria*. Padova, Comune di Padova.

Puig Cuyàs, R. (1995) *Ramon Puig Cuyàs; Dibuixos de taller (Workshop Drawings)*. Barcelona, Hipótesis and Renart Edicions.

Ramshaw, W. (1998) *Wendy Ramshaw: Jewel Drawings and Projects*. Barcelona, Hipotesi.

Ramshaw, W. (1998) *Picasso's Ladies: Jewellery by Wendy Ramshaw*. Stuttgart, Arnoldsche.

Ramshaw, W. (2008) *Wendy Ramshaw: Colour Field*. Cambridge, MA, Mobilia Gallery.

Schliwinski, M., & Eickhoff, J., Eds (2005) *Peter Skubic: Spiegelverkehrt*. Munich, Galerie Spektrum.

Simon, M. & Sørensen, G. (2001) *Liv Blåvarp: Jewellery 1984–2001*. Kristiansand, Sørlandets Kunstmuseum (Art Museum of South Norway).

Skubic, P. (1995) *Der Kosmos des Peter Skubic*. Leipzig, Grassi Museum.

Staal, G. (1993) *Manfred Bischoff: üb ersetzen*. 's-Hertogenbosch, Museum Het Kruithuis.

Zellweger, Z. (1999) *Christoph Zellweger: 1990–1999*. Sheffield, Sheffield Hallam University.

Zellweger, Z. (2007) *Christoph Zellweger: Foreign Bodies*. Barcelona, Actar.

van Zijl, I. (2000) *Gijs Bakker: Objects to Use*. Amsterdam, 010 Publishers.

# Index

CPSIA information can be obtained
at www.ICGtesting.com
Printed in the USA
LVHW101642231020
669661LV00007B/219

9 781845 207694